Beyond the Horizon might be Better

SOLA AMURE

Published by Goldcrest Books International Ltd
www.goldcrestbooks.com
publish@goldcrestbooks.com

ISBN: 978-1-913719-94-4

To all who strive for a better future.

With best wishes
Larry 2025
February 2025

Sola and Olu
Lagos, 1954

Preface

My becoming a Cambridge-educated medical doctor is not all it might appear to be, to a casual observer. My struggles, from taking A levels in Norwich, obtaining a bachelor's degree from Bristol before obtaining a PhD from Cambridge, all combined with my abusive childhood caused by people I trusted, made me the person I am today.

I enjoyed helping people when I was a doctor and now feel that I might help others to realise that, in many cases, giving up should not be an option, hence the title of this book.

If one keeps one's eyes fixed on the destination, despite its lack of clarity, there is a chance that the unseen destination is closer than one thinks.

The deaths of people very close to me caused me all kinds of problems and in one instance, I actually considered taking my own life. This feeling of despair was not helped by the fact that I had considered suicide as a young child.

Sitting at home in England reflecting on my decades working for the National Health Service, my mind drifts back to my beginnings in Nigeria and the UK and the long and bumpy road that has brought me to where I am today.

To say that I had a clear view of my eventual destination would be false. However, I am pleased to say that I somehow survived the journey. Knowing what I know now, I am not certain that I would like to do it all again.

There were occasions when I almost gave up writing this book, but my thanks go to all those people who lifted my head when it sagged so that I could focus on the horizon.

1

One of my Yoruba names is Olusola which means God has blessed me, and a few weeks short of my sixth birthday, life took an unexpected turn.

My father took me to live with his own father, James. Father had not discussed this move with my mother; it happened without her knowledge while she was in hospital giving birth to her fourth child, Adebo.

Grandfather lived in a very big house in Lagos. It had to be large to accommodate him, his many wives and the children who still lived at home.

I had so many uncles and aunts that it was impossible at first for me to remember all their names. I could only see my teenage uncles' faces by looking up all the time.

Grandfather was a fearsome figure who did not allow anyone to stray too far from the rules he laid down for his household. He was a big naturally imposing man who wore long flowing robes and was never far away from a whip or cane. His whip resembled a walking stick without the curved end. It stood propped up in a corner, visible to all, and was used to dispense summary justice. Anyone with any sense did their very best to behave appropriately.

It seemed that only the male children received beatings, though I myself was never introduced to Grandfather's whip.

Life in pre-independence Lagos in 1958 was fun from my perspective. I loved sitting outside the house and watching the traffic and the people go by. The engine noises from the cars and the motorcycles sounded like jumbled up music that required somebody to take charge of its organisation. The car drivers and motorcyclists obeyed the traffic lights and only showed their frustrations at being stopped by hooting their horns continuously. Cyclists rode on the non-tarmacked and dusty ground next to the road. They were responsible for raising dust that, depending on which way the wind blew, came straight into our faces. The people spoke loudly and mostly wore brightly coloured clothes. Nigerians by and large still wear such coloured clothes. I now wonder whether the bright chromatic canvas induced a state of happiness, since the people rarely complained about their lot in life. I loved seeing all the important-looking people coming in and out of the house to visit Grandfather James. Because my grandfather was chief of the clan, most of them bowed or prostrated fully in his presence. They must have been people of some stature though because they all wore shoes.

We children went daily, in a family group, to the communal standpipe in order to draw water. When the neighbourhood children saw us coming, they ran away, even when, in some cases, they had been waiting patiently in line for a while. They feared being beaten up yet again. I could understand them fleeing from us but failed to see why they left their pails and plastic bowls behind.

Our family never waited in order to draw water. In fact, we had the run of the street whenever we chose.

Being the youngest member of our troop had its disadvantages though. Some of the children from other families took their revenge by slyly kicking or slapping me when they knew they could get away with it. After a few painful encounters I learnt that I must not stray too far from my uncles' sight.

My parents and three younger brothers, Olu, Bode and the recent arrival, Adebo, lived about one hundred miles away in the city of Ibadan and visited Lagos infrequently. I confess that I did not miss them – at least not at first.

Some things about my new life were different from what I had been used to in Ibadan. For instance, using the toilet allocated to the children in Grandfather's house was difficult for such a young person as me. Urinating was easy as we boys just stood by the side of the main road and did the business. I watched the urine as it disappeared slowly into the sand and sated its thirst. Making its way through my body, the urine did not burn or sting, but on cold harmattan mornings it appeared to emanate steam. Harmattan is a seasonal wind which blows across western Nigeria every year between November and March. The harmattan seasons were extremely cold due to the dry winds blowing in from the Sahara Desert. I remember my mother rubbing Vaseline on my lips in order to prevent chapping, as the nights tended to be very cold.

Going to proper toilet though was a different matter. The toilet was at the back of the house and consisted of elevated brickwork with a circular hole in the top. I utilised my limited life experience to manage to stand on the upper bricks and I wondered whether the designer had children of his own. In the end, I managed to find a rickety wooden step that I could use to gain access to the flat top.

Once up there, there was no way that I was going to allow myself to slip and fall through that forbidden hole. Fortunately, I did not possess shoes and was able to make sure that all ten toes gripped as tightly as a lizard's claws.

On occasions, I forgot to take my bottle of water with me like everybody else did. I must have appeared interesting to any onlooker as I walked away, wide legged, and made my way to remedy the situation. Absence of toilet paper was the order of the day!

Grandfather used to tell me stories that made me laugh. I sat on the floor in his parlour as he told me tales of the things *he* did when he was young. He regaled me with his recollections about how naughty my dad had been when he was young and how he sometimes had to admonish him – with a meaningful glance at the whip in the corner of the room.

I studied his face when he told me of instances when he'd sometimes had to punish my father. He said that this was the only way to make sure that he concentrated on his studies and didn't go bad. There were times I failed to listen closely to the things he said because I was so intrigued by the amount of hair sticking out of both nostrils. Some were not as black as others. He wore Nigerian tops known as *bubas*, which were shaped in such a way that his extremely hairy chest was visible above the V-shape. The full local attire consisted of trousers, *buba* and *agbada*. The latter appeared larger than required from my perspective, as the wearer was always throwing the excess material over one shoulder or the other.

He laughed out loud when relating stories about the village where he was born. The sound could be heard throughout the house, rolling like a wave. The loudest laughter, accentuated by his shoulders juddering up and down like a jackhammer, accompanied his accounts of the villagers seeing Europeans working for the British government for the first time. Some ran away because they believed that the albino visitors must have sinned in an earlier life. Despite the introduction of Christianity, many still preferred to believe in idols. Others were inquisitive and gingerly approached them in order to stroke the pale skin. Grandfather had left his rural village and travelled to the capital in order to find a good job and earn some money.

Grandfather was tall and handsome. He always carried something in his left hand which resembled a fly swatter. It had a firm handle composed of many interwoven colours, and its head was made of what looked like animal hairs. He loved swishing it about like a handheld fan for no apparent reason.

Father, whose name was David, was the eldest of six children born to the number one wife Julie. Julie was very short in height and always had to get help removing pots from a high cupboard. She was plump with a rounded face. Her face reminded me of a smooth, ripe mango fruit. Her stern expression melted away once she started to talk, and completely disappeared the moment she smiled. Maybe this is why Grandfather James married her. The other wives looked up to her and everyone seemed to know their place in the hierarchy. The younger wives did most of the housework, cooking and cleaning, and had more nightly visits from Grandfather than the older ones. Grandfather's English name of James was due to the fact that Christians were given a Christian name on being baptised.

When he smiled, he looked a picture with his perfectly set white teeth appearing to glint as if they had a private battery supply. I wondered whether he brushed those teeth using ground coal rubbed on with his fingers, as we children did sometimes. On the few occasions that I witnessed him angry, I couldn't believe that I was looking at the same person as his whole face took on a different appearance. It was like the difference between night and day. The whites of his eyes went on temporary holiday on these occasions. I admit I never liked or felt comfortable with the redness that replaced them. These occasions reminded me of the noise made by a boiling kettle sat on a work surface just before it started to whistle. It meant that someone was in big trouble.

Grandfather was wealthy by the standards of the day. He owned a tailor's shop not far from where we lived. The shop was small and had five or six sewing machines in it. There were cloths of different colours hanging horizontally on all four walls. It was difficult to see the brickwork behind them.

The sewing machines all had pedals that were moved to and fro by foot. They all had long, thin, metal bits on which the cotton threads, wrapped round a wooden core, were inserted through a hole in the wooden section. In one corner, on a table, lay outfits that were ready for collection. In the daytime, the shop was busy and usually had four or five people crammed in, working. I watched as they sweated and the beads coalesced before falling onto the dusty concrete floor. The solitary and noisy ceiling fan did not appear to be useful.

One Sunday afternoon, I entered the shop when an older uncle went to fetch something for Grandfather. I began climbing the rolls of cloth on one side of the room. From my perspective, they looked sturdy but I soon discovered my eyes deceived me. One of them gave way and came away from the wall. I somehow managed to twist in mid-air and landed on one of the machines. It was not my lucky day as I fell on one of the machines with no thread on its spool. The cold metal, with its pointed apex, had no difficulty penetrating the skin in my groin. My screams would have woken up anyone.

My uncle appeared and surveyed the scene. He lifted me upwards gently and stood me on the floor. He raised my shorts and saw the blood trickling down my left leg, right down to my foot. I looked down and saw this red liquid disappearing between my toes. The pain in my groin was terrible. I cried as my uncle carried me all the way home. Grandfather drove me to the nearest clinic. The kind doctor wearing a spotless white coat, gave me an injection for the pain while I thought the last thing I needed at that moment was another pointed metal object entering my body. He also gave me some liquid to drink for the pain. He brought out what looked like a needle and thread and joined my split skin together. I wondered whether he too was a tailor. When I looked at the wound later, it was very near to my scrotum. The pain eventually went and my skin healed, leaving a scar that is still present. The experience with the doctor and the calm manner in which he reassured me, relieved my pain and made me better impressed me a great deal. His white coat conveyed to me a sense of unblemished kindness and purity. I began to think that when I grew up, I would like to be like him.

One sunny afternoon, I strayed too far from home and was cornered by some of the local boys. The initial approach was verbal.

'Look, here is the posh boy.'

'He is alone,' said a second.

'Talk your fancy English, posh boy,' said the third one.

Even at my young age, I sensed danger, and glanced round furtively, looking for a means of escape. There was none. I knew that I could not outrun them. I was about to be introduced to my first taste of real physical hurt. Having learnt the language by the time I was eight years old, I begged and pleaded in Yoruba, but to no avail, and the next thing I knew, my head made an involuntary rapid move to my right. Almost at the same time, I felt a sharp stinging sensation on my left cheek. It reminded me of the pain I always felt when holding a rose stalk without adequate care. It really hurt and I had a strange taste in my mouth that I had never come across before. I staggered as if unwell and a second boy, standing behind me, kicked me hard on my right side just above my waistline. The third boy raised his leg and I could distinctly see the patterned lines on the sole of his right foot travelling straight towards my chest. At some point, the foot was close enough to almost obscure my view of the boy's stocky frame. The impact sent me backwards and I landed flat on my back.

I looked up in confusion at three faces laughing at me. I wasn't laughing. I failed to see the joke. I resolved not to cry and show weakness. I staggered to my feet and was promptly back on the ground, aided by another kick. This one scythed my legs as if they were corn stalks. People walked by and minded their own business while ignoring my cries for help.

I looked round for an escape route. They appeared to relax for a second as I lay on the ground. I sensed an opportunity. I was quicker getting up the second time and my little legs ran as fast as they could carry me towards home. I heard them chasing me. Fortunately, when I rounded the corner and was on the road our house stood on, they stopped because two of my uncles, Lanre, aged thirteen, and Wale, aged barely fifteen, were outside the house smoking cigarettes. If they were smoking, then Grandfather must be out.

I ran to the elder of the two and clung to his skinny leg. He struggled and shook the leg so violently that he managed to throw me off. By this time, the tears of relief were flowing because I had arrived home safely.

'What is the problem with you stupid boy?' asked Wale the older uncle, looking as if he and his clothes required a good wash.

'Some boys beat me up,' I replied, in between replenishing my lungs with much-needed air.

'Did they see you cry?' shouted the younger uncle.

'No,' I sobbed.

'You are too weak and letting the family down,' screamed Lanre bending down towards my face. I felt the saliva followed by the whiff of his bad breath.

The older one grabbed me by the back of my neck in a way that I had seen chickens being handled just before their throats were slit with a sharp knife. He dragged me into the house like a toy doll and into the bedroom he shared with two others. A third uncle, Biodun, was sitting on a bunk bed, drinking palm wine – the local alcoholic beverage – from a gourd. He was told that I had let the family down by crying in front of my assailants. He looked at his younger siblings and then down at me. The palm wine had done part of its job because the whites of his eyes were pepper-red.

'You are too soft and you need to be toughened up,' said Wale. His grip tightened on my neck.

'Yes, you have eaten too much butter,' said Lanre.

I realised what they were talking about at that point. Anyone who had been to England and had lived there was deemed soft and was said to have eaten too much butter. I had been born in London through no choice of my own when my father was a student at Bristol University, and they held this against me. Grandfather sent Father to England to study for his A levels in Norwich prior to starting university. He met my mother in London through mutual Nigerian friends. Mother was a student at Pitman's Secretarial College.

Before I realised what was going on, I was grabbed by two of my uncles, one on each arm, and shoved down onto the hard concrete floor. I struggled but decided that there was no way that I was going to get loose.

I saw Biodun jump down from the top bunk, stand up, unzip his trousers and kneel astride me. I had absolutely no idea what was going to happen. Wide-eyed and unblinking,

I stared at them. Something was thumping rhythmically in my chest in a way that reminded me of having run very fast. One of the other two forced my mouth wide open and the one astride me calmly used my mouth as a toilet. The urine felt hot and I remember that it had no taste. Biodun's aim was straight and true, despite my attempts at struggling by moving my head from side to side. I was spluttering and by this time, I struggled without success.

I noticed some redness in the stuff that came out of my mouth, which to my surprise, was also coming out of my nostrils. Even as they tortured me, I was wondering how come my mouth and nostrils were linked. I was convinced that some damage had been done. These three people were laughing. They thought it was funny. All I wanted to do at that point was to kill them all. I was totally confused as these people were my relatives. I had hoped that they would protect me. I felt something leave my body at this point. I appeared to abandon my physical entity to cope by itself.

When it was over, they warned me in no uncertain terms that if I told anyone what had happened, next time would be worse.

What had happened was bad enough, and my childhood experience up to that point could not let me imagine what could possibly be worse. At that moment in time, it felt like someone had entered my life uninvited and switched all the lights off.

I went to my room, got the bottle I normally took to the toilet and rinsed my mouth out the best I could. The liquid that I spat out contained what I assumed was blood and I must have accidentally bitten something in my mouth when I was being attacked. No matter how much I rinsed and washed, I couldn't get rid of the experience. I went to my raffia mat bed, lay down and sobbed. With nobody to help me, I felt totally isolated and abandoned.

In the following days I found it difficult to eat and no longer wanted to go and watch life go by on the street anymore. My once happy life now resembled an old balloon days after a party. Before all this, whenever I chanced to look in a mirror, my cheeks looked full as though I had large gobstoppers permanently stored in my mouth. Now, my once chubby cheeks were no longer present. I did not have too much body fat beforehand, as I never walked when I could run. What little I had, went the way of my cheeks. I made a conscious effort to avoid those three uncles from that day on. I hid whenever I saw them coming my way. I wanted to tell Grandfather James, but their warning was foremost in my mind.

Some weeks after this assault, my parents came to visit and my father decided to remove me for two reasons. One, my bones were sticking through paper-thin skin with both cheeks concave, and two, my skin colour had changed. More importantly the whites of my eyes were yellow. Father knew, because of his medical knowledge that I had developed jaundice. He never enquired about how I could have caught this disease and I didn't offer an explanation to him.

I don't know why I became jaundiced. Was it the assault by my uncles, or was it that I drank from the bottle I used for toileting? As there were no taps or soap in the toilets, I wasn't sure how hygienic the bottle really was.

I never told anyone about my experience at the hands of my uncles. I just wished that they would pay for it somewhere along the line.

I was to learn that fostering children to relatives was common in Nigerian society. Living with relatives was deemed safer than living with a total stranger. On occasions, children did stay with close family friends who were of similar social standing. The reason was usually that both parents were abroad or had to study while having young children.

On rare occasions we visited our maternal grandparents in Yaba, a suburb of Lagos. Grandfather Thomas always looked distinguished in his suit, tie and waistcoat. I hardly ever saw him without a pocket handkerchief. He worked high up on behalf of the British government in the Ports Authority and lived in a very grand-looking house on Herbert Macaulay Street. The street was named after one of the early nationalists fighting against British rule. Mother told me later that Grandfather Thomas worked so closely with the British government that he and Grandmother Toyin had invitations to the Queen's coronation!

The house they lived in had a short drive leading to a gravel-covered circular parking area surrounding a well-tended flowerbed. In front of the house and on two sides were beautiful flowerbeds with different coloured roses and hibiscus flowers. Grandfather was much lighter skinned than many of his fellow Nigerians. He owned a black British-made Morris car in which he sometimes took us children for rides on Sundays. He possessed a faint black moustache, which stood out against his light skin.

Grandmother Toyin was much shorter than her husband and, unlike him, didn't smile much. She did however, give us tight hugs associated with a rare smile. She was very kind to us and when we were not visiting, they lived alone in the house. Mother was their only child, which might explain the genuine love Grandmother showed us. While Grandfather Thomas was always dressed in western attire, Grandmother Toyin was invariably to be found wearing multicoloured Nigerian clothes. These consisted of a petticoat, a top not dissimilar to the bubas men wore, a wrap worn around the waist and tied as one would tie a towel nowadays, all topped up with a headwear called a *gele* in Yoruba. She possessed a lot of shiny jewellery and wore some most of the time.

Both grandparents travelled regularly for holidays with my mother to England and had a place they rented in Penywern Road, Kensington. When Mother was christened, they named her Lily presumably because Grandmother Toyin loved flowers and had beautiful ones in her large garden.

2

In 1961 when I was nine years old, my parents decided to return to England for Father to study for his postgraduate qualifications. One night I overheard them discussing the move through our bedroom wall. Father told Mother that my siblings and I could not accompany them for money reasons. By this time, there were five of us children. I had mixed emotions as on one hand I did not want to leave my brothers, and on the other hand I looked forward to a less oppressive home environment.

We were split into pairs and one pair, Bode aged five years and Adebo, aged three, went to live with a doctor friend and his family in a very grand house in Ibadan. It had a private hospital on the lower floors and residential floors above. Bode had a smooth complexion and always looked studious. He was thinner and didn't climb trees or charge around like the rest of us. He also had fewer scars than Olu, Adebo and me. I had a thin and wiry frame. My body, especially my legs, had multiple scars. My elders loved to describe me as a cheeky whirlwind. Olu and Adebo took after Mother in being plump and filled out.

The youngest, my sister Yinka, travelled with our parents, but my immediate brother, Olu, eight, and I went to live with a relative, Kola, who had a clerical job in Ibadan. Olu was much quieter than me; he didn't say much. I felt an urge to look after him because he tried to avoid confrontation whenever possible. Olu always had a look on his face like he was trying to figure out what someone was thinking.

Ibadan is located in the western part of Nigeria, and our home was part of a small community consisting mainly of white painted bungalows. Across the road from the house was the primary school we attended. I made friends easily and got on well with my fellow students.

Not many households had cars parked outside, and the majority of residents travelled on the overcrowded and sweaty public transport. Why many of the men wore white shirts, I did not know, as I surreptitiously observed the coffee-type stains in the armpits when I walked past the queue on my way to school. I could not figure out why anyone would willingly go about smelling like a mixture of boiled eggs and cooked beans.

At Kola's house, things were progressing well until they changed abruptly, like the onset of one of the weekly power cuts we had at the school compound.

'Get up, get up now.'

The command sounded distant, as if in a dream. The words registered at a higher decibel, and to convince me that I was not dreaming, I felt a sharp pain in my side. A decent night's sleep was like winning the top prize in a raffle.

I struggled to open my eyes, and then looked from the shoe up to the owner's face. The guardian's flared nostrils resembled the end of a double-barrelled shotgun. About to be accused for something I didn't know yet, my heart began racing in fearful anticipation. Being kicked and beaten was becoming a way of life in this household.

'Where have you put it?' Kola shouted, the whites of his eyes tomato-red.

'What?' I replied, wildly attempting to unscramble my thoughts in case the answer was somewhere in my subconscious. Not easy to do for a nine-year-old boy.

'The money, it's gone,' came the reply in a voice loud enough to disturb neighbours in the next bungalow. He sprayed me with saliva, most of which entered my eyes. Standing up did not warrant the further kick. My brain was attempting to handle both the kick and my blurred vision. I did not attempt to wipe my face, and, as a result did not see the fist until it was impossible to react to it. In no time, I was back in contact with the floor I had just left. I decided it wiser to stay sitting down.

'What money is that sir?' I asked, remembering to show due deference, as is the custom.

'The money you stole,' he screamed, his face now down at my level. I honestly thought that I should headbutt him. I looked around in confusion and desperation for help despite knowing it wasn't there. By this time, the rest of the guardian's family had gathered in the parlour, presumably to watch the equivalent of a Christian being thrown to the lions. My brother, woken up by the commotion, sobbed, barely audibly, and shook in a corner of the room. The wife of the house asked me to give the money back.

'But I don't have it,' I replied, my voice breaking as I became aware of fluid pooling in the crevices of my lower eyelids. One blink would send it cascading down in parallel lines down my face. I must not blink, as I hated letting him know that he had got to me.

A firm and painful twisting motion on the ear, and I was standing again. Nobody, it appeared, noticed the questioning look on my young face. The painful grip still on my ear propelled me towards the front door. I blinked in the daylight feeling like I felt when Kola drew back the curtains of our bedroom on a bright sunny morning without warning. I struggled to focus through misty eyes that were still attempting to regain function.

'Give me my money, you thief.' People in the neighbourhood did not look kindly upon anyone called a thief. They acted as judge, jury and punisher. As I recalled seeing innocent people bloodied by indiscriminate stoning and beating, I confessed immediately.

'I will take you to where I've hidden it.'

With the grip on my ear loosened slightly, I walked across the road towards my classroom. My confused mind was all over the place. All I could think about as I walked along was my mother. I could do with a comforting hug just then. Why was she not there for me? My life seemed as if day had turned into night in a way similar to the total eclipse of the sun that I saw while living in Lagos. I did not understand the science at the time, but I was excited to see the day turning dark gradually. The young children were advised to look at the sky by observing the sun's reflection in a bucket of water. It was stressed to us that this was in order to protect our eyes. As is the way with children, some looked directly upwards and subsequently damaged their eyes. I felt that my life was suffering a similar kind of damage.

Walking to the school, my intestines sounded louder than I have ever heard them. The noise coming from my stomach was so loud that I convinced myself everyone in the group could hear it.

I must have looked odd wearing nothing but underpants

that nobody else realised were slowly getting soaked as the group crossed the road, dodging a water tanker that had arrived early to deliver to the school. I led the troop like a mother duck: head of the house, his wife, their four children and my younger brother followed at a respectable distance.

Walking into the empty classroom, I went straight to my desk, barely giving the goats in the corner a second look. I opened the desk looking for the money. I was not surprised to find it empty. I winced as he punched me in the solar plexus, which made me suddenly remember that I had put the stolen money elsewhere. Out we all marched to the back of his house, to look under the water tank. I convinced my guardian that the money was there. The area under the tank was sodden and was home to green plants lying flat, having no leaves or other visible forms of support.

Keeping money under the tank would indicate, to normal people, desperation, stupidity or both. However, no one could accuse our guardian of being a right-thinking person. He then kicked me hard, over and over again. His aims were true, using either foot. I knew I had to find the money, and quickly.

Following the fifth such place that I led them to, the guardian told me that he had to go to work, and on his return, I would suffer to such an extent that all lies would willingly vacate the mind. I felt that I had suffered enough by then. I felt like a spider attempting to climb up the side of a smooth bath.

Mentally, I became a spectator peering over a stadium fence, separated from the action. This was good because it limited the level of pain that I could feel.

Later on, when I was alone following a punishment, the pain appeared to hurt more than it did at the time.

I returned to tidy our bedroom ready for its normal daily use. By now, alone with my brother and my thoughts, the tears were in full flow. I could find no satisfactory explanation for my present predicament. More physical pain had been deferred for the time being. There is a Western Nigerian saying that he who cleans up the faeces remembers the experience far longer than the one producing it. A fair amount had already been shovelled into my rapidly filling memory bank in my short life.

My brother and I found life difficult, and we realised fairly quickly to what extent. Kola slapped us frequently without warning. On occasions, it hurt to comb our hair, as the comb travelled over our uneven scalps, painfully negotiating excrescences caused by yet another smack into a wall.

On the rare occasions the reasons for such punishment were offered, they made no sense. Kola's favourite was that I reminded him of my father – a relative who had done better in life than him. Olu and I often discussed how much we envied the living arrangements of our siblings. Lying in bed most nights, I tried to figure out how the different guardians had been chosen. Olu and I longed for happier times. He was more reserved than me and just got on with things in a quiet, unquestioning manner.

Kola had a lowly clerical job in town. He was tall and thin and the only times I ever recall seeing him smile were when he was hitting me. His trousers never reached his ankles, exposing his dirty socks, and his open-ended sandals looked too large for him. He had three vertical lines carved on both cheeks. Those lines differentiated tribes in days gone by. They prevented attacks by another clan. I was intrigued by the apparent roughness and depth of the scars. I had to be careful not to be caught staring at the hairs that poked out from the recesses of the scars.

School on the day that I had been accused of stealing money, was non-existent for me, as I spent an inordinate amount of time thinking about what fate awaited me later. There was no consolation in the fact that I hadn't taken the money in the first place. Going from one false hiding place to the other had only given me respite from the punishment. I wanted to be with my parents. Did they have any idea of what we were going through? They would surely treat me better than this, I thought. Nothing lasted forever. I knew that there must be an end to any problematic situation. My understanding and acceptance of this fact saw me through many difficult times.

At six o'clock or thereabouts, the unmistakable chug of Kola's motorcycle engine seared through my whole being. I felt that I was about to be cored like an apple. My fear drilled deep into my bones and shook my marrow like loose pipework. I had no idea what punishment was coming, but whatever it was to be, I wished it would stay away.

I heard the stabiliser grate on the concrete floor of the passageway. I imagined him taking off the khaki-coloured helmet, heard the footsteps as they made their way towards the back door. I started sweating, my mouth was dry and my tongue felt too large for its home. I listened as the wife said something to him, unable to make it out. When he entered the room and appeared to reach out, I instinctively closed my eyes and stiffened my body, expecting the worst. Instead, I got a clout round the head, which I sensed was not malicious.

'Don't worry,' he said. 'My wife found the money'.

No apology, no explanation, nothing. That was to be the pattern of things as he was never wrong. The wife, Bunmi, a cook at the primary school, stood behind her husband with arms folded. Her face had the sort of look that telegraphed regret at missing out on more entertainment. Her arms reminded me of those of Popeye's, except that she had more hair. Her shape brought back memories of a very large egg. She was marginally taller than she was wide – but only just. She did not say much, but when she did, she had a habit of talking in a very quiet voice. A voice that was incongruous with her physical appearance.

I loved school because it got me away from home, and I liked learning. I was like a parched sponge in the presence of water, ready to absorb any new piece of information. The classrooms appeared huge to me. The wooden desks and chairs were arranged in rows, four across and six deep. Each desk had seating for two students. The horizontal grooves at the upper end prevented the pens and pencils from rolling off. The inbuilt inkwells were never used as far as I could recall, as everyone used pencils. The scratches in the desks informed us about who had sat at them in years gone by. The dust covering the concrete floors, not helped by passing traffic, and trampled mostly by bare feet, would have been a problem for those with a dust allergy. The blackboard had a reflective sheen thanks to repeated polishing with a duster.

The windows, lacking panes or wooden surrounds made the rooms cool, something much welcomed in the heat of an afternoon.

Before the teachers arrived for lessons, some brave souls, mainly boys, used the windows for access and exit. A leap, a step on the ledge and onto the floor worked in many cases. Those unfortunate enough to misjudge things on the way in ended up bleeding or in hospital. Some exhibited permanent reminders of their exploits whenever they grinned. Jumping to the outside and misjudging at least gave the luxury of the face and chin landing on grass. I did not attempt this exercise especially since the rooms lacked doors making it easy to just walk in.

Olu, previously plump, was now thin like me. The doctor looking after our two brothers asked us one day whether we were being fed properly at Kola's house. He was a very distinguished-looking man. He had obtained his medical and obstetric qualifications in Edinburgh. He reminded me of Grandfather Thomas in that he was always dressed in a suit and tie over which he always wore a sparkling clean medical coat. He always stood upright; I never saw him slouch. His stethoscope was usually to be seen dangling from one of his white coat's side pockets. His breast coat pocket always had the tops of three pens visible. He never allowed his hair to grow longer than a certain length and it looked immaculate. His command of English was very good and he sometimes used words that I didn't understand.

After we informed him that we only ate after Kola and his family had eaten, he looked annoyed. Our skeletal frames, lacking little flesh to support, must have convinced him that something needed to be done. I heard him asking his wife what was Kola doing with the money he was being paid to look after us? The doctor and his family made sure that Olu and I were well fed whenever we visited them in Oke-Ado where his house and hospital were. Oke-Ado was a bustling part of town with street vendors selling almost anything one could want. They all shouted what they were selling in an attempt to gain attention. The lucky ones showed their gratitude by adding a little extra of what was purchased which encouraged return visits.

After about three months of living with Kola, and without any explanation we were informed by Kola that we would be going to England to live with our parents. Having left England when I was a baby, I had no recollection of the place. Olu and I were so happy to be leaving Kola's house. We both felt that things could only improve in our lives. We hoped to be proved right.

3

The day we left Ibadan, we were informed that we would be going to Lagos, the capital city at the time. The puddles in the potholes from the rain of the night before were throwing shards of bright light in our direction. It felt as if the rain had washed away our recent past life and a new future beckoned. The mid-morning sunshine was almost too bright for my eyes causing me to squint. Excitement overtook us, and our emotions ran away and saw the beauty of our destination as we imagined it would be.

We travelled to Lagos with another unknown member of the family. Grandfather having many wives had its benefits. It was only after we had left Ibadan and St Luke's Primary School behind that I realised that we had not said our goodbyes to Kola and his wife and children. This thought, similar to a very light feather, crossed my mind and left before it could settle. An early morning flight from Lagos meant an overnight stay locally. The very small and battered brown suitcase we shared had space to spare, despite holding the worldly possessions of two young boys.

Happiness ensured that neither of us got much sleep in our shared bed at the hotel in Lagos. The food, the surroundings with beautifully laid out flowerbeds that we could see from our bedroom window, made it one of the happiest days of our young lives so far. We felt free and had little fear of being told off or hit without warning. We had each been given brand-new patterned pyjamas, a world away from sleeping in our underpants. That bed was so different from our sleeping arrangement at Kola's house that we could have slept through the next day. Before we could get deep into proper sleep, it seemed that a hotel porter was waking us up. There was no time to be bleary-eyed due to the massive doses of excitement coursing through our veins. I had to shake my head a few times to make certain that it was not a dream.

I also had to remember not to squat on the rim of the toilet bowl. I initially climbed onto the seat's rim before I realised that it wasn't necessary. I laughed out loud and the relative in charge of us wondered what was happening, as I was alone in the bathroom.

I couldn't stop smiling as I showered, watching the water coming out of a proper overhead unit. It was a far cry from using an empty can of Ovaltine to take small scoops of cold water out of a metal bucket in an open courtyard at the back of Kola's house. Nobody walked past, gawped and laughed.

The clean white towels that we were provided with resembled bed sheets and were soft too. Breakfast of fried eggs and bread was devoured in no time at all. I felt good, especially as I would not be doing the washing up.

We travelled to the airport with another man who turned out to be yet another relative, whom we had never met or heard of. He could have come from outer space for all we cared as I felt so happy to be leaving our recent home. The car journey was all a blur, with my thoughts having raced ahead. Olu and I could not hide our excitement on reaching the airport. We wandered everywhere, looking for nothing in particular. The place teemed with people appearing to be in a rush to get somewhere. Many had suitcases, with quite a few looking less battered than ours. Almost everybody seemed dressed for a party, in clothes of all the colours of the rainbow. The bright lights lying horizontally across the ceilings reminded me of the sensation I felt on waking up on bright sunlit mornings. I saw more white faces at the airport than I had seen in many years.

Some invisible person announced our flight and our escort walked us right up to the steps of the plane. The aeroplane seemed huge. I could not get the whole thing in my field of view and had to turn my head from side to side. The letters BOAC were written large on the side. The escort had some words with one of the stewardesses; we rushed up the stairs and were soon shown to our seats. I got the window seat without any argument. I wanted to see outside, somehow believing that I would have sight of land throughout the journey.

The stewardess that had been spoken to earlier was very beautiful. Her hair was long, shiny and held in place by a green band at the back of her head. Perched at an angle on her head was a hat. I convinced myself the hat would fall off the moment she leant forward. When she looked at me, I could not get over the brightness of her eyes. They resembled green buttons with perfectly round black centres. The blackness contrasted with the pure white background of her eyes. I could not imagine that those white areas could ever change colour to red or crimson. There was not a single blemish on her face. She looked so kind I guessed she would have made a great mother. The hat never moved despite her bending down to make sure we were securely fastened in our seats. She brought us bags full of presents, with one including a model of the aeroplane.

Looking out of the window as the plane's speed tried to pin me back in my seat, houses and vehicles rapidly became much smaller, and were intermittently hidden from view by clouds. The clouds appeared to float in the air, and some did not reach as high as they appeared from the ground. Soon, it was difficult to make anything out clearly. Once I realised that there was little to see, I settled in my seat to talk to Olu and occasionally play with the puzzles in my bag of presents.

At one point, I felt sick and called the stewardess over. She was very kind and gave me a bag to be sick into should the need arise. I managed to stay fine, and not require the bag by swallowing furiously. In a few minutes, Olu fell asleep, missing out on nothing much. Sleep was the furthest thing from my mind, as I did not want to miss anything during the trip. I no longer had a watch having managed to lose it when it slid off my wrist without me realising, so the passage of time had little meaning. I ate all the food that was offered without wasting a single morsel. I drank lots of soft drinks too, especially as it came free of charge, leading to numerous visits to the cramped and noisy toilet.

A voice I assumed must be the pilot's informed the passengers that we were over Italy and would soon land in Rome. There had been a similar message when we stopped off in Kano in the north of Nigeria. Those who wished to stretch their legs could do so, but they had to make sure they returned in time for take-off. Sure enough, looking out of the window, I could see the sea, buildings and land again, and before long, the plane made contact with the ground to the sound of screeching tyres. The smoke from the tyres was impressive, and within a few minutes, the plane came to a stop.

The beautiful stewardess came to ask us to wait for a while, to allow the grown-ups off first. Her soft eyes had the sort of fixation that prevented us from doing otherwise. Sometime later she led the way down the steps. I could not recall much of the journey to Kano or Rome, where the plane was refuelled both times. I did remember the exceptional sensation as the plane took off and landed as I was forced back and then made to lurch forward involuntarily. The painful sensation in my ears did not bother me at all.

Once outside the plane, the cool January air forced a sharp intake of breath. The cold air hurt the back of my throat. It was very different from Lagos. I walked down the steps, taking great care to hold onto the railing because those steps seemed huge and the tarmac appeared a long way down. After a short walk across the tarmac, we entered the airport building. The toilets were totally different from the ones we used while living in Ibadan. They were clean, no need to squat, although my initial reaction again was to do just that. I soon sat down properly when the plastic rim cover started groaning and squeaking under my feet. Gaining a good grip was difficult because of my brand-new *Bata* shoes, which were still taking some getting used to. I could not believe the absence of flies, although I still had an urge to look out for them.

Olu and I were looked after by the stewardess and given more food. We ate our slices of cake and washed them down with more soft drinks. It did not take long for our plates to be cleaned. Anyone could be forgiven for thinking our behaviour was to prevent someone taking the food away. When the stewardess came to ask how we were getting on, her smile showed a set of perfectly aligned white teeth. The colour of her red lipstick stood out against the whiteness. With the second helping of cake and drinks, she brought a serviette, which to me resembled a large handkerchief, and wiped icing and cream from both our smiling faces. If this was the sort of lifestyle we could look forward to, it couldn't arrive fast enough.

Soon, it was time to continue the journey, but not knowing in which direction to walk in this huge place, we remained in our chairs. We were relieved to see the stewardess come back, and as we travelled down identical-looking corridors, were glad that we had not been required to find our own way.

Back in the air, I was totally engrossed looking out of the window, despite seeing nothing in particular. On occasion Olu leant over to see as well, and his attempts made me feel momentarily guilty for hogging the window seat.

The stewardess came to tell us that we would soon be landing in London, information that only served to heighten our excitement. We had not seen our parents for a long time and looked forward to seeing them. As for the city of London, I had left it at an age where I had long since forgotten landmarks I might have seen.

The plane landed to the familiar screech of tyres and came to a stop near the terminal building. I watched as a man drove mobile steps to the aeroplane doors and somehow appeared to lock them onto the body of the aircraft. The stewardess asked us to wait for people to get off before attempting to do the same. My emotions, taut as a catapult rubber pulled to its full extent, somehow remained under control. So many questions I wanted to ask. Where did the man with the mobile steps hide his cigarette? Would I recognise our parents? Where were we going to first? These and many questions tumbled without answers in my mind. It was much colder outside than it had been in Rome.

Olu and I somehow received our battered suitcase. I cannot recall how we ended up being suddenly handed over to our parents by the stewardess. Mother and Father were instantly recognisable. My concerns about recognition had been unnecessary. Both parents wore gloves and had coats that reached below the knees. Father had on a grey hat that made him look taller than I recalled. He had grown sideburns since we last saw him and they actually made him look very approachable. Mother hugged us in rapid succession, while Father appeared in a hurry to leave the airport. Mother looked as if she was feeling the cold despite being well wrapped up. She couldn't stop smiling and running her hands over our heads. She asked so many questions that we couldn't answer them all. Father, on the other hand looked stern and appeared to glance continuously at his watch. He didn't smile or engage in conversation. He was rubbing his hands together despite the gloves and I thought that he was shivering a little.

In the taxi on the way to the hotel, Olu and I kept looking out of the windows. Snow was not something that Olu had seen before. He could not take his eyes off it and asked Mother what it felt like to hold. Everyone appeared to be smoking invisible cigarettes. It was not until Mother explained that it was not cigarette smoke, but the effect of exhaled warm air hitting the cold that I understood. Mother pointed out the hospital that I had been born in some ten years before but my height made it difficult to see out of the window easily.

'Sit down,' said Father, in a voice that brought back memories of Kola. I complied quickly.

The rest of the day was an exciting blur as we narrated our journey to Mother. In fact, events after leaving the airport contributed to our getting a very good night's sleep. We shared a bed with Mother, lying on either side of her.

Some days later we travelled to Bristol in a white car, a rugged looking beast called a Zephyr. I still remember the car's registration: 110 OAE. I sat in the spacious back with Olu and we could not reach to touch each other with outstretched arms no matter how hard we tried. Home in Bristol, where Father was studying for his doctorate, was a three-storey building above a bookstore on Whiteladies Road, at the junction with Blackboy Hill. The store was named after the owner, Mr Harold Hockey, a true gentleman in the proper sense of the word. The few times I met him, he radiated warmth and kindness that I had seldom seen before. How he ever came to rent property to a black couple remains a mystery to me. I remember seeing signs in those days saying 'Blacks, Irish and Dogs' were not welcome. At least the blacks received top billing, as Olu continually remarked. Seeing this sign every time we walked past really upset me, as I could not understand why someone that I had never met hated my family so much. Maybe if they met me, they might even like me. This thought made me decide that when I grew up, I would try not to judge people I had never met.

Blackboy Hill was off Whiteladies Road, just at the point where the road forked. The front door to the house was at the bottom of the hill. On entering, the small room on the ground floor provided some storage space, with stairs immediately to the left. The first floor housed the sitting room, or parlour as Father insisted on calling it, and the dining room and kitchen. The second floor had two small bedrooms and the toilet. The uppermost floor housed the attic, which had two small beds in it. This was to be our bedroom for almost two years.

I was intrigued by the names of the two roads that we lived on. Why Blackboy and Whiteladies? What was the connection, if any, between the two? I found out later on, as an adult, that the names were unlikely to be related to the history of the slave trade of the nineteenth century. The story goes that in the early 1700s, Clifton was a tiny village on the top of the hill above Bristol. There may also have been a field of snowdrops that became known as the 'white ladyes' and subsequently Whiteladies Field. Someone then built a big house on the site that became Whiteladies House. After this, it is thought that a pub was built on the hill, and in those days the road that led to the pub was named Blackboy Hill after the name of the pub. As it happens, the docks where the ships from Africa used to arrive were not far away from the house we rented. This could have been a reason why some people connected the slave trade with the street names.

The inside of the house looked amazing, with running taps, pull-chain toilets, and a black and white television. Exploring the house was fun, and we agreed that just sitting in the bay window watching people and traffic go by made for interesting viewing. On the few occasions that we ventured out, the cold was terrible and we couldn't wait to get back home. Olu and I could not believe the difference in our circumstances and hardly stopped grinning. Father's behaviour prevented us asking any questions, the most important being 'Why had we been brought to England?' Father was just as distant as I remembered him from living in Ibadan.

The first school we attended was Amberley House School on Apsley Road. The head was a formidable and scary, to the young students at least, Miss Smith. She was short and had her brown hair long enough to rest on her shoulders.

The ends were cut neatly horizontal. She always wore a tweed skirt and a white blouse that looked starched and well ironed. Her shoes matched the colour of her hair and were very clean. She had a habit of staring at you when she was in conversation. The stare was such that you felt that you could not look away. Students felt rooted to the spot when spoken to by Miss Smith.

This was a prep school. Olu and I did well, obtaining good reports. Looking back, it became clear to me that we then went to St John's School in Bristol for financial reasons. With

Father studying, Mother took a temping job with the railway offices in Bristol, in order to earn extra money.

Again, school was fun and we enjoyed ourselves. St John's had a walled playground and all the children appeared to love playtime. Everyone received free bottled milk before running riot. I hardly got enough milk because of a bully. His name was Robert, and he resembled the Billy Bunter that I read about in comics. His overhanging tummy hid the belt on his shorts from view. His cheeks possessed a reddish hue, regardless of the ambient temperature.

No one argued with Robert, and nobody dared to call him Bob unless seeking trouble. He demanded milk from some of the children, including me. For some unknown reason, he never took Olu's milk. No one felt brave enough to mention anything to any teacher. Robert seemed so large that thoughts of resistance were futile. He once sat on top of me, causing me difficulty in breathing properly. From then on, whenever he wanted my milk, he got it. I wondered whether the milk was like petrol in a car to him and perhaps he couldn't function properly without it.

The two Johns were much nicer guys. English John and Italian John sometimes stood up for me when Robert tried something outrageous in their presence. Italian John had an odd-looking upper lip, which seemed like it was not joined up properly in the middle. When I became older and more informed, I realised that what Italian John had was a cleft lip. The scars indicated signs of previous surgery. He was taller than me and quite slim and always looked smart in his school uniform. The upper lip shape was more pronounced when he spoke or smiled, and John seemed to be always smiling. His parents both worked for the Italian government in England.

English John was shorter and wore spectacles that resembled cycle wheels without the spokes. His eyes appeared much larger when I looked at them through his glasses. Whenever he looked at me, I could not understand why John's left eye always appeared to be looking in a different direction. Yet the right eye did what it was supposed to do with no trouble. Again, it was many years later that I realised that English John had a medical condition called hypertropia. One of the associated problems with this condition is the presence of a squint.

As the only black students in the school, Olu and I must have stood out like beacons. Fellow students, if they noticed, did not comment on this fact much. As far as the other children could see, Olu and I were just another two kids they could play with.

Lunchtime became a source of amusement for some of my teachers. At the age of ten, while accepting that I should have understood certain things, my spoken English could have been better.

'You children must learn not to waste food,' said one of the teachers, her voice matching her features in being soft and welcoming.

'You'll have me to deal with otherwise,' continued one of the cooks wagging an index finger.

Her demeanour did not encourage small talk, and most students avoided drawing her attention. Even Robert did not mess with her. The rectangular lady, as some students cruelly referred to her, made sure that no one wasted food. Many children, including me, had to stay behind to finish lunch, trying very hard not to be distracted by the happy sounds emanating from the nearby playground. Some of us soon correlated a short playtime with leaving food on the plate.

I became confused having to eat food that I did not want, and for reasons I did not know. Then one day, it all became clear.

'Would you like some more food?' asked the kindly-looking teacher as usual.

'No,' I replied.

'Are you sure?'

'Yes,' I replied, my face lit up like a new bulb by a sense of satisfaction, staring at my already clean plate. Until that day, my answer to that second question had always been No. For some reason I had assumed that my second response had to reinforce the first.

However, once I had rectified my error, I arrived in the playground at the same time as my friends. I could join in the games without suffering from an abdominal stitch later.

We led a carefree life and had a decent home life, even if Father seemed somewhat preoccupied. He went off to the medical department in Bristol University and got on with his research. The rest of the family rarely saw him, as on many evenings, he worked late. Olu and I got on very well with our mother. She was always good for a laugh with us and she understood our childlike sense of humour. Our father, on the other hand, rarely smiled, at least not in our presence. Looking back after all these years and knowing what I know now, I ask myself to what extent was his behaviour genuine or did he try to suppress the real person?

Mother was always there when we got back from school. We managed to keep ourselves occupied at home by playing games such as Ludo and Snakes and Ladders or by watching television. Sometimes, we asked Mother to take us to the Downs just up the road so we could fly kites and play. Olu and I loved the wide open spaces on the Downs. We could run around and not barge into anyone. On our way back home, we stopped sometimes at the fish and chip shop at the top of our road. We also loved reading comics - *The Dandy*, *Beano* and *The Eagle* among the regular material.

As well as researching for his MD, Father was also studying for the Membership of the Royal College of Physicians, and the Diploma in Tropical Medicine from Liverpool. He had his hands full.

When he and Mother travelled to Liverpool for one of his exams, Olu and I went to stay with a nanny and her family in Southmead. They had looked after me in the early 1950s while Father was a medical student and Mother was working to supplement the family income. She and her family now had two-year-old Yinka to look after, some eight years since doing the same for me. Both of our parents had jobs and as Yinka was too young to have started school, she required looking after. Nanny and her husband Bill, both white British, lived on Wilton Close, a quiet road in Southmead, Bristol. It was on this road that I learnt to ride a bicycle. Their daughter Maggie was slightly older than me, and we got on really well. Maggie had very curly fair hair and loved drinking milk. Her socks never seemed to roll down to her ankles as ours did.

After a bath in shared water made bearable by occasionally adding kettles of hot water, we children all had tea. Tea usually consisted of a sandwich or two followed by pudding. By five o'clock, looking clean and feeling full, all four children were dressed and ready for bed. There was no television, so evenings involved reading and playing games like Ludo and Tiddlywinks. Nanny read to us on occasions. She always wore plastic-rimmed glasses and they appeared to be sufficient for seeing at all distances. I seem to recall that, unless we were out of the house, Nanny's flowery apron never left her front.

Bill was a genial man who was extremely handy about the house. He worked in a local factory and always arrived home after we children had finished tea. Payday was Friday and Bill handed over the unopened brown envelope. Nanny took out the cash, counted it, and gave him his weekly pocket money.

In those days, men knew their place. The rest, she kept for housekeeping.

Before and after eating, he was attached to a cigarette, held in calloused fingers stained brown with years of smoking. Despite his heavy smoking, Bill never had a day off work. He wore a boiler suit that was so stained with grime and dirt, its original colour had disappeared long ago. Before dinner, he had a bath, and then after eating left to join his mates at the pub, no doubt to wash his food down with a pint or two. I couldn't believe the colour of the bathtub after Bill's bath. He always seemed to return from the pub before Nanny went upstairs to bed. Most nights though, we never heard him return. By the time we got up in the mornings, Bill was at work and had probably already been there for a couple of hours.

We had fun living in Southmead. Olu and I loved the area and were glad that we had other children to play with in the street. The street was a cul-de-sac making it safe for us to play. We exuded innocence and enjoyed a lifestyle not possible on Blackboy Hill. Yinka, being much younger, did not join in playing with Maggie and us.

Olu and I had mixed emotions when our parents turned up to take us home. Life appeared great at that moment. Just as we got ready to leave, Nanny mentioned the fact that we had appeared hungrier on that visit and had eaten all her bread. A statement proffered without malice. It was true that we had eaten a huge amount the night before, but that was probably because we had worked up a healthy appetite by running around and expending energy. Father smiled, a smile I could tell from experience was not from the heart. He smiled without showing his teeth.

Goodbyes said, we thanked Bill and Nanny for their hospitality, and our family clambered into the Zephyr. The journey home was difficult. Father said that we had disgraced the family. How could we have eaten so much that it was noticeable? That was the first shot across our collective bows. Throughout the journey and his monologue, Mother did not say a single word. I pondered whether she was as scared of him as we were.

4

Life at home and at school continued in a routine fashion. Robert still drank my milk. We went for walks during which I was fascinated by nature including all kinds of birds. I couldn't name the different coloured birds that we came across, but I became mesmerised watching them fly high up in the sky. I wondered what it was like to fly and wished that I could too. How did they obtain food and did they have problems with their parents too?

We played games on the Downs, read comics, and watched television once back home. *Sunday Night at the London Palladium* was a favourite as was *The Black and White Minstrel Show*. Compared to all the blacks that I had seen previously, the black characters did not look quite right to me, but I could not work out what the problem was.

We loved listening to the radio playing songs by Cliff Richard, Gerry and the Pacemakers, Shirley Bassey who was from Tiger Bay, Cardiff with Olu's and my favourite being Millicent Small who sang *My Boy Lollipop*. Mother and

Father appeared to take reflected pride in the fact that Shirley Bassey had a connection with Nigeria in that though born in Wales to a white mother, she had a Nigerian father.

Just up the road from Harold Hockey's was a newsagent, located at the crossroads before the Downs. Olu and I visited this shop on many occasions, usually to return empty lemonade bottles. For two or three returned bottles, a three pence piece came back as our reward. The coin felt and looked heavy, with its multiple edges. Father did not appear to mind us going to the shop on our own. We sometimes wondered whether he did not realise or was too preoccupied with work. We decided on occasion to take comics in lieu of money. Our comic collection soon grew, and we even managed to do some swaps at school. Both Johns introduced me to philately. I enjoyed swapping stamps in the school playground. At that age, I was sufficiently aware to be proud of my Penny Blue.

I accompanied Mother to our local launderette on quite a few occasions. Once she felt that I was sensible enough, I was allowed to go on my own. I hung on so tightly to the money for the machines, and for buying the soap, that opening my hand on arrival hurt sometimes.

Olu and I often looked longingly at the toys in Woolworths near our house, despondent at the fact they would require quite a lot of empty lemonade bottles. As we thought we did not have many toys of our own, we decided to get some. The fact that we had no means of paying did not seem a major problem. I was aged ten, and with a brother of barely nine, we went into the store and helped ourselves to what we wanted. No sooner were we outside the store than my thoughts were intruded on, when without warning, I felt a firm hand on my shoulder. The touch was firm in a way that I knew made attempting to run a non-starter.

'Where do you boys live? Do you have a receipt for those toys?'

45

Olu's and my head moved in unison as if under the control of a puppeteer. Our eyes tracked the brightly coloured yellow tie upwards. Just above the knot was a stubbled chin, supporting a face completely devoid of humour. The jet-black eyebrows, arched in a way that they resembled the letter V for victims, pointed at us. Why wasn't Woolworths like some other shops, where you asked for things, which were then brought and handed to you?

Fortunately, Father was not there when the shop assistant took us home. Mother did not tell Father on his return. She had known Father longer than us, and had possibly worked out that there were times when she needed to save us from punishment. Being from a different type of family to his, she might also have realised that getting the authorities involved in family matters would not be appreciated by him. The stolen goods were returned, aided by some physical propulsion from Mother, and we apologised to the manager. That was the end of the matter and we never attempted to take things without paying again. Once we realised that we were not getting more toys, we stuck to playing with those we had, and reading comics acquired by returning empty bottles.

In November of 1962, we knew of friends who were allowed by their parents to build guys and stand in the street asking 'penny for the guy'. Olu and I understood the significance of Guy Fawkes Night, as school had discussed the gunpowder plot in history lessons. Both parents were out, so I decided to make some money. Telling Olu to make sure that he let me back in when I rang the doorbell, I ventured out into the cold and damp air to make our fortune.

Everything went so well by just saying 'penny for the guy' that I wished every month was November. It was a lot easier than hunting round for empty lemonade bottles. Furthermore, it was more lucrative. People willingly put money in the green plastic bucket I had borrowed without permission. At least, that was until a woman came along and demanded to see the guy. A slight problem lay in the fact that I did not have one anywhere. My looks must have assured every other donor in a way that failed with the security guard in Woolworths and this woman, who was not going to part with her money without a fight. I was just as determined that, having stopped to question me, I would try very hard to answer her, aware that it was an impossible task. Her black-rimmed spectacles with their equally thick lenses did not prevent the invisible rays from her fixed look from unnerving me slightly. However, I determined not to be beaten.

'Where... is... the... guy?' she repeated pausing between each word.

'Just on the other side of the hill,' I replied in a voice full of conviction.

'Show me,' she said, calling my bluff.

I had never until then played poker, but double bluffed by inviting her to come and see it.

'As we had only one guy between us, my brother and I decided to split up and ask for money for the shared guy.'

This was the explanation I offered as we walked up Blackboy Hill together past our front door. At the top of the hill, I began shouting for my brother.

'Mike, Mike,' I called out. The spectacled one was right behind, looking from left to right and all around. If anyone named Mike had acknowledged the calls, I do not know who would have been more surprised. I knew my brother was at home, and he definitely was not called Mike. After a few fruitless minutes, we had both had enough, looked at each other, and declared an unspoken truce.

'I told him not to move from here,' I said, still pretending to search.

'No guy, no money,' she said, and turned on her heel to leave. I watched as she appeared to shrink walking down the hill. The last thing to disappear was her bright blue headscarf, oscillating from side to side.

The spectacled one notwithstanding, we thoroughly enjoyed counting the takings under the bed sheets, aided by a flickering torch. We talked in low, hushed voices to prevent Father and Mother from hearing downstairs. Total takings for the evening came to just under two guineas. I loved the word guineas, having first come across them on finding out the cost of my elocution lessons. In those days, I had trouble pronouncing words that began with the letter 'o'; I always put the letter 'h' in front of them even though the written words lacked this extra prefix. My parents, for reasons unknown to me, felt that proper diction was important and paid for lessons. Even at that age, I appreciated the financial sacrifice. I could have paid for a lesson or two with my share of the takings. However, thanks to Guy, we had no trouble getting a decent supply of comics and sweets for the next few weeks.

The winter of 1962 came soon enough and despite being prepared for the cold, it seemed to penetrate to our bones as if we had no clothes on. Our matching pyjamas stood no chance against the temperature in that attic. Keeping our feet warm involved wearing socks to bed. Olu sometimes wore two pairs. It took a while to stop shivering once in bed. The hot water bottles did make a difference, but only just. Olu and I made sure we emptied our bladders before getting into bed as getting up in the middle of the night to use the toilet was plain foolhardy. Going down the stairs to the toilet on the landing was not easy in the darkness either. Regardless of whether we got up in the night or not, both hot water bottles laid discarded on the floor in the morning like something shed during an animal's moulting process.

We avoided having a bath or shower most mornings. The usual order of things involved a tepid bath using a flannel. Wearing many layers of clothing reduced the effects of the cold once we left the house. After breakfast, we went to school, hands and neck completely covered. Trusted with finding our own way to St John's Primary School, we never got lost.

Playing in the school playground was difficult in the snow and ice. All the children had steam-like air coming out of their mouths and nostrils while talking and breathing. I remained intrigued despite knowing the reason.

Olu and I were afraid of the snow as we thought that we could just sink into it and never be seen again. Olu's thought on this possibility made me smile when he said that there shouldn't be too much trouble finding us because of the contrast in colours. Both parents seemed less bothered possibly because they had travelled to England regularly since 1949 as students in Norwich and London.

I even managed to fall in love with one of my fellow students. She was, in my eyes, very beautiful. She had red hair, freckles, and looked great in her grey socks with black shoes. Her pleated skirt matched the colour of her socks. Our paths first crossed properly when she stood up for me against Robert. I had handed over the bottle of milk to prevent getting squashed but had apparently done it slower than Robert would have liked.

Janet possessed a bubbly character and an infectious happiness. No matter how bad anyone felt, whenever she was in a group, there were no long faces. She was about the same height as me. I fell in love but in truth had no idea what the word meant. All I knew was that she was great fun, and looked pretty with it. One day I bought her a present from Woolworths, which, on receiving it, made her give out a sound of genuine delight.

Her freckled face beneath the red fringe appeared even prettier. When she hugged me in thanks, I stood with arms hanging limp by my sides as if they were broken clock hands stuck at the half-past-six position. This was more than I expected after buying a copy of *Bunty*. After she had let go, I stood rooted to the spot, blinking in utter disbelief. If that was the reward for buying her favourite comic, maybe next time I should buy a month's supply, or an annual. Eventually, feeling and movement returned to my limbs after another friend ran past, giving me a playful tap on the back. I could hardly concentrate on anything in class for the rest of that day.

As I had a good singing voice, some of my fellow students and I got picked to go to the BBC studios not far from our house. The television station was doing a recording. It pleased me that Janet was also in the choir. The broadcast was in black and white, and it amused me greatly to see myself on television. The episode led to my joining the choir at Bristol Cathedral. I remember wearing what I used to call a dress, which possessed a neck resembling something that Francis Drake might have worn. For the remainder of my time at that school, I felt a bond with Janet, despite having no real clue what she thought of me.

I had been trusted to go alone to the launderette with the family's washing. Fortunately, I managed to retain the instructions from Mother as they were not repeated or written down. One Saturday morning I went to do the washing alone as usual, as Olu was never allowed to go with me. Having completed the tasks successfully, I folded the clothes carefully and put them in a now clean pillowcase that we usually used to ferry the clothes to and from the launderette. I left the launderette, turned left and began the slow climb towards home with the pillow slung over a shoulder. I walked past Woolworths, Apsley Road, and was about one hundred yards or so from home, when I became aware of a woman's voice.

'Excuse me, young boy,' said a woman sitting in a car that was being driven at a pace attempting to match my walking speed.

As I could not hear what else she said, I stopped. She motioned me closer to the van. It resembled a VW camper, the ones with a compartment in the front for driver and front passengers, and a sliding door on the left side so that pavements were easily accessible. The fading yellow colour, interspersed with the brown of rusting stood out to me. This woman was now leaning almost out of the car, her left hand held firmly to the vehicle - should her grip have slipped, she would no doubt have fallen.

'What is your name?' she asked.

'Sola,' I replied, as I observed the matted and dry-looking hair, and the gap in the row of upper teeth that her top lip failed to cover. She tried not to smile and I only saw her remaining teeth when she spoke.

'That's right, Sola,' she echoed while totally failing to get the accent right, her mouth appearing to drool as if she was about to eat her favourite meal.

'Would you like help with that pillowcase?'

Before I could figure out why someone I had assumed was about to ask for directions, was asking to help, she said, 'Your parents have asked us to bring you home.'

I looked at the man in the driving seat. He looked as if he had not shaved or washed for a long time. He did not say anything and kept both hands tightly on the steering wheel. His white knuckles contrasted with the pink of his hands. He stared straight ahead. He appeared oblivious to the conversation that his partner was holding. I looked back at her, and the outstretched right hand that was attempting to help me into the van. Inside the van, I could see what resembled bedding, camping gear and other detritus. As if a starting gun had been fired, my brain started computing and the result was recall of the sentence, 'You must never go anywhere with a stranger,' which both parents had instilled in us from the time they thought we could understand the message. These two people in the van were definitely strange.

At this point, my brain sent urgent one-way messages to my legs, and I began to run as fast as they would propel me. My head was lifted to an extent that I became aware of seeing the sunny and bright blue sky. I did not look back, passing familiar landmarks without noticing them, and arrived at the house panting, with my heart and head pounding in unison. Running up the hill was tiring, something I only became aware of once I reached home.

This experience brought to mind the signs we had seen in windows advertising vacancies for Bed & Breakfast. I remembered the sentiments expressed about blacks. From discussions with our mother, I was already aware that there were people out there who might not have our best intentions at heart.

With hands on my knees and bent almost double I explained to Mother, with my story punctuated by sharp intakes of breath, what had happened. She listened carefully before asking about the washing. Oh dear, I thought, I must have left it on the pavement in my haste to get away. When Mother and I returned about twenty minutes later, the pillowcase I had dropped was still on the pavement. I sometimes wondered in later years what would have become of me had I got into that van. This story would never have been told. My brother listened patiently as I related the incident to him repeatedly. He said that *he* would never ever get into a stranger's car. The experience did not put me off going to the launderette. The one change in me was that whenever I was alone on the streets, I made sure that my gaze was fixed firmly on the pavement. I avoided eye contact. My young mind came up with all types of scenarios that might have happened had I entered that van. We had seen news reports on the television about children who went missing and were never seen again. Thinking about this was scary.

We loved living in Bristol; Olu and I just could not get enough of the Downs. We also enjoyed going to visit the Roman baths in Bath on school daytrips. The impressive expanse of the Downs allowed games to be played there. We played cricket there once, having gone with the school. The game looked so easy that I felt I could bat all day if given the chance. I never forgot the first ball I ever faced. It came down at quite a respectable speed. I watched it all the way and was still watching as it travelled up the bat, straight into my face. I was very lucky not to lose any teeth. My once-white top changed colour rapidly as my lips swelled to a size I would not have thought possible and bled onto it. That was my first and last serious attempt at cricket. I listened to all the tips that followed advising me on how to avoid a similar fate in the future. I did not fully assimilate them. My mistake apparently, was to have the bat angled upwards instead of downwards. This made it easier for the ball to rise and give me an unwanted kiss.

On getting home, I must have looked awful because both parents expressed sympathy.

Sometimes, while our parents were busy doing something important, we visited Southmead and were looked after by Bill and his wife. Nanny was surprised to notice how much less we ate, frequently asking whether we were hungry. We always replied that we had had enough to eat, trying very hard not to torture ourselves by looking at the inviting spread on the blue-and-red chequered tablecloth. Those times were difficult as the hunger was real, having expended a lot of energy running around.

Bill and Nanny took all four of us to the seaside when the weather allowed. Yinka and Maggie just loved splashing around at the water's edge. We boys couldn't get enough of the beach at Weston-super-Mare. We and Maggie, when she was not in the water, ran around all day, stopping only to have ice cream and eat the picnic that Nanny had prepared.

We enjoyed building sandcastles, and singing loudly at the top of our voices, oblivious to the many gazes directed our way. Cliff Richard's 'Summer Holiday' was a favourite. We had no problem getting off to sleep following such hectic days. We treasured these days out, as they rarely happened with Father and Mother. He had been her first and only boyfriend, and possibly from a lack of experience, she felt unsure how to behave towards him. She and her parents could not contemplate the relationship not working out. Besides, from what little that I could glean from an overheard conversation, it was not a planned wedding. In retrospect, I am certain that Mother, a few months into her twentieth year on her wedding day was afraid of him and possibly treated the relationship like an egg and spoon race, except that she was not in it to win it. That egg must not be allowed to fall off that spoon, no matter what.

Father worked hard because he had returned to England for post graduate qualifications. Even I could understand that. What Olu and I could not understand was why the family lacked many relaxing moments together. If not for school and visiting Southmead, there would have been little reason to leave the house as a family. We only ever went to the cinema once in the two years we were in Bristol. We saw a Saturday matinee of *The Pirates of Blood River*. Certain scenes frightened me so much that they forced me to shut my eyes tightly. I had a few weeks of bad dreams before my nights reverted to normal. We don't know how or why we were able to see a film, but it never happened again in England.

Apart from the escapade at Woolworths, attempting to shop with no money, I rarely got into trouble at school or at home. Of course, like many youngsters, we did the occasional naughty thing, but nothing serious. Olu and I never had fights, especially as he always avoided confrontation. No fights with anyone at school, and no trouble with any form of authority. We had to learn by exploring our surroundings, find the boundaries, so as to know the limits of protective safety nets. Some of our friends crossed beyond acceptable boundaries and required discipline. I learnt from friends of their being banished to their room or having things they loved confiscated for a short period of time. We longed to be like other children, able to act with our parents the way we noticed them doing at going home time. They couldn't wait to tell them what sort of day they'd had and we did our best to emulate them. I studied hard and did well at school. Olu progressed well too.

Christmas of 1962 came and went, devoid of any kind of what I thought of as a proper celebration, apart from a stocking hanging on a door handle with a few toys inside as the equivalent. I do not recall any special meal or acknowledgement of the festivities. Upon talking to them, I realised that my schoolmates had totally different experiences. January came and it was back to routine; going to school, coming home and finding things to do for amusement.

Before long, it was time for me to sit an exam called the 11-plus. I had an idea from some of my teachers that this exam was critical for the future of those taking it. This importance was completely lost on me. The school prepared eligible children including me, for the exam by teaching us the sort of things that we needed to know. It was important that English and arithmetic were well studied. History, especially English history, was important too. Revision as such was not something that I did much of for the exam. It made sense to me that people had exams in things they had been taught. I looked forward to the examination, as I loved being tested at school. In no time, the exams were upon all of us. Fortunately, I found that the questions barely stretched me and I ended up quite pleased with my efforts. When the exam ended, I had to wait like everyone else for the results. They would come via the school.

We continued to visit the Downs for walks and running around aimlessly. These visits coincided with spending more time at home with Mother. Olu and I played rounders with other children, but I studiously avoided cricket. We flew kites, which had been cut out from shapes in various comics. Those were carefree days. Such expenditure of energy went quite a way towards ensuring that we slept well at night. Olu and I often talked about our brothers in Nigeria. We imagined what they might be getting up to at any particular time of day. We never had a chance to correspond with them in any way. At least we managed to see Yinka now and then, but I failed, for some reason, to develop a sibling relationship with her like I had with Olu.

Our days at home consisted of reading, playing and watching television. School was an added extra, something we loved doing.

'Sola,' Mother called out after school one day.

'Yes,' I answered with my eyes darting from side to side like an overworked pendulum in anticipation of getting told off. I racked my brains to try and recall a misdemeanour.

'You are a good boy,' she said, her lower face completely bisected by a wide grin. I never realised that lips possessed such degree of flexibility.

I exhaled gently through my mouth and nostrils more or less simultaneously, happy in the knowledge that no problem was forthcoming.

'You've done it,' she went on. The lack of expression on my face must have told her something, as she went on to explain.

'You have passed the 11-plus.'

'Oh,' was all I could say in response. Why was she so happy that I had passed an exam that was not that difficult? Had I failed, then what? After conveying the good news by telephone to Father she looked quite pleased with me. Seeing how glad the news had made her, I began grinning. The twitching at the edges of my mouth as I grinned confirmed to me that my grin was not natural. I hoped that she did not notice.

Some of the exam questions had been, to me, ridiculously easy. When was the Magna Carta signed? What date was the Battle of Hastings? These and other questions had not caused any trouble at all. Some of the answers had been learnt, I told Mother, from reading comics. 'The Bash Street Kids' had Plug answering a question on the Battle of Hastings, for example.

'Do you know what this means?'

I shook my head slowly from side to side. All I knew was that it meant proceeding to the next stage in my education.

'You have a choice of grammar schools,' she explained. As she was still looking pleased, I deduced that going to grammar school must be a good thing. The alternative, which Mother explained, virtually decided future career paths and prospects, and that was to attend a secondary modern.

'We will sit down together and choose,' she said.

Since my geographical world only extended a short radius from the house, my input was going to be minimal. I was totally surprised by one piece of information though. Mother told me that as I had performed well in the exams, I was going to be awarded a fountain pen. That was the first prize I had ever won in a school.

All the children loved the last few weeks of school,

especially as lessons were few and far between. All my friends had passed the exam too, including English John and Italian John. I did not know how Robert got on, and there appeared to be no one brave enough to ask. Janet had also passed, but it was sad to realise that we would all be going in different directions. Life at that time seemed to me like different passengers getting on a bus, and as each person reached their destination and got off, few looked back at the remaining passengers.

Mother had helped me choose possible grammar schools to visit, and after visiting a few, we had both agreed that Brislington Grammar School was the one. The last day of term at primary school was an odd affair. Most of us felt upset at the fact that some might never meet again. I wrote down the telephone numbers and addresses of the two Johns. Shyness prevented me from asking Janet for her details.

During the summer holidays, I travelled on buses with Mother to familiarise myself with the route and the correct fares.

Mother still had her part-time job at the railways, meaning she could not accompany me to school on a regular basis. Getting to Brislington Grammar School involved taking two buses, one of which was the number 1A. Getting to the first stop was easy, as this was visible from the parlour window. Despite having to change buses on the journey, I managed never to get lost completely in all my time at the school. The bus conductor in his or her uniform and cap soon came to recognise me, and they were very friendly. I loved sitting on the upper deck of the buses and enjoyed the vantage point that allowed me to see and notice things not visible from lower down.

Brislington Grammar School was a long bus ride from home; it especially felt like that in the autumn. It was one thing going when we had longer daylight, but quite a different matter in the dark. Peering through bus windows covered in condensation in order to see my stop was not easy. On a couple of occasions, I did miss the stop by one, and had to retrace my steps, but it wasn't that far. Going to school was made more enjoyable by the fact that very near the school was an ice-cream factory. After school, some of the favoured students were given ice lollies and other cold treats by an Italian who worked at the factory. I wondered, but never dared ask, if he was related to John. The end of the day worked out well in that there was time to visit the factory, eat the offered ice cream and still make the bus.

The students at school were all allocated to 'houses'. I became a member of Blackwell House. The uniform made me proud, with its smart cap and the black, yellow and green striped scarf. I still wear the scarf almost sixty years later. People noticed me, giving me a sense of satisfaction, especially as I was the only black student at Brislington. Passing the exam was a good thing all told.

My schoolwork was very good and I got good grades in all assessments in my time there. I could not have been happier. The not-so-good times from my past had more or less been crowded out by the current experiences. My form tutor encouraged me and told me that he had no doubt I would fulfil my potential. 'Fulfilling my potential' was such a good phrase that I resolved to do all I could to ensure it came true. I interpreted it as meaning that not only would I fill it, but it would also be completely full.

I devoured novels at a rate that would make anybody think they were about to be officially banned. I could not get enough of Biggles, Tarzan and almost any Enid Blyton. The Famous Five became heroes; I loved reading about all the escapades of the young boys and girls. I had a soft spot for Ian Fleming, and in time managed to collect all the James Bond books written by him, including *Colonel Sun*, which was completed by a ghostwriter after his death.

Grammar school was great and I loved acting the grown-up. I could do up my school tie without help. There was no Robert to terrorise me, but on the downside, there was no Janet either. I enjoyed the academic side of things as well as taking part in the various sports on the nearby school field. I tried most sports and loved doing so.

I loved playing football for the House, my favourite position was on the wing wearing number 7. Even though I was nowhere near being the best player in the team, I managed to score the occasional goal. I showed a lot of enthusiasm. I most likely burnt off more energy than my teammates as I wanted to be involved in every move. The scars on both legs testified to my tenacity and eagerness. I was temporarily upset one day when I overheard the coach telling someone that I had only played as there was nobody else available.

Father continued with his work and seemed to be doing well from what Olu and I could see. Our young minds did not realise how difficult it must have been to study simultaneously for the Doctor of Medicine (MD), Membership of the Royal College of Physicians (MRCP) and Diploma in Tropical Medicine and Hygiene (DTM&H). Father had returned to his alma mater for the Doctorate, but had to go to Edinburgh for the Membership, and Liverpool for the Diploma.

He was a clever man and Mother was hopeful that he would obtain all three qualifications before returning to Nigeria. To us, he was a peripheral figure whom we did not miss in the way some children might miss a parent.

Olu and I were always inquisitive and this led us one day to decide to discover how a watch worked. Taking the watch apart was very easy; reassembling it proved to be more problematic. After what seemed an age, we decided that we had succeeded in putting it back together, and replaced it on the table. Something told us that things were not quite right, but as it looked just the way it had prior to our intervention, we felt shakily confident. Our confidence was not built on a solid foundation.

A couple of hours later, we peeked at the watch and to our combined horror, time had stood still! Fate was against us, as the next day the family had to travel to Edinburgh and the watch was to be an integral part of the exams Father would be taking there. Father hardly ever wore a watch, a factor that had allowed us easy access to it. We watched in the morning as he put the watch on his wrist without checking the time. The cases were packed and placed in the boot of the white Zephyr. Olu and I sat in the back, with me on the left side behind Mother. The journey to Edinburgh seemed to take a very long time. Boredom came quickly and easily to us boys as there was little to do. I could not even attempt reading as I developed a feeling of nausea quite quickly, leading to an irresistible urge to vomit.

I sensed trouble when in my peripheral field of vision, I saw Father shaking his left wrist and placing his watch to his ear. I felt almost sick watching the rhythmic movements, as my gaze followed the oscillation of wrist to left ear and back. Shake, look and listen, but I knew that no amount of coaxing was going to get that watch working.

'Have you children touched this watch?'

'Yes,' we chorused without hesitation.

'Why?' he asked, looking back at me over his left shoulder. At that moment, it flashed through my mind that I had chosen the wrong seat.

Why? I asked myself. Children sometimes did things for reasons that adults couldn't understand. Had he forgotten some things that he might have done when younger? I realised that no answer was ever going to be sufficient. Looking at the large rearview mirror, I could see the whites of Father's eyes had suddenly turned a pinkish shade of red, and the usual gap between the iris and the eyelids increased, resembling an odd type of fried egg. I wished that he would keep his eyes on the road. He then said the watch was to act as a timer during the exams, so that he could allocate the time evenly.

'Sorry,' I said in a very quiet whisper, to be rapidly copied by my brother in an even quieter tone.

'Sorry, is that all you can say?' came the shouted retort in a tone and decibel many orders of magnitude greater than ours. The car weaved from side to side as we drove. Attempting to drive while looking back and shouting did not appear safe to me.

'Look out,' Mother shouted suddenly. She had noticed that we were just about to hit the car in front. Father slammed the brakes on and everyone was thrown forward. The backs of the front seats prevented Olu and me from joining them in the front.

That car journey was not enjoyable as we were constantly reminded of how bad we were. This was the second shot across our bows, and again, it took place in the car. Apart from being prone to travel sickness, I also had a small bladder which seemed to respond to stress by becoming smaller still. I was so afraid after the explosion from Father that I could not ask to stop for a toilet break. I sat with legs tightly crossed and hoped that Edinburgh would arrive soon.

5

Some weeks later, a letter arrived informing Father that he had passed and could now write MRCP after his name. He seemed happy enough and the family felt pleased for him too. Things do come in threes, because the DTM&H diploma arrived from Liverpool, and after a viva voce, words that meant nothing to Olu and me at the time, the Doctor of Medicine was awarded for his thesis on duodenal ulcers.

Despite having successfully completed what he came to England for, he still worked hard in the laboratory. Circumstances dictated when and how often we saw him. In my quieter moments, I was glad at the way things worked out and did not lose sleep over the lack of more contact. We came home with muddied faces and cheeks, holes in the knees of our trousers and, depending on the weather, there might be muddy footprints all the way up the carpeted stairs. Sandwiches and broken wristwatch apart, we hardly ever got in trouble, especially with Father. He treated us three children equally, with Yinka as the only girl just shading it.

Never being part of any discussions involving us, Mother called us to the parlour one afternoon after school and sat us down.

'We will be going back to Nigeria at the end of the year.'

I felt like an outsider, banished to the periphery. It was like being a kite at the whim of the wind and the guy holding the ends of the string.

'Aren't you happy?' she asked, noticing the lack of emotion on our faces.

'I suppose so,' I replied, my facial expression at odds with my statement.

Later on, when we were alone, I asked Olu what he thought about the prospect. He shrugged his shoulders in resignation, punctuated by a deep sigh.

'I am going to miss my new friends from school,' I said, focusing on nothing in particular. I sighed long and hard as well. The decision meant that I would be collecting more names and addresses.

Within a few weeks, the house was filling up with brown tea chests and we gradually began to pack our belongings. We often overheard Mother and Father talking about the upcoming trip. They planned to send the majority of the luggage ahead by sea, with the family following later on in another boat – a liner. That thought excited us, as we had never been on a boat of any type before, and we were at an age where we could appreciate the experience. We felt torn between looking forward to the experience of travelling on a liner and being sad at leaving our friends.

We kept catching our fingers on the sharp metallic bits of the chests. This limited the amount of help we could give. As each box was filled, it was sealed and large name and address tags were stuck on, then it was placed in a corner ready for collection. We could see that the chests were destined for

Ibadan, which made for animated chats in the privacy of our bedroom as this meant we would soon be reunited with Bode and Adebo. We were returning to the town that held minimal fond memories. The address on the labels said University of Ibadan.

Olu and I found it difficult saying goodbye to our friends in anticipation of our leaving. We had no idea when we would be leaving England. I thought it must be easier for Olu as, being quieter he had made fewer friends. Some friends repeatedly asked me how much longer before our leaving.

Everyone resolved to write regularly like penfriends, except the chances of exchanging visits would be remote. Every day became like those counting down to Christmas or a birthday as we anticipated the trip. Our joy, on occasions, was tempered by the thought of no longer seeing people we had come to know and like. Being late in the year, days appeared to go by rapidly, just like the blurred trees we saw from the car when driving down a country road. The weather had started to turn colder. Mother had given us Christmas stockings the year before, and we assumed this year would be just as much fun in that respect.

Back in the real world, the new term progressed and the weather, unrestrained by time, marched on in its purposeful manner ensuring that I needed to peer harder out of the bus windows to make sure I didn't miss my stop. Just as I was getting used to recognising landmarks in the winter to help spot where I should change buses, Mother announced suddenly that we were leaving for Nigeria sometime in the middle of December.

When Father informed us Lagos was our destination we were confused. He explained that the ship docked there, and we would then travel by road to Ibadan. The information came across in a curt manner. I sensed something but could not identify it. At half term, we managed to get addresses from some friends, and, for me especially, the most important involved getting up-to-date addresses for Italian and English Johns. I still could not bring myself to ask Janet for her address.

Mother told us that we would be travelling from Bristol to Liverpool, to get on the ship that would take us home. We soon noticed that conversations in the household, by then, had become one-way affairs. Something made us feel that we could not ask too many questions. Olu and I were getting good at understanding a new language, one that was transmitted mainly by looks.

I felt sad on my last day at school, realising that I would probably never see any of these guys again. I managed somehow to fight off the tears, at least until I was safely on the bus home for the final time. A woman in a matching green hat, coat and dress sitting nearby asked me what the problem was. I replied that there was no problem, hurriedly wiping away tears with the sleeve of my blazer.

That blazer was never going to be worn again. No more football for Blackwell House either. No more questions about whether the man on jars of *Robertson's* jam was a relative. No more sitting on the polished floor in the gym for morning assemblies, listening to Johann Sebastian Bach's *Jesu, Joy of Man's Desiring* or Beethoven's *Für Elise* while waiting for the headmaster to arrive. No more free lollies either. I found that moment extremely difficult.

The family visited Southmead for the final time, to collect Yinka. She did not seem to feel the same way as Olu and me. At the age of four, this was to be expected, and it seemed that she stayed happy so long as someone looked after her.

We all said goodbye to Bill, his wife and Maggie. Father was matter-of-fact in his behaviour and shook hands with

Bill and Nanny. Olu and I managed to resist the offer of something to eat.

Back home, Olu and I perched on a shared chair looking out of the window as Father sold the Zephyr to one lucky person. The car had never given us any problem in the two years that we had travelled in it. When he came back upstairs, he asked us to come away from the window. The tone of voice told us that the quicker this order was obeyed, the better.

The train journey to Liverpool left no concrete memories. We arrived at the docks in the middle of the morning. Thick coats, gloves and scarves covered all available space on Olu and me. The gloves failed miserably in their function. Everybody I saw was wrapped up warm against the biting cold wind. Most of the coats and gloves people wore were dark in colour, mirroring the miserable weather.

Father and Mother dealt with paperwork while we marvelled at the sight of the ship. On its side was written *Aureol*. Olu and I could not get over the size of this vessel. It was white and had a bright yellow funnel. Soon, all the passengers embarked as names were called out in alphabetical order, and the Amure family was shown to our cabins. Olu and I shared a cabin, with Father, Mother and Yinka in an adjoining one.

Before the ship had even set sail, our excitement, like an unseen battery, boosted our energy levels. There seemed so much to explore. We visited the dining room, the library, the shop and other places of interest. We could not work out how the water in the swimming pool had got there. Olu suggested that it must have taken a very long time ferrying buckets of water. The narrow corridors were lit by a luminance that always appeared as if it was living on borrowed time.

On meeting another passenger in the corridor, both people had to slow down. Olu and I soon slowed down to a crawl after being told off for running by a total stranger. He spoke to us in a manner that suggested we had better comply. He was dressed smartly in a black suit and a blue tie. He had a brown hat on. Heads bowed at being admonished, I could see my blurred reflection in the stranger's shiny black shoes.

The smell of disinfectant hung in the air. Someone appeared to have been a little liberal with the cleaning fluid. Our cabin was small but appeared cosy. What was more, it was much warmer than the attic. We had bunk beds and a small sink in the corner. I commandeered the top bunk and got it without a fight. Olu did not argue, and just placed his gloves and scarf on the lower bunk.

The ship's toilet had no window just like Kola's and Grandfather's toilets.

The first time we ate in the dining room, there was so much food that Olu's and my eyes almost popped. Our family shared a table, with the food laid out on a nearby long table covered by a white cotton tablecloth. All passengers served themselves from this table. My first visit was tentative in the extreme, until a steward told me that I could have as much as I wanted and could keep going back. After looking at Father's features to make sure that no message was forthcoming and that the roof was not going to fall in, I soon got the hang of things. I can't remember how big the dining room was, but there seemed to be many people present whenever we went.

Olu and I did manage to explore the ship, especially as Mother realised that, short of going overboard, getting lost would be difficult. Our love of reading took us to the library, a place that Father never minded us visiting, and we enjoyed standing on the upper deck, despite seeing nothing but water most of the time. The cold wind forced us to view the world through partially closed eyes. The ship stopped off at various ports, and passengers were allowed off the ship to explore inland. We kept worrying about the fact that the ship would sail without those who had ventured ashore, so we stayed on board. My favourite stop was Las Palmas, where Olu and I looked through the ship's railings to marvel at what went on nearby. Seasoned travellers threw coins over the side and we watched in utter amazement as children, mainly boys not much older than us, dived in after the money. They had nothing but shorts on and disappeared for what seemed an age. Once the heads broke the surface of the water, the boys held up the coins as if to say 'Look, we found them!' Their beaming faces with huge smiles reflected both satisfaction and delight. As the ship sailed south towards Africa, the weather got warmer; and passengers wore clothes more in keeping.

The journey was great and we resolved to remember as much of it as possible. We looked forward to Christmas, as it was going to be spent at sea.

'How many people who are not sailors do you think spend Christmas at sea?' I asked Olu.

'I don't know,' he said with a furrowed brow.

I did not really expect a response.

Olu and I, like most children, wanted to explore and discover things, and one day we ventured further afield. We wanted to go beyond our sector, and we did. Not knowing our way around unfamiliar territory rapidly became a problem, and we got lost. Olu became concerned, but I knew that getting truly lost on a ship was impossible.

By the time a steward returned us to our cabin, time had moved forward a couple of hours. As we approached the cabins, I noticed the streak of light on the passageway carpet and realised that our parents' door was ajar. I knew at that point that there was no way that we could easily sneak back into our cabin without being seen. On hearing our voices, Father came to the door, asking all sorts of questions. By the time the next question in a rapid sequence came out, the previous one stood in a queue in my brain waiting to be assimilated, never mind getting answered. The main question appeared to be asking where we had been. Since we had got lost, we could not tell him.

'We got lost,' I answered in mitigation.

'Who said that you could go out?' he asked. The telltale sign of the whites of his eyes changing colour due to increased blood flow caused me to sense trouble coming our way.

'No-no-body,' I replied, stammering. I sensed things had got to a worrying stage, as I did not usually stammer. I glanced past Father's arms and caught a glimpse of Mother standing behind him and shaking her head from side to side. Any form of support would not be coming from that quarter.

'Nobody!' Father repeated, to my total and silent discomfiture. I almost closed my eyes, as his right index finger was pointedly jabbed inches from my face.

'You are both staying in your cabin tomorrow night as a punishment.'

Tomorrow night? Why not punish us tonight? I thought.

Anyway, why punish us in that manner at all? Then it suddenly dawned on me in a way similar to suddenly solving an easy crossword clue. It just so happened that the day of our escapade was Christmas Eve, and the next night was to include a party for the children, with games, Father Christmas and giving out presents. Our punishment was to miss the Christmas dinner and party. We were learning that away from England and its laws, things were going to be different. We were returning to an environment where neighbours minded their business, and children were treated like possessions. I recalled the treatment I endured at the hands of Kola.

After dinner that night, I apologised to Olu for dragging him out and causing him to miss the Christmas dinner and party. It took me a long time to get to sleep. Punishment was one thing, but forcing someone to miss their food was on a different level. We would just make sure that we stuffed ourselves at the lunch table the next day.

The following evening Father and Mother locked their cabin door and left with Yinka. I half expected us to be called for dinner too. About an hour later, Mother, to her credit, came to make sure that we were fine. She did not bring any food for us. Being punished in such a manner was to stay in my mind forever. I hoped that this was not a foretaste of our future life. We had been in trouble for eating too many sandwiches, breaking the wristwatch and going for a wander on a ship. Surely, it couldn't get worse, could it?

The next day, the few friends that we had made on the ship asked where we had been the night of the party, and as far as I could recall, I told my first meaningful lie as opposed to a bluff. I said that we had felt queasy and had not been up to it. Lying did not come easily, and I felt extremely bad.

I had an urge to go after those children and tell them the real reason, but did not think that would have gone down well. Some things were best kept in the family. Unlike the psychological hurt, the feelings of disappointment from not attending the Christmas dinner party would soon fade.

Arriving at Freetown in Sierra Leone was a memorable moment. We were not allowed to leave the ship, which ensured we hung onto the railings watching youngsters no older than us, diving into the water to retrieve money thrown from the ship. Having seen this sort of thing in Las Palmas, I asked Mother about the children.

'Some of them have to do this sort of thing to earn money,' she explained.

'You mean like pocket money?' I asked.

'No, they are sometimes the ones earning enough money to feed their families.'

Serious poverty was not something that Olu and I had seen close up, having been fortunate enough to have been born into a family possessing a decent income and lifestyle.

'Those children have no choice but to do what they do, or else they might not survive,' Mother explained.

Olu and I went quiet as we digested this information. I could not understand why the children all seemed happy, possessing wide grins as they went about their business. The memory of the diving boys stayed with me for the rest of the journey as I tried to figure out how they could stay underwater for so long.

One bright sunny morning, I spotted land from the breakfast table. Not long afterwards, I knew the ship had arrived in Nigeria as I could see the sign that said Ports Authority, Lagos. For a while, I wondered whether Grandfather Thomas would be there to meet us. I wasn't surprised to find that he was not there. After all, we hardly contacted him or Grandmother Toyin while in England. Getting off the ship was a bustle, and it was sad to leave what had been our home for the past couple of weeks. Looking back from the quayside, the liner appeared larger than it had done in Liverpool. My mind retraced the places the ship had visited and I recalled nothing but fondness, the odd hiccup notwithstanding.

A man that Olu and I did not know met us at the docks. He said he would be driving us to Ibadan. Thanks to Grandfather's position in the community, he could have been another relative. This person, dressed in multicoloured flowing Nigerian clothes and wearing sandals covered in brown dust, took our family to a waiting car. I was struck by the amount of hustle and bustle going on at the quayside. Merchants were selling almost anything that a person could need. There were many different colours compared to England that I felt calm and optimistic.

The journey to the new house in Ibadan took a couple of hours. The heat was in complete contrast to the cold of England. I was sweating without having done anything strenuous. I never sweated in this way back in Bristol. The car's interior was even hotter on the journey. I kept imagining what it must feel like to be a chicken in an oven. Father sat in front next to the driver, with Yinka on his lap. Mother, Olu and I sat in the back. The identity of the driver remained a mystery despite my listening carefully for any clues.

There did not appear to be the same orderly arrangement we saw in England, as people seemed to move in different directions at the same time, and a few appeared content to sit beneath trees doing nothing in particular. My brain had to readjust to seeing faces of a different hue to those it had been used to recently, and the background noise was louder than in England. People appeared to have an inclination to shout.

The women seemed to be doing more than the men. Some were carrying wares on their heads, with their hands free, while at the same time carrying a baby in a sort of hammock on their backs. The babies sat with their legs visible on either side of the woman, and each one was bound to its mother's back by material tied in such a way that held them in place. The women called out at intervals as they went along in an attempt to attract attention, and to tell people what they were selling. Those with wooden boxes, their goods visible through the glass sides, felt the need to shout just as loudly.

There was a lot more human activity in Lagos, as well as more brightly coloured clothing.

At our new home, we five children were reunited, and for the first few weeks, filled each other in on what life had been like in our respective locations.

Bode and Adebo appeared to have had a great time. We four boys did not dwell on the fact that we had not spoken to each other in two years. Olu and I said that our time in England had not been too bad either.

When the two of us had a chance to be alone, Bode asked me if living in England had been as good as we said.

'When we first met you, you did not look that happy,' said Bode.

'England went fine, but … I think we are in deep trouble,' I replied. He seemed to be studying my facial appearance. He must have noticed something because he probed for more information. His eyes narrowed as he looked at me as if seeking clues.

'We both got lost on the ship and got punished by being prevented from eating Christmas dinner.'

A few weeks short of his eighth birthday, Bode nodded slowly and screwed up his eyes even narrower. I wondered whether he could still see out of them.

The new house was set back from a main road, with reasonably sized gardens at the front and back. We children appreciated the fact that there was enough space to run around and play, safe from the hazards of the road. A door led from the sitting room to a fair-sized kitchen which in turn opened out to a large back garden. At the back of the kitchen was a raised area with cement flooring, where the houseboys and girls sometimes sat. The boys' quarters were nearby.

I never knew why they were called boys' quarters when females lived there too. There was a houseboy, a housegirl, a gardener and a driver. The latter two did not live in the quarters but went home, and arrived early in the mornings. The houses of the well-heeled had these quarters, with each building having two or three bedrooms. They all possessed a shower room and toilet, as well as a room that could be used as a kitchen.

In front of all these rooms ran a covered passageway or corridor where the staff could sit when they were not in their rooms or on duty. It also provided cover from the rain and sun, and if the rain was light, they stayed dry.

From the back garden, some offices could be seen towering over the thick boundary hedge; these buildings housed a government secretariat. A roundabout, which seemed huge, was also visible from upstairs. Back in the house, upstairs had four bedrooms. Our parents shared one room, Yinka had one to herself, and the four boys were two to a room sleeping on bunk beds. The house, despite its size actually felt small.

By the time Father started work at the local university hospital, he had got rid of the sideburns and was clean-shaven. My brothers and I thought it made him appear gentler and kinder. He always wore a suit and his Bristol university tie for work. Things went well until the day I managed to knock a wooden carving off a shelf. I looked at the numerous pieces on the wooden floor, realising that unlike the watch in Bristol, its demise was not in doubt. The stern telling off from Father indicated to me that things would be different to our experiences in England.

Our family lived at Awolowo Avenue for a couple of years before moving to another house on the university campus as Father gained promotion. Life appeared good for families in the professional world, as the people employed by us carried much of the weight of running a home. Their duties included washing, driving, shopping and cooking, through to looking after the children. I disliked the way some of these boys and girls were treated but was powerless to do anything about it. A particular act that really upset me involved the fact that someone might be called to fetch an item that was only a few feet away from the master. I felt that this was not right. If another person had less education, it did not warrant looking down on them. Some people ended up in a particular life situation owing to a lack of opportunity. It did not seem fair then to ill-treat them for something over which they possibly had little, if any, control.

To their credit, the employees never complained, but that did not excuse the way they were treated at times. They never wore shoes, and those who could afford slippers had to take them off on entering the house. Visitors on the other hand, when they came, were allowed to keep their shoes on. I found it difficult watching fellow humans being treated badly.

We children only wore shoes for school and church. Sometimes, unable to see every object on the ground, we managed to stand on nails or broken glass while out playing, which then left a trail of blood.

6

We all had to get used to starting yet another school, my fifth in almost twelve years. The International School was brilliant, run by British and American teachers. Every child attending came from relatively wealthy families, and it had a large number of children of diplomats. I enjoyed going every day; learning was fun, especially Latin, Logic and English Literature. I had great difficulty getting to grips with declension but managed to negotiate it successfully in the end. The school had great teachers and discipline was of the highest order – no one wanted to visit the headmaster's office.

The grounds covered a large area, with classrooms situated in a block at the end of a long, tree-lined drive. Located on the approach from the school entrance were tennis courts and volleyball courts, with a football field nearby. Situated around this central point stood the dormitories for boarders, with the tuck shop conveniently located on the ground floor. Round the corner from the tuck shop and behind the dormitories was a covered area. Stored here were many mattresses on which all the students were expected to lie after lunch for a siesta. I appreciated siesta as a respite from the unrelenting sun.

There were some concrete steps along the front of the dormitories, on which everyone sat each morning for school assembly. Beyond the steps opposite the dormitories were six music rooms equipped with pianos and other instruments a student might learn to play. Nearby stood the dining room with three sides open to the world. The dining room had tables with metal benches to sit on. Round the periphery, we had four water dispensing machines.

Sited well away from the classrooms, dormitories and sports areas, stood buildings in which the teachers lived. The houses looked fine; they had boys' quarters too. Each dwelling possessed a very neat garden at its front. I assumed the gardeners employed by the school maintained the beauty. The school had everything, and its students were the envy of those from other schools. I radiated a level of pride in letting everyone know I attended that school.

I excelled at school, scoring high marks in all subjects. My progress pleased my parents and it seemed that nothing could go wrong. Home life was very satisfactory and we were living life, as most of our friends did, without a major care in the world. Not being allowed friends to visit us at home did not present a problem. With five children in the family, we played amongst ourselves. Furthermore, the employed staff boosted our numbers and we involved them in the games we played on occasions. At least, everyone played together until we were advised by Mother not to cross the line between master and servant.

We became six children when another sister arrived, but our joy did not last long as she died. She did not even make it to her first birthday. My siblings and I knew she had died, but not one of us had any sort of explanation from either parent.

The fact is that she had some kind of illness and succumbed to it. I still do not know what happened after all these years.

Affection for school and home was in equal measure, just as it had been in England. Unknown to any of us children, especially me, things were about to change.

Being boisterous was part of growing up and we were no different from other children as far as we could tell. One day, I jumped through a window instead of coming through the door, leaving a footprint on the sill. After all, the goats and fellow students at St Luke's did it. No big deal you might think, but you would be wrong. When Father found out what I had done, I knew trouble was nearby just by observing his face. He did not ask me any questions, and being ignorant of what was coming, I remained standing in front of him with a blank expression. Then Father uttered the words that would become a feature of my life.

'Sundayyy!' Father called, loud enough that Sunday could not fail to hear. The houseboy duly appeared as if ethereal. He stood with his arms behind his back, barefoot, waiting for an order. Sunday was short and stocky, and whenever Mother called him, he always replied, 'Madam.' He never responded to Father in a similar way, he just appeared silently like a figure from deep fog. He had light skin, and sported a moustache. He looked to be about late twenties and you always knew when he had been in a room because he left a strong smell of body odour. Both armpits of his shirt possessed the familiar watermark caused by stale sweat.

'Sir?'

'Go and get me some whips,' he ordered in a calm but firm voice. I stood wondering what the heck was going on. Sunday dutifully went to comply, obviously aware of what was being asked of him.

'Take off your clothes,' ordered Father. My mind went into

action. What if someone came in while I was naked? Anyway, why should I be taking off my clothes? It seemed a very odd request. My mind refused to provide an answer, so I did as I was asked, especially since the tone of voice gave me few, if any, options. I left my underpants on, only to be told that they had to come off as well.

Many more questions engulfed my twelve-year-old brain as it rapidly became more confused. I could not believe the change in my circumstances in such a short space of time. I had lost any state of orderliness I possessed previously. During the process of attempting to find answers, and without warning, I felt a sharp, stinging slap on the side of my face. The force was such that it propelled me against the nearby solid wall, which stopped further movement. For the first time ever, I saw flashes of light as my head banged against the wall. The pain was terrible and there was nothing that I could do about it. I was rapidly getting the message, and undressed completely as fast as I could. By this time Sunday had reappeared clutching a bundle of freshly cut branches that bordered the garden. He had even managed to strip them of their leaves and smaller sprouting branches. I took in the smell of the freshly cut sticks. The first couple of lashes from Father merely tested the integrity of a whip, as he did not want them to snap prematurely. I obeyed without understanding. Could I be dreaming? This couldn't be real! Confusion, anger and sadness felt like heavy weights that somebody had transfused into my muscle fibres pinning me to the floor.

'Lie down on the stairs' he screamed. By this time I was totally confused about what was happening. My mind had gone as naked as my body. It was like my mind had a parallel entity, with one part trying to figure out whether this was a bad dream, and the other casting fearful wide eyes at the whips which must have numbered over a dozen. My eyelids became taut as they reached the limit of their possible excursion.

As I lay on the stairs getting a closer than usual look at the frayed carpet, the lashes came down onto my bare back. Some strokes seemed to hurt a hundred times more than others, as they struck already broken tissue. The beating went on until all the whips had been worn down to little more than stumps.

The rest of the family looked on in silence. No one attempted to intervene on my behalf. I kept hoping that a visitor would arrive and end my plight, but no one came. Those minutes contributed to making it the worst day of my life to date.

If I had committed murder, I thought, any punishment would have been deserved but this was different. After what must have been a quarter of an hour, the whips ran out. I gathered up my clothes and struggled painfully up the stairs. I lay on my bed, confused and all I could do was cry.

For the next few days, lying on my back was impossible, and just as the scabs were healing, something would happen that caused them to come off and bleed. This usually happened at times when I took off my top, not realising that the scabs had stuck to the clothing. For many weeks after, I could see the faint dark brown spots of blood on the wall leading up the stairs. Father never mentioned anything about the beating, and there was no explanation regarding why it was felt necessary to be so brutal for a minor act on my part. No matter how much I reflected on it, I failed to come up with a satisfactory explanation.

Apart from anything else, how could I modify my behaviour if there was no explanation regarding any punishment? True, I had climbed through a window, but I needed to be told what was so bad about it and why I should not do it again in the future. It was not as if I had hurt anyone. Against my natural instinct, I told some tall tales at school to explain why it hurt whenever someone tapped my back in a playful manner.

For some inexplicable reason, it was no longer good enough to obtain good grades, and I had to do better. Ideally, Father informed me, I should be in the top three of the year group at each assessment. Was this the same man with whom we had lived in Bristol? What had changed? There were no more exams taking his attention, although he did work hard at his job. He failed to come home in time for his meals sometimes. Did he feel more confident in Nigeria that he could get away with his behaviour? After all, the two countries differed in many ways.

Our lives as children became more difficult and we boys began to be really scared of him. He would punish us for no obvious reason. Yinka, the youngest, being the only girl, was spared and had no problems. I received most of the punishment being dished out because I was the eldest and someone had to be made an example of. The rationale was that if I behaved properly, my siblings would follow suit. I was not convinced about this. The few friends that we boys had could not visit us at home. They all soon learnt that the best time to visit was when both parents went out.

I used to be able to mentally remove myself from the present, and this ability returned full time. The beatings were so severe that the only way that I could survive them was to block things out mentally. I became so proficient that after the first couple of strokes, I was no longer present in spirit. I ran away from my physical being, leaving it to suffer alone.

Marrying up with the mental anguish came later. The body by then had no choice but to join me. Sometimes, I received a double dose of punishment in that following a beating, I was made to stoop, sometimes naked, in the corner of a room.

Whoever came up with the idea of stooping was clever. The

first few minutes did not present a problem, but as time went on, things became unbearable. The stoop involved standing on one leg, with the trunk flexed so that the index finger of the corresponding limb touched the floor. It did not look much, but after five or ten minutes the whole body began to wobble and shake in the manner of a rickety wooden bridge at the mercy of strong winds. This scenario was accompanied by the danger of falling over.

The whole point being that to fall was deemed a failure, which incurred further punishment. The only thing that I could do was to concentrate on the task in hand. Looking at the pool of sweat dripping off my forehead and onto the polished brown wooden floor in front of me served only as a kind of timepiece. I watched as the sweat disappeared slowly down the gaps in the interlaced floor coverings.

To make matters worse, I could not swat the flies buzzing round my exposed nether regions and face. Separating body and mind was no good under these conditions, as the prevention of tipping over required combined maximum concentration. This punishment was simple yet devastating.

It was very difficult knowing what to do to avoid being beaten as, sometimes, innocuous actions were reasons enough. One day during a family lunch, all I did was to look up. Our eyes met, which was enough to warrant a beating. I was accused of eavesdropping on the conversation that he was having with Mother!

'I don't understand what is happening,' said Bode one day. Bode had a handsome face, fronting a sharp intellect. I still tell him today, that he is the most intelligent of all of us.

'I don't understand it either,' I agreed, eyes still puffy from crying following another beating.

'Maybe you should try and behave. Don't do things that will get him upset,' Olu suggested. I looked at him and said nothing.

'No real father would treat his own child like that,' said Bode.

'Do you think we are not his real children?' Olu asked.

'Maybe we are adopted', I concluded after recollecting being farmed out to Kola and Grandfather James.

'That must be it,' said Bode, nodding, appearing to weigh up the chances of us all being adopted.

The more the beatings increased, the more I became determined to live as normal a life as possible. I must try to not offer opportunities that would anger Father. No amount of reflection on my part provided any answers regarding why my life was the way that it had become.

After Father got another promotion in mid-1965, our family got allocated a larger house on the university campus. The family moved to the new house and that was that. All the domestic help moved with us. The new house came with larger boys' quarters and garden. Mother's love of gardening was obvious as she kept the garden immaculate. Brightly coloured flowers grew in the beds. Mother's favourite flowers were her roses. She loved sniffing their scent. Vases with an array of beautiful flowers also adorned the inside of the house.

We boys shared rooms, as we had done previously. That move took us nearer to the school. My schoolwork had started to suffer and my grades were dropping from A's to B's and then to C's. School became both an escape and a chore. It got me away from home, but my performance there dictated the sort of home life that I had. Life started getting even more difficult.

Despite the numerous friends that we made at school, they were not encouraged to visit us at home, and only came round when they knew it was safe to do so. Some played the game according to whether they were friends at any given moment in time. Many times, I was forced to bribe fellow students with my pocket money to prevent them visiting the house. Father had this belief that anyone coming to your home, or telephoning, must be asking for the return of money owed or some other bad reason. Olu, Bode and I all assumed that his growing up in Grandfather's house in Lagos must have had a role to play in this erroneous supposition.

The engine sounds of all three cars became familiar, and we all recognized the noise that accompanied deceleration, ensuring that everyone disappeared in seconds. Play was more often than not outdoors, in case any telltale signs were accidentally left indoors. Anyway, it was easier to hear the cars when outside.

It was while living in this house that I received another serious beating, this time in the study. The study was off the dining room, with its entrance directly behind Father's chair at the dining table. The two doors to the study had angled horizontal wooden slats and opened inwards. The study's bookshelves looked impressive with many medical books and journals on them.

My crime? Father came home from work one day, and without warning asked a question on a topic that had not even been taught at school yet.

'What is Boyle's law?'

Never having heard of the guy, this was a difficult question. I could not answer it. His eyes went a salmony pink and I knew what was coming. However, he provided me with a possible chance of redemption. The chance came when he instructed that I learn all the laws in my chemistry textbook written by Holderness and Lambert. The slight problem was that all these laws, nine or ten in total, had to be learnt by the time he returned from work that evening.

Mother must have felt sorry for me as she continually asked whether I had memorised all the laws yet. I sat, furiously committing them to memory. To help, Mother held the book and asked me all these laws in order. Boyle's Law, Charles' Law, Dalton's Law of partial pressures, Gay-Lussac's principle and so on.

By the time she had asked me to recite these laws multiple times, I had become word-perfect and ready to shine in front of Father. I could recite all the laws perfectly, with no idea of what they meant. The learning was in isolation, as the class had not yet reached this stage of the book.

I had dinner while mumbling these laws over and over in my mind. I always ate very well but did not gain much weight. My brothers and I wore khaki trousers or shorts most of the time, as the material was deemed hardy. My legs, coming out of the bottoms, resembled a pair of brown pencils.

Those legs suddenly started shaking at a fine frequency, with my knees banging each other like silent cymbals, as I registered the car's engine and knew that the critical moment had arrived. Father came into the house without as much as a hello to anybody, and asked where I was. My heart began pounding, straining to escape its leash. My tongue went dry, feeling no more comfortable. I walked into the sitting room from the kitchen where I had just finished eating, and before I could gather my thoughts, out came the question.

'What is Boyle's law?'

'The vol-vol-ume of a given mass of ga-gas' and then I went blank. Further questions came, shouting out requests for answers to the other laws. By this time, if you had asked me my name, I most likely would have got that wrong too.

'Sundayyyy!' he screamed in a musical sort of way.

In an attempt to justify why I was being treated this way Father said that everything possible was going to be done to prevent me from turning bad. My paternal grandfather had several wives, with Father being the eldest of all the children.

He had been brought up this way and had convinced himself this was the reason he was successful. He did not consider the fact that children might be different as individuals.

We boys knew that he had it in him to be kind and gentle: all we had to do was look at our sister's treatment. We knew, from comparing our lives with our friends, that not all children were treated this way. Even those who were disciplined had a modicum of love interspersed with it. A little amount of love, like some salt sprinkled on food, makes things better.

The parlour, into which the front door opened, had wooden flooring with strategically placed mats around the place. The floor was so shiny, especially after being waxed and buffed, that on occasions, those with shoes slipped. The chairs were set in a semicircular pattern with the television as the focus in a corner.

We boys were allowed to watch television sometimes. The one proviso was that we could not sit on the cushioned chairs. We had to sit on the floor with the houseboys and girls, when they were allowed to come in and watch ethnic plays. The only people allowed to sit on the chairs were Father, Mother and Yinka. When both parents were out, we boys felt like kings sitting in those chairs. The moment we heard the noise of the car engine, we jumped off the chairs, rearranged the cushions, and quickly sat on the floor.

If we happened to be in the garden and heard the car, any visiting friends would disappear through the boundary hedge. They realised that to be caught playing was to place us in physical and psychological danger from being shouted at. However, just being told off did not happen often.

I maintained my love of books, and after the beatings, would go to my bedroom, and read while lying on my front.

As things got worse and lacking a trusted confidant, I started to keep a diary which I wrote in code. There were symbols for all the letters of the alphabet. I was the only person who could read its contents. The diary was black, thin and rectangular in shape. The wooden bedroom floor had one or two loose slats. The space under them provided a good hiding place. At the very front of the book, in code, were my perceived top ten ways of committing suicide as a means of escape from my home environment. The first method was that which I deemed the least painful. Being the son of a doctor I had access to drugs like tranquilizers. I could wash down 30 or more phenobarbitone tablets with a bottle of his favourite drink, Bristol Cream sherry.

Running out in front of a lorry was sure to succeed, however I did not feel brave enough for that. Barely fifteen years of age, and I harboured such thoughts!

As things got worse at home, they mirrored my studies. The poor results then got me into more trouble at home, leading to even worse performances at school. I could not see a way of breaking this cycle.

When in Bristol, I had become dry and stopped wetting the bed. Now, I was in my teens but this became a problem once more. Most mornings, I would wake up early, the smell and the tell-tale cold feeling indicating disaster. Under the bed sheet would be a patch of urine. Having got up early on such days, I turned the mattress over. Fortunately, it never seeped through on to Olu in the bunk below. He seemed to feel sorry for me and never minded being disturbed. The two of us had become closer having been together at the teacher's house, and then in Bristol. Turning the mattress over and placing a towel over the patch to speed up the drying process did not really help. Mother had a nose for smelling things and she could pick up the ammonia smell before she entered the room.

Mother gave me every encouragement to help me become dry: reduced fluid intake after a certain time in the evening, ensuring that I emptied my bladder just before bed and Mother waking me up before she went to bed. When everything failed to work, Mother decided to use the problem as a punishment, hoping it would be therapeutic as well.

I stood in total amazement one morning, when as a punishment, Mother insisted that I wore a placard to school, on my front and back. I could not believe what was being planned. That day, I went to school accompanied, to make sure that I did not tamper with the placard, which read, on front and back, in bold, black ink, 'I AM A BED WETTER'. This kind of treatment was not one that I had ever come across in any school I attended. Some of my fellow students appeared confused when they saw me get out of the car. Father was well known on the campus and apparently had a good reputation. I did often hear that he went out of his way to be kind to other people's children. I couldn't figure out why there appeared to be two personas inhabiting the one physical body. As soon as the car had left the school, I removed the placards carefully and kept them in my locker ready for the return home later that afternoon. Even at that age, my embarrassment was complete and plain for all to see. Having always fancied myself as a handsome boy with an eye for the ladies, that day was one where I returned home and looked at the front of my diary with intent.

7

At times, when I was alone and in a reflective mood, I accepted that I was not going to win any prizes as the best child in the locality. In my defence, I reasoned that I reacted to the prevailing circumstance in the same kind of manner as depicted in Newton's third law which states that every action has an equal and opposite reaction.

A driver was allocated to drive us to school; it was relatively easy for me to convince him to teach me how to drive. Our driver, Cornelius was tall with possibly the darkest hair I had ever seen. He always wore hardy sandals made from old car tyres. This type of footwear was common among those with limited financial means. Cornelius loved wearing light colours and Bode and I used to joke that the black head and footwear resembled bookends as found in Father's study. I used to sit on a pillow, peering over the steering wheel; Cornelius was surprised how quickly I caught on.

Reaching the pedals involved a to and fro piston-like movement that intermittently reduced my height below the steering wheel top. At home on some evenings, I marvelled at how brave or foolhardy my driving on the university campus was, where almost everyone knew Father. I wonder whether some chose not to tell in order to save me.

Once we had safely got out of the drive in the mornings, the driver pulled over and we swapped seats. By the age of fifteen, I was driving to school regularly. The only thing that interrupted me, were the occasions when my back was still raw. I took great pride in being the first student to start the trend of driving to school.

There were some special days at school. One morning, we all sat as usual, on the steps waiting for morning assembly. Our white British headmaster was Mr Gillespie, a distinguished-looking gentleman, who wore half-rimmed spectacles and looked over the top of them to see things in the distance. Students soon learnt to recognise the look indicating they had misbehaved. On such occasions, he leant his head forward like a cockerel about to fight and stared unblinking through narrowed eyelids, with pursed lips, while at the same time holding both hands behind his back. Most of us tended to behave.

On this particular day, he announced that the school had an important visitor from America. Who could the visitor be? I had heard of John F Kennedy when we lived in England. Something had been said about the possibility of there being a third world war. I remember the older people feeling scared at the time. However, it could not be him as he had died in tragic circumstances. Olu and I were too young to experience the same depth of fear as the adults, possibly because we had no comparable reference point. Sonny and Cher and James Brown were names that I knew. However, it was none of these. When the visitor walked up to the front, I did not recognise him. He had a helper bringing up the rear, carrying a heavy-looking cardboard box.

'Good morning boys and girls,' said the head.

'Good morning, Mr Gillespie,' we chorused.

'We have an important visitor at our school today, and he has brought some presents for a lucky few.' Some of the American students began murmuring, and from the look on their faces, they obviously recognised this man. He appeared very important.

'Can you please give a round of applause for our special guest, Mr Charlton Heston.'

I joined in with the clapping, still with no idea who this man was. Mr Gillespie went on to explain that Mr Heston was an actor and had recently been in a film that had performed very well. The film was called *Ben Hur*. The head saying the title of the film nudged a dormant cell that recognised this piece of information, and some latent memory stirred in my brain. I knew of the film, but to have a major film star standing in front of us in our school was a lot to take in. Mr Heston must know Hollywood, and probably knew other American actors that the other students and I had only ever heard of. People like Jimmy Stewart, Kirk Douglas and Gregory Peck.

The whole thing impressed me a great deal. The fact that he chose me to be one of the people he spoke to, and who was lucky enough to get a signed copy of the book on which the film was based, made me extremely proud. I could not stop grinning and I felt like my head had become a fraction of its normal weight. It felt extremely light as I walked about. I held on to the book for the rest of the day as if it had been glued to me.

My meeting with the great man acted as a spur to succeed and to try very hard to fulfil my potential despite the huge odds against it at that moment in my life. Another word of wisdom from the great man came as I received the advice that instead of asking famous people for their autograph, I should strive for a position where people wanted mine. Some of my close friends say that is why I became a doctor, because I got to sign prescriptions for people – a kind of autograph signing, they reasoned.

Lacking an approachable father figure to talk to at home, and not trusting that anything said to Mother might not migrate towards Father, I confided in a Voluntary Services Overseas (VSO) teacher from England. He was approachable, something aided by the fact that he always dressed informally and looked less scary than many of the teachers. At first, he found it difficult to believe some of the things he was being told but soon changed his mind when faced with the physical evidence. The VSO young people did overseas work for fixed terms. I confided in Peter safe in the knowledge that he would not be around in Nigeria forever. It was like telling secrets to someone you knew had a finite time left in this world. Peter looked sympathetic and always tried to help any student he could see was having a difficult time at school. He even suggested once that we should get help from the authorities.

I told him quietly, but in a firm tone of voice that the way of life in Africa was totally different from that in England, and unless he wanted to have me seriously hurt or worse, he had to promise to say nothing. The obvious look of fear on my face as we discussed matters must have convinced Peter of my terror. Peter did not seem happy that he could not tell anyone what I had told him. It must have been difficult for him, but he agreed in order to protect me. After all, he had been shown some of the bruises on my back following a beating. Had he been in England, there would have been no question regarding informing the authorities. I felt sorry for the obvious dilemma I caused the poor man. However, a problem shared is a problem halved, and some weight was lifted from me. Peter must have realised that Nigerian culture did not always rate children as much they did in the west, and girls were valued less than boys. Boys were seen as a means of earning an income as unpaid workers. Girls, at least in some families, were only seen as being of value when it came to receiving a dowry on their getting married.

It got to a stage where fellow students realised how petrified of my father I had become. Some took advantage by asking me to do things that I would not have agreed to under normal circumstances. All some had to do was threaten to telephone the house and ask to speak to me. Such an innocent action would be enough to land me in deep and hot water. Father would ask why anyone would telephone me at home. Did I owe them money? I never did understand why he felt that money had to be a major reason for someone asking to speak to me on the phone.

Before the beatings began, I rarely told lies, but this was something that I tried to become proficient at as time went on. In most cases, it did not matter whether I lied or told the truth as I got punished anyway. Lying at home was not discouraged, and some lies became part of the family history as it were.

Life at home was tense, especially when both parents were in. Some not very good things were done and said, orders given without explanation, and obeyed without question. It resembled what I imagined being in the military would involve. Obey without question. You could be forgiven for thinking that I had no functioning brain. I was always being threatened with having all my books confiscated and being forced to learn a manual job. Being sent to learn carpentry was a favourite.

When things were said, they were meant to hurt, and they did. My life gradually resembled having a slow tyre puncture that one couldn't fix.

As I got older I began to wonder what type of person I would turn out to be. I already had a short fuse and it didn't take me long to react aggressively to what I considered a slight. This led to my getting into fights at school. My problem with keeping dry at night was not helped by my home circumstances. Thinking about ending their lives was not something that I ever heard my siblings and friends mention. The truth is that we are all wired differently, and each person has a different level of tolerance.

Discussion with some of our friends showed that our home life did not reflect theirs. We relaxed at mealtimes when neither parent was present, which happened a lot as Father was invariably at work doing what he enjoyed. Mother felt that she had to wait for him so that he did not eat alone.

When the family did eat together, things were distinct and separate. There were six chairs around the table. The upper end of the table had a lovely, patterned lace tablecloth on with china and silver-plated cutlery. The glasses sparkled when the sunlight coming through the window hit them. The lower end of the table was covered with plastic sheeting, with matching plastic plates and cups. The sunlight had no chance of reflecting off these.

The upper end housed Father, Mother and our sister, while the lower half housed Bode, Adebo and me. As if that was not bad enough, there were two sets of food. One lot was presented in beautifully decorated bowls, while the other had been served in the kitchen before being brought out to the table. There was a definite demarcation in every respect.

The food at the upper end of the table had the finest ingredients and was cooked solely for three people. The food at our end of the table had coarser ingredients, which were not as expensive to buy, and which was also served to the driver and the houseboys and girls. The fact that Yinka could be treated in a way that we boys considered normal, meant that somewhere in Father's being was a gentle and capable parent who could do the right thing. We concluded amongst ourselves, that there must be two different fathers in the physical manifestation we perceived as one. My confusion was a major problem as I found it difficult to reconcile the two personas. Did his having only a single sister from Grandmother Julie influence the way that he treated Yinka?

The palpable fear we boys had could have explained what led to a very sad situation at home one day. The incident involved Olu. We had been out playing when both parents were out, and during the afternoon, a sick-looking dog had bitten Olu. We rinsed the wound the best we could using the outside garden tap, put a plaster from Father's study on it and thought no more of the matter. A few weeks later, the car that was supposed to collect Olu and me from school was delayed, and Olu said that he felt unwell. I should have stayed with him, but because I lacked patience at the time, I left for home on foot, leaving my brother behind. He did not look too well as I left.

Olu remained sitting on the steps at the front of the school, waiting for transport. More than fifty-four years later, I can still vividly see the way he looked as I left for home. Unless people have experienced similar situations, they cannot understand the genuineness of me saying that if I could turn the clock back, I definitely would. There are few things that I regret, but my actions that day are at the top of the list.

The next time that I saw him was after he arrived home from hospital, sweating profusely in the bunk bed below. He looked and sounded in pain. I was aware of both parents coming in to check on him through the night. I drifted in and out of sleep, catching bits of conversation, and on waking up in the morning noticed that he had gone. I cried a lot that day.

All that we boys were told was that he had died, and no further information given. None of us children knew what he died of. We boys had our suspicions and knew that the commonest reason for a dog looking ill in this part of the world was rabies. This became the foundation of my wariness of dogs. I missed the confidential chats that Olu and I used to have.

Bode, Adebo and I missed him a great deal, and often talked about him. I lost my best friend when he died. My personal situation became worse as I had no other close family confidant. My aggression towards fellow students who upset me became more pronounced.

I did not even know where Olu's resting place was. Sometime in the middle of the night, he was moved and that was that. He hardly came up in conversation within the whole family after his death, and the situation under which we lived precluded any questions, never mind discussion. I found it very odd that no mention of Olu was ever made in our house. It was as if he had been a visitor who had left to go back home!

I came to hate school holidays and would be in fear of what fate might befall me at home. For a couple of terms Father dished out punishment in the form of a short beating for all the boys every morning before school. The rationale being that we were bound to do something wrong at school or had done something he was unaware of. Getting the punishment in early covered the potential that we might misbehave. By extension, if we had done something already, then we received punishment for it.

Outdoors, we played cowboys and Indians using homemade bows and arrows that were dangerous, if only we had stopped to think. What if an arrow mistakenly hit someone in the eye? This became a distinct possibility once we decided to emulate William Tell as seen on television. Not having an apple, we used whatever we could find, such as a mango. This is an example of what could have earned us a beating had he known.

During one school holiday, I borrowed a bicycle from one of my friends and went for a ride around the university campus. On my return, Father was waiting with questions.

I could see the telltale signs of increased blood flow to his eyes. His nostrils flared as if held open by a pair of tongs. My legs began shaking, telling me that they would not be able to support my weight if I got off the cycle as planned. I decided to stay on the bike with both feet on the ground either side of it.

'Whose bicycle is that?'

I looked round for my friend whose bike it was and pointed.

'Give it back right now, and I must never see you borrow someone's bike ever again.' The friend gave a weak, supportive smile as I slid off the bike and pushed it forward the short distance to him. He would not be smiling if he realised what was in store for me.

'Sunday, go and get me some whips, and once you have done that, soak them in a bucket of water.' At that moment I had no idea what the significance of the water was but I would find out soon. I followed Father into the house meekly, heading for the study without waiting to be asked.

'I am not ready yet. I will deal with you after I have eaten.' I was so stunned at this that I convinced myself everything was a dream. He was going to eat first, while allowing the whips to soak. The point of soaking the whips then hit me in a manner similar to the feeling I got when banging my forehead on a low door beam. They would become more supple and less likely to break and disintegrate easily. It increased their life span. However long it took for him to eat was too long a time from my perspective. Calmly eating knowing what he was then to do, opened another window on his ability to be cold and calculating – a dimension that I could never have thought existed. I could understand spur-of-the-moment anger followed by action, but this was something of a different magnitude.

After the beating, I lay on my bed, which had become a regular port of call following these events. Many thoughts went through my adolescent head. Should I fight back? Should I run away from home? Should I mock him, pointing out that the worst that he could do was to kill me and that I wasn't afraid to die? If I left home, where would I live, and who would feed me? Perfecting my ability to separate my body and mental states helped greatly, and there were even occasions when, after he had finished beating me, that I stayed on the ground not realising it was over.

The study was the usual place for the punishments. I sometimes wondered what effect blood had on wooden flooring and on the books on those shelves. I never knew the answer. Nowadays, as I watch episodes of 'NCIS' based in America where a chemical is used to determine the presence of blood at crime scenes, I imagine that the study would have lit up like a Christmas tree once luminol was applied. From Father's point of view, borrowing the cycle had been a worse crime than the possibility that I might have been involved in a traffic accident.

The first day of a new term was one of the better days that I had in Nigeria. It heralded a reduction in the amount of time that I spent at home. Since my schoolwork was going nowhere, I decided that I might as well enjoy myself. I joined a poker school and was soon losing money to some of the older boys. I did not win many decent pots and convinced myself that the games were rigged in their favour. Being too stupid and naïve, I failed to spot anything amiss. As I never had enough pocket money, settling any debts was going to be difficult.

I embarrassed myself by asking family friends for money, and when this route did not provide sufficient funds, took to hiding around the school to dodge my biggest creditor. This guy was bad and needed minimal excuse to beat anyone up. He was tall, and had a face scarred from previous fights. His shirtsleeves were taut, struggling to contain his biceps. I never saw him smile, even as he counted the money he was owed. Nobody messed with him, as being a person of few words, he punched first and explained later. I was surprised to later discover that he was a relative of our family. This fact did not make any difference to him, though.

The more I gambled, the more they fleeced me. I lost seemingly impossible to lose hands. I needed to make money fast. That was when I hit on the idea of charging for matchmaking.

I did have a way with the girls, and soon realised that the best way to get a girl interested was to make her laugh. Laughter somehow made people more receptive to an approach. However, to get the chance to impress, there had to be some sort of initial dialogue. I had worked out that the dialogue could be initiated by some activity that prompted conversation, and if any boy was too dim-witted or shy to even manage this, that was where I came in.

Word soon spread among the boys that I could bring people together, and if they played their cards correctly, the immediate future might be assured. I knew many of the girls, and so was able to assess the success rate of any task. As I could not be personally involved in any kind of relationship, I had little problem making an approach to any girl. I stood to gain financially if things worked out, and that was the spur. I always carried out rudimentary research to make sure that my plan could work, as it was not in anyone's interest to attempt something bound to fail. I charged one pound for the prelims, and if I thought that there was a chance, charged more.

I had various schemes to get a face-to-face meeting between suitor and unaware love. These ranged from asking the girl straight up what she thought of the guy, through promising them a share of my earnings, and my *pièce de résistance* was finding and hiding something of value to the girl. The aim of this was to get an agreement that whoever found it would get a reward and earn her lasting gratitude.

I never took anything that I considered too precious, as there was no point having the girl in an unreceptive state of mind. Once the call had gone out asking for help, I handed over the 'lost' item to the potential suitor and it was returned to its rightful owner. This allowed the finder the ability to nudge open the door of access, and what was more important, the ability to show off by refusing to accept whatever reward had been promised. Whatever happened thereafter was up to the guy. I had earned my money.

There was another ploy that I used sometimes, but this was reserved for those I judged to have less than the full complement of what was loosely termed common sense. These guys were so stupid that subtlety, a word whose meaning was alien and which they could not even spell, was lost on them. One such boy always made me laugh by constantly writing 'someone took to their hills'. With boys like this, I tried harder to ensure success. I arranged for a big fellow student to 'threaten' the girl and the suitor came to her rescue. Unknown to the potential suitor, there was no way that the big guy would ever harm the girl.

The suitor would arrive, tear a strip off the much bigger

guy and save the girl. This was usually sufficient to impress the girl in question. Feeling indebted, she usually agreed for at least one date.

In this way, I was able to gamble more than I should have done. I did not win many big pots but I loved the game and the way it made me feel. We always played by a student's bed in the dormitory reserved for the boarders. After school, I was invariably to be found playing poker. Being strongly attached to the game, I found it difficult to be pulled away, and this behaviour got me into trouble one day.

Father had arrived to collect Bode and me from school because the driver had been delayed collecting the younger ones from the university primary school. Bode was sent to fetch me, and he came to the dormitory to say we had to go home. I asked him to tell Father that I was busy in class doing an extra physics lesson and would walk home. Thinking no more about this, I concentrated on inadvertently losing more money.

A few minutes later, I heard a familiar voice. 'So this is the physics lesson?' I looked up and standing there looking less than pleased, was Father. I could so easily have emptied all my bowel contents on the spot. Without another word, he turned and left, leaving me wondering why Bode had brought him to the card game in the first place. Looking at Bode, I could only assume that having seen my plight in the past and what punishment could befall him, he felt it prudent to do as he was asked. He was hardly ever subjected to beatings, and he always managed to obtain good grades at school.

I gathered my satchel and followed quickly down the spiral staircase to the car, a huge white Oldsmobile. Father loved big cars and the Oldsmobile was an American beast of a car. The back seat could have accommodated six or seven children sitting in a row, in my estimation. My mind and thoughts arrived home ahead of us and had already previewed the scenario. As I sat in the car, my thighs encouraged my knees to join them in banging noiselessly like cymbals at an odd frequency. I could not prevent them attacking each other. I desperately needed to sit on the toilet. Not a word had been spoken on the way home and I was grateful for the size of the car because I was not within reach of a slap or any form of hitting. On getting home, Father walked as far as the front door and turned to say to Bode in a loud voice. 'Tell your mum he was gambling, and told me he was in a physics class.'

As soon as I got within reach of Mother, I had a slap on the side of my face that knocked me sideways. I really must learn to stand my ground I thought, as my head travelled east. At least there was no wall against which to bang my head on this occasion. Mother hardly ever resorted to whipping. Her punishments were limited and in the main involved verbal or quick hits. Had I not known better, I would have been forgiven for thinking my name was 'bombastic fool'. This was a favourite saying of Mother's. There were other times, not too many, that Mother must have felt genuinely sorry for me, because she tried to punish me in order to prevent Father having to do it his way. In a funny way, I did feel sorry for her. In fact, Bode did as well. To me, she was like a fly struggling after being caught in a spider's web. While alive, the fly was at the spider's mercy. The spider possessed the upper hand knowing that the fate of the fly was in its hands, as it were. No amount of struggling made the fly's life or its future any easier.

Once she had assimilated the fact that I gambled, she decided that I needed to be punished. Father had, by this time got in the car and gone back to work. Mother had to punish me to save me from a worse fate. My punishment involved another innocuous-looking activity.

Nigerians in those days did not have easy access to blenders. They had traditional equipment that did the job just as well. We possessed a grinder at home which consisted of two parts. The base was a hard stone that was extremely heavy. It measured approximately forty centimetres by thirty. The second part was what one could describe as a cylindrical stone, which was also heavy. This measured about twenty by ten centimetres. If either was to drop on a foot, you could guarantee a fracture. The way this contraption worked involved squashing whatever needed blending, such as onions, peppers or tomatoes, between the two stones. The cylindrical part was held down by both hands and a forwards and backwards motion ensured the crushing of the piece of food on the larger stone. The crushed part, usually a vegetable, somehow moved up the larger stone, ready for collection at the top end. One could think of it as being like a mortar and pestle found in chemistry labs or pharmacies of old. The difference was that the motion was in a horizontal meridian rather than vertical. The Yoruba name for it was óló (or law – phonetically).

Mother found another use for the equivalent of the pestle as a means of punishment. The task was to hold the heavy stone on the flats of both palms with outstretched hands. Like the stoop, the pain only came after about ten minutes or so. The penalty, usually a slap, kicks or, on the odd occasion, a flying slipper, came when the arms dropped, which invariably happened as fatigue set in. For real fun, I heard stories from some of the housegirls where the arms were held over a hot plate or the flames from the gas cooker, so that any dropping of the hands soon brought on pain of another kind. Fortunately, I was never offered this option.

I had to hold this thing without dropping my arms, which was a virtual impossibility. Why ask someone to do something you know is bound to end in failure? I would have preferred a beating; at least that had an end to it – either time or the whips ran out. That particular day, her ploy worked because I did not get beaten after Father arrived home in the evening. The quivering wreck that greeted his return was enough to spare me.

The family went to church every Sunday, wearing our Sunday best. We boys loved this as it allowed us to wear decent clothes that were not school uniforms, or the regulation khaki shorts and shirts we wore at home. Khaki was apparently the chosen material of choice as it was hard-wearing and being the sort of children that they thought we were, the material could not be bettered.

Whenever we were fortunate enough to be bought new clothes, I would spend ages wearing them around the house and looking at myself in the mirror. Bode, Adebo and I wondered but never dared ask why the only girl was allowed to wear cotton and suchlike.

I did not remember much about church or what was said on most Sundays, as I was more interested in the fact that I had decent clothing on. Going to church gave me some respite from the suffocating atmosphere at home.

There was one more house move to come, as Father got promoted yet again. All the children were happy and visibly proud when he became a professor. Our friends could see the happiness on our faces. We learnt many things through osmosis, as little was told to us formally. My schoolwork and grades were inverse to Father's success, but for some reason, I was sometimes promoted to the next year regardless of my grades. At sixteen, I was poor at school, and with a year to go before sitting the General Certificate of Education exams, things looked bleak.

Our new house was bigger with a corresponding sized

garden. Straight up the stairs led to a toilet next to a bathroom. Bode and I shared a toilet with Adebo and Yinka. We boys used to occasionally steal the much softer toilet roll from the parents' toilet. I used to think that the same architect must have designed many of the university lecturers' houses. There appeared to be so many similarities in some of the layouts.

Turning right at the top of the stairs past our parents' bedroom led onto a balcony through a wooden door. Father and Mother's room possessed a window overlooking the balcony. It had mosquito netting, which prevented us seeing in, but more importantly kept the mosquitoes out. The balcony overlooked the big garden. At one corner was a tree that grew right up to the edge of the balcony. At the end of the balcony was a bedroom that was home to Bode and me.

Father did not let up on asking any of us boys questions out of the blue. My youngest brother, Adebo, was sitting on the floor watching television one evening when Father asked him a question. He wanted to know how many yards in a mile or something like that. The poor boy knew the answer but surprised at being asked this question unexpectedly, could not answer correctly. My guess was that he probably would not have been able to name the first letter of the alphabet at that moment. He paid for his apparent lack of knowledge with a beating. That was one of the rare occasions that I saw, without the aid of a mirror what a mess my back resembled after a beating. I felt sorry for Adebo. He probably did not have a hiding place such as the ability to separate physical from mental states. The poor boy subsequently decided that it was safer not to watch television when Father was around.

We boys tried everything to be what we considered normal, and desperately wanted to be like other children we came into contact with. We bore little, if any, malice but on a personal level, I felt that I could have responded physically as I grew older, with the ability to cause some serious harm. We felt like unwanted and irritating appendages which could not easily be shaken off. Why have children if you were going to abuse them? Was there some kind of thrill obtained from the beatings?

One day, Father went to visit his dad in Lagos and we boys knew, again by placing ears on alert, what time he expected to return. When he had not arrived by eleven o'clock that night, we were all worried, and sensing Mother's anxiety, everyone waited up looking at every car that drove past the house. Every headlight could have been him until they failed to slow down and drove past our entrance. The family's collective anxiety was not helped by the fact that it was raining heavily, with thunder that shook the whole house to its foundations, and lightning that lit up the sky like expensive fireworks. The trees bordering the boundary stood out like sentinels watching out for Father's return when lit up by the lightning.

At almost one o'clock in the morning, he eventually arrived. Everybody's relief was palpable, and all felt that we had done the right thing. His reaction was to ask why the children were still up and whether Mother thought that he was a child, unable to look after himself. As far as we boys were concerned, that was it, and we never again worried about what time he returned from any trip. We escaped beatings that night only because it was late and he was tired, and Sunday had long since gone to bed. Only once did he ever go and fetch whips himself as far as I can recall.

Despite my best efforts, my schoolwork continued to suffer and I became frustrated as a result. I knew that I had ability and it was awful that I could not express it. Because of the situation at home and being unable to fight back against injustice as I saw it, I became unable to accept the smallest perceived slight outside of the home.

One day, a fellow student made some derogatory remarks about Father. I asked him to retract the statement and when he refused, I punched him in the chest a few times. I punched so hard that my knuckles ached for days afterwards. Unfortunately, for me, a teacher spotted the attack and I was marched to the headmaster's office where I received a severe reprimand and given one hundred lines to write. I flatly refused to write anything and when asked subsequently where the lines were, I confessed to not having done them.

The headmaster's response was to double the lines to two hundred. I was determined not to write those lines, feeling aggrieved that the guy who upset me had gone unpunished. I knew that eventually the lines would reach a number that was completely impractical. Sure enough, Mr Gillespie recognised that there was no way anyone was going to write close on one thousand lines, and suspended me for one day instead. This would not have mattered except that I was given a lift home on the school bus and Father was at home. For some unknown reason, I did not get a beating as usual. The advice came that fighting was out and that I must never do it again. I wondered whether Father had taken some pride in having someone defend his honour and good name.

Within a few weeks, end of term arrived again and a feeling of cold dread came over me. At such times, my whole body felt like something recently removed from a freezer in order to thaw. I was going to be at home, and more importantly, sitting in my satchel was my school report. I had already taken the liberty of gingerly opening the envelope and reading all the not-so-nice things that the teachers had said about my lack of application. I even managed to get a bad report in physical education.

No sooner had Father read the report than he called for Sunday. I made my way to the study before being asked. I undressed completely and waited. Looking round, I could not help thinking it was ironic that there I was in Father's well-stocked study, its walls plastered with certificates, because I had not done well in my education. From the one-way conversation that accompanied the beating, a not unusual occurrence, I found out I was to get the tariff for the suspension added to the current one. Fortunately, I reached my state of dissociation fairly quickly, and became a peripheral part of proceedings.

On this one occasion, however, dissociation was going to prove inadequate. When the last whip had become a discarded stump, and the beating would have finished under normal circumstances, there was more to come.

For reasons not apparent to me, Father appeared angrier than normal. Maybe he had had a bad day at the office. What happened next jolted me from my comfortable state as a psychological bystander and dragged me rapidly back to the present. This was most unusual because, having completely left my physical self to suffer, I did not normally return until it was all over. There was a noise that was a cross between something snapping and something tearing. Never having heard this before, I wondered what it was. Out of the corner of my eye I caught sight of it.

Coming down in an arc, ready to make contact with naked skin, was the whip substitute. I felt it before it made contact and closed my eyes tightly to steel myself for the searing pain that followed. Although I could not see it at the time, I was convinced that a fine spray of bloody mist flew off my back as contact was made.

All of a sudden, I noticed a ray of light entering the study. Out of the corner of my field of vision, I saw a silhouette in the doorway. I then heard a voice saying, 'David, oto, otito.' For the first time ever, Mother intervened to stop my beating. I was very surprised at this, and, more to the point she used his first name as she told him that it was enough, and he should stop. For a woman who was normally subservient, this came as a shock. My screams might have been enough to jolt her into action, as she probably did not want another dead child. However, I don't know whether Mother's intervention was instrumental in bringing the session to an end or not.

Father had picked up the chair at his desk, broken one of the legs off, and was beating me with this. I realised at that awful moment that I was in serious trouble of a totally different magnitude. There was no way this instrument was going to be worn down to nothing in the same manner as the whips. As hard as I tried, my physical and mental entities decided to stay together on this occasion, providing each other with moral support.

The pain was different from anything that I had ever felt before in any aspect of my life. My screams must have been heard in every house on the street. As there was nothing that I could do, I had to take the blows.

As luck would have it, I was to be proved wrong because even the wooden chair leg couldn't cope. It broke under the force that was being applied to it. Afterwards, as I looked at the blood-spattered wall, I wondered how bad things could get. My blood had even splattered onto the spines of some of his textbooks. I picked up my clothes with swollen, sausage-shaped and blood-stained fingers that had been hit without my registering it, I wondered how much longer I could continue living in that environment. My diary again got a much closer perusal that evening.

Back in my bedroom, I looked at my back in the full-length mirror and realised that this beating was different. Instead of the linear skin breaks, there were areas of circular skin loss, some as large as two centimetres across. They appeared, in the mirror, to possess sheen. This time round, I reckoned that I would need to lie on my abdomen for longer than usual. Bode and Adebo felt sorry and expressed sympathy. They were glad that they were not the eldest, because they understood the rationale was that making an example of me would help make them behave.

That night as I lay sobbing in bed in agony, my back stinging as if hot pepper had been rubbed in, I overheard Father telling Mother next door that since I did not wish to study, my textbooks should be confiscated and I should be sent to be a carpenter's apprentice. That, apparently, was a sign of failure in the circles in which he moved. Mother actually turned up to confiscate the books which were to be burnt, but left without the books and without explanation. Getting to sleep that night was difficult and every time I moved in the night, I became reacquainted with the pain.

8

The holidays dragged by and the start of term could not arrive soon enough for me. We surreptitiously played with friends when the opportunity arose. My back did heal, but in a totally different way from normal, and I did not get the satisfaction of peeling off dried strips of healed skin as many could not be reached by hand. This healed scar felt much rougher in texture.

By this time I had become proficient at driving and provided that I knew for certain where Father was, I would borrow the car keys and take my brave and foolhardy brothers for a spin. We carried out many escapades, fully aware that they were wrong. We made sure that we hid them from Yinka, because it reached a stage where we felt she could not be trusted not to tell Father. Yinka was and is a kind-hearted person, but we did not want to take the risk of her being unwittingly used as a Trojan horse.

Our fear was such that for some things, we were extremely careful and for others, less so. On rare occasions, I did wonder what would happen if Father had caught me driving. Deep down, I was mentally prepared for the worst. I always wrote in my diary that the worst that could happen was that I would die from another beating. Being mentally prepared to die, the prospect of getting caught doing something seen as very bad actually held little fear for me. My love of reading inspired me in many ways. I loved John Bunyan's poem named after its first line, which I could totally relate to 'He that is down needs fear no fall'.

At the age of sixteen, little had changed, and we were still being treated in the same way; a demarcated life in all respects, and it was awful. If we boys had been pets, we would have fared better, so long as we did not suffer the same fate as a dog the family owned in 1959. Father reversed the car over it without realising it was there. Everyone was heartbroken and we never had another pet.

The things that sometimes got us into trouble were the things one would expect of teenagers. Having an untidy bedroom, running around the garden shouting, or receiving a telephone call or a visit from friends. My brothers and I were never allowed to go to any friend's party, leading to a constriction of the small circle of friends we had; they soon stopped inviting us. The only person who was allowed to attend parties was our sister, who only had to ask Daddy for things. She even managed to go swimming with him on a few occasions. We could only look on in envy.

The family must have had relatives because everyone has them; the main problem was that we were prevented from seeing any. Father appeared overprotective for reasons we did not know. We could understand, up to a point, possible reasons for running to our bedrooms, and keeping very quiet, as asked, when visitors came calling. Some Nigerians believed that others were envious of success and did all they could to harm any achievements.

The houseboys and girls had been programmed to tell visitors that the whole family was out. No one seemed to consider how this was so when the three cars were all parked out in the drive. Father, it seemed, trusted very few people including his relatives.

One day, some visitors arrived from Lagos and were inadvertently allowed into the house. I could hear voices and I recognised one or two of them. A familiar voice expressed disappointment that no one was at home but offered to sit down in the sitting room and await the family's return from wherever we had gone. Father and Mother were hidden in their room and everybody else had gone into similar hiding, except yours truly. I had to put a face to the voice I thought I recognised.

Going on all fours, I crept from my room onto the balcony, so that I could crawl beneath the mosquito-netted window of our parents' bedroom. I was soon on the landing, went down the stairs, and peeped around the wall. Lady Luck must have been busy, because I was spotted.

'Look, it's Sola,' someone said with obvious relief. I was invited downstairs to greet them all and it was then that I knew to whom the voice belonged. Grandfather James had come visiting and his son did not seem keen to see him. Having spent some time in the past with Grandfather at his house in Lagos, I remembered how I really loved to be with him. He had so many wise sayings and I learnt a lot from him. He was tall and still looked distinguished in his traditional flowing robes.

He was just as good looking as I remembered, and the similarity with Father was striking. Fortunately, he had no facial or tribal marks. I think Father would have done this to us had he had it passed down in the family. He still carried that fly swatter with its multicoloured handle.

Once my cover had been blown, Father felt the need to come down too and he made some excuse for the misunderstanding. I was oblivious to any frostiness in the meeting, just said my hellos and goodbyes to the visitors and returned upstairs. Before I left, I saw my father prostrate in order to show respect for Grandfather as was the custom. In that moment, it was as if I could see myself in a mirror as I pondered the fact that he must still be fearful despite being a married man with a family.

After the guests had gone, Father called for Sunday who went and did his duty. I was totally confused as I failed to understand what I had done wrong. Luckily, as it was the school holidays, I did not have to be embarrassed at school yet again. The embarrassment was to come anyway, and in a completely unexpected manner.

Following the beating, I picked up my clothes as usual, only to be ordered to leave them alone. Father then called one of the housegirls, who had just finished washing some clothes, and I was made to go and hang them up on the washing line in the garden. The housegirl, Deoti, came from a village in Western Nigeria. She was very beautiful and had very light skin. Her bottom caused me all kinds of problems whenever I looked at it. Whenever she smiled, the gap between her two upper central teeth resembled a miniature door leading to a mysterious and dark room. She tried unsuccessfully to get me to have sex with her. It was all I could do to resist. What would Mother have said? We were not even allowed to involve them in our games!

The clothes went on the line, and my tears could have done a good job of washing them all again. What kind of life was this? Completely naked, bleeding and bruised, I hung the clothes out as instructed making sure the wooden pegs did their job. I was all too aware of the neighbours' children watching through gaps in the various hedges as word spread.

Beaten, humiliated and looking forward to the sanctuary of my bed, I was thrown when Sunday was again summoned after I had hung all the washed clothes on the line. No more surely. There could not be any more. I decided instantly that if he beat me again, I would definitely have to end my life, as I felt that it had zero value at that moment. It felt like a show on which the curtains had come down, except that the actors were still putting on a show behind them. There was to be no more beating though; the next phase of the punishment was further humiliation.

Sunday was instructed to take me for a walk around the campus, still without any clothes. The whole experience was demeaning and I resolved that were I ever to be a success in life, I would try to make sure that I lived as far away as possible from those people who had seen me humiliated.

As I walked round the streets, I kept my gaze firmly on the ground, in a vain attempt to reduce the chances of being recognised. We boys could not understand why Father appeared not to consider what his colleagues might think upon seeing his son walking around the university campus with no clothes. I could not get over the fact that the cause of the current punishment was because I went and greeted a blood relation. I never saw Grandfather again, and this saddened me.

The start of term seemed ages away but arrived on cue. My life assumed its happy state again. I was able to see my friends, and not worry as much about being asked questions to which I did not know the answers or was too scared to answer correctly. I joined the school theatre and enjoyed Shakespeare because we had to study Macbeth and Twelfth

Night for the GCE. On occasions, I could relate to the feelings of Malvolio from Twelfth Night following his humiliation.

I was given a small part in Bertolt Brecht's The Caucasian Chalk Circle. I enjoyed acting although Father never saw any of my acting. Unknown to Mother and Father, I joined a school band and played the bass guitar, then, wishing to improve, I signed up for music lessons. When Father found out, he immediately cancelled the lessons.

Science, maths and the like were more important from his point of view. I regretted very much not being allowed to study music. I stayed in the band and learnt to play by listening to original songs and then learning to play by ear. I sneaked out of the house on some occasions in order to play at events. The bandleader played the clarinet beautifully, and the sound that emanated from the instrument had a lifelong effect on me. Our group needed a name for the band, and after some deliberation, we agreed on the name The Paragons. I don't know whether those listening to us ever saw us as being excellent or not. Much later, in my early sixties, I took clarinet lessons and managed to pass grade four examination. I loved playing the clarinet until I developed some left-sided facial weakness, possibly due to high blood pressure which put an end to that aspect of my life. The good thing is that I at least managed to learn and play an instrument I consider one of the best around.

For gigs, I had to devise ways of sneaking out of the house without being seen or arousing suspicion. Bode's and my bedroom was at the end of the balcony and so leaving the house did not present too many problems. I had to get Bode's agreement, as, without this, the chances of being caught increased. Part of the deal allowed Bode to go with me when I felt it was appropriate. I used to hide my clothes in the boys' quarters or in the garage. Before leaving the house, we made

117

sure that the landing light was off, so that we could climb down an adjoining tree to freedom. We also made sure we locked the bedroom door and took the key with us. It would have to be something special for either parent to use their key to enter our bedroom if they thought we were asleep. I sometimes placed a couple of pillows under the sheets in case either parent came calling. I had seen this ploy on a television film I watched.

On returning from the gigs I relied on Bode ensuring the balcony light was still off on my return. If either parent had turned on the landing light before going to bed, things were tricky but manageable. I climbed the tree while listening out for voices, and then, once over the railings, walked with my back to the wall, under the offending bulb, till I reached the wall of our parents' bedroom. I then crouched and snaked along on my belly till I had passed their bedroom window, before gingerly standing up and safely entering my bedroom, and locking the door.

Father did have an extremely loud snore once he was fast asleep, and this sound informed me that I should be safe. That tree allowed us boys to go away to evening events without being caught, with Father having no idea what went on. On informing him of these escapades many years later, all he could do was laugh.

With exams approaching rapidly, I studied as hard as I could while keeping an eye out for a severe beating that could come at any time. Aged seventeen and about to sit GCE exams, I pondered the fact that I had slipped behind my classmates at Brislington. I had been put back a year, because Father felt that my educational standard was not of sufficient quality.

The GCE exams were graded in order of excellence from 1 to 9, and aggregate totals for the best six subjects calculated. Grade 8 was the lowest pass mark. Depending on the scores achieved, the grades ranged from Class 1 for a total score between 6 and 24 through to Class 3 with the worst score for this being an aggregate of 48. An aggregate higher than 48 was deemed a failure. I made the mistake of trying to cram for history on the day of the exam and was surprised to find that I could hardly find five questions to attempt out of a choice exceeding twenty. History seemed to offer such a wide scope to be able to spot questions, or so I thought. The class studied history from 1763 onwards, including the reign of George III. Needless to say, the plan backfired and I got a grade 9 in history. I passed Latin despite having problems understanding some of the language structure. These two subjects notwithstanding, I managed an aggregate that put me in Class 1 – just.

Father was still not convinced that I was serious enough about my studies, and matters were not helped when I shattered my left knee attempting the hop, step and jump at school. I ran up and hopped without trouble but taking the step placed extreme pressures on my left knee joint. I heard a massive crack not dissimilar to the noises made by some people biting hard on chicken bones. Searing pain arrived not long after the noise. I had not experienced similar pain since being beaten with the wooden chair leg. What remained of the left knee joint failed to complete the jump, and I crumpled to the ground in severe agony.

A couple of teachers carried me to the sick bay but I knew already that this particular injury required more than a couple of aspirins and an Elastoplast. Father was summoned and, apart from the times he drove us to or collected us from school, he rarely visited the place. Being a doctor, he assessed the situation, and decided that I required hospital input as soon as possible.

I was taken to the University College Hospital in Ibadan,

where one of Father's colleagues had already arrived, having been notified by him. The hospital smelt of disinfectant and appeared sparsely decorated. The orthopaedic surgeon looked at the X rays, concluded that I needed an operation, and booked theatre. He summoned another friend, an anaesthetist, and I went to theatre. As I slowly counted to ten as instructed, I was soon out for the count. Following the operation, I went home in a plaster of Paris cast and on crutches.

I had great difficulty easing the itch beneath the plaster but I was very happy in plaster as it prevented me from getting up to much trouble, and so less likely to get beaten. I discovered that I could resolve the itching issue by borrowing one of Mother's knitting needles and gingerly pushing it down the space between my skin and the plaster. The relief was wonderful. I thought that there are few things more irritating than an itch that cannot be scratched.

My ending up in a cast did not improve Father's mood in relation to me. I fell short of the standard he wanted for me in the GCE. I realised that the school was expensive, and like any purchase, Father would like to feel that he obtained his money's worth. He threatened repeatedly to send me to yet another school, a less expensive one.

This school had a reputation as being the worst in the county. As a secondary school never mind as an educational establishment, not many people knew how it even managed to get local government approval. Students from other schools avoided these students whenever their paths crossed in town. Their reputation preceded them. No one messed with the students at Boys High College (BHC). If at all possible, I did not wish to go to this particular school, having heard so many bad stories. I resolved to try and impress Father.

Some months later, in late 1969, I was at home and felt

hungry. Both our parents were out and I could not ask anyone for food. I assumed that it was fine to help myself to food from the pantry. I walked in there, looked around at foodstuff neatly arranged on shelves. I marvelled at the two different coloured buckets containing gari, a derivative of cassava, blue for parents and green for the children and the staff. One contained fine gari and the other coarse. I looked at the packets of Uncle Ben's rice. I compared them to those containing various bits of unwanted ingredients such as very small stones but dared not even touch the better tasting stuff. They allowed us to eat Uncle Ben's on special occasions such as Christmas or birthdays.

In the end, I opted for taking a can of sardines in oil. I opened this and ate it with some bread, sharing it with Bode. Hunger sated, I thought no more about this natural act until Mother asked a question.

'Who took a can of sardines from the pantry?'

'It was me,' I confessed without a moment's hesitation.

How did she find out? As I pondered, she provided the answer.

'I always count food in the pantry to make sure that none is stolen.'

I convinced myself that my eardrum had burst as I could hardly make out the words bombastic fool as I staggered from a slap. Despite the pain and confusion, I assumed that her palm must have made a tight fit over my left ear as she hit it, creating a vacuum. The pain was bad and shaking my head vigorously did not get rid of it.

Hit for eating at the family home. What the hell is going on I thought. What was the big deal? This was not necessary, and before I could organise my thoughts to attempt some kind of mitigation, she disappeared, only to return a few minutes later with a razor blade in her right hand. Now what? I would

121

never have guessed what was going to happen next if I had been given all of eternity.

She beckoned both Bode and me over. I went first and was baffled when she placed her left hand on my chin to steady my head, and calmly made three cuts in my lower lip with the blade. My eyes, by now wide open in terror, ached as they converged in an attempt to focus on the blade. Bode had the same treatment and then to cap it all, she applied red chilli pepper to the still-bleeding wounds. As if that was not bad enough, we were then instructed to go and stand in the blazing sun with lips exposed to its burning intensity. The pain was not that bad really, having already climaxed at the point when the blade made contact with flesh.

Was Mother behaving like the victim of a bigger bully whom she couldn't fight, and so took things out on those weaker than her? I had seen this sort of behaviour at school where a bully's victim looked round, noticed a smaller student possibly grinning, and after asking what he was laughing at, beat him up. Kind of bullying by proxy.

We don't know how long we stood in the sun for, but the punishment was sufficient to act as a deterrent. I never took anything again without asking her first. But the slap, cutting and pepper, and standing out in the sun did not satisfy Mother. I then had to go to school with another placard on my front and back with the words 'I AM A THIEF' written on both sides. I found that humiliation was something that I never became accustomed to. No matter how many times a given situation had arisen, it still hurt to be belittled. Many years later I read about the early life of Rudyard Kipling and was surprised to find that he had been ill-treated by his foster mother in Southsea, Portsmouth in the late 1870s. What stood out to me was the fact that his foster mother made him walk round the local streets wearing a placard that said

'I AM A LIAR'. I don't honestly know whether my mother read books about Kipling, but I do know that ill-treatment of children was not unusual in those days either.

I was not surprised to find that my studies did not improve to Father's satisfaction. I ended up at BHC and the experience was one that exceeded anything that I could have imagined. Embarrassment prevented me from telling any of the few friends I had, when they asked. The college was awful, backward and a total waste of time from an educational point of view. The owner was also the headmaster, and people believed that he established the school just to make money. The college pass rate in any external examination barely threatened 10 to 15 percent.

The classrooms stood in a whitewashed building lacking doors and windows. In almost ten years since living with Kola, little had changed, and animals still ran in and out of the classrooms. The desks were so old that leaning too hard on them risked their collapse. It was bad enough coping with the chance of getting cut by the rusty nails holding some of them together.

I was convinced that very few, if any, of the all-male teachers had recognisable qualifications. The spoken English of the teachers was abysmal never mind that of the students. The first-year students of this secondary school contained students in their late twenties and early thirties. Any other school would have eleven-or twelve-year olds. The school provided a uniform of sorts, made of khaki. I possessed one of the few pairs of shoes in the school.

The classrooms lacked modern amenities such as electricity. Teachers wrote on old-looking blackboards using white chalk. The noise that accompanied the chalk meeting the board jarred my teeth to their roots. The students competed for the space in the classrooms with the local goats. Some two hundred yards from the classrooms were the dormitories. They were cramped, filthy, and had to be shared with the teachers. They had no electricity either so any necessary reading had to be done before dusk, or that was it. I possessed a torch that I used for reading in bed at night. Because I owned some decent textbooks, the teachers sometimes asked to borrow them. I made sure that I read them too, if only to show that I did not belong there. I helped some teachers by writing letters for them in acceptable English, usually applying for better posts. Any replies had to be read for them and translated by me into Yoruba.

If Father wanted to teach me a lesson, I was learning fast, but I was not going to be broken.

The college lacked proper communal toilets and urination was done anywhere handy, and defecation done in a latrine lacking doors and in full view of all and sundry. Crouching over a hole in the ground, with the most sickening nostril-tearing stench wafting up was bad enough; huge flies with bright green bodies and enormous looking eyes, attracted by the smell, did not make the visits any easier. The buzzing noise they made drilled to my core such that I thought our bodies were on the same frequency.

Braving the toilet at the height of the heat was asking for trouble as snakes sometimes loved hiding just inside the entrance. Early evening was the best time to go, as the temperature was more bearable. The corrugated iron roof turned the toilet into an oven during the day, possibly baking the effluent awaiting removal by the council.

I was the only one with access to toilet paper. Everybody else went into those toilets clutching pieces of newspaper, or more commonly, large leaves torn from nearby plants. No one bothered to wash their hands either, and some could not understand why I took a bottle of water and soap with me to the toilet. I shook my head in amazement as I watched some of my fellow students pay repeated visits to the toilet as a result of food poisoning.

The headmaster lived in a big house just down the road from the classroom buildings. He also had a business that involved heavy lorries transporting building materials around the city. I cannot remember how it came about, but one of his lorries needed moving and the driver had gone home.

'Can any of you drive?' The headmaster asked one afternoon. He was dressed in traditional clothes made of expensive white lace. The outer garment, almost as big as a medium-sized bed sheet, covered him from the neck down. Its size made it necessary to occasionally pull up the excess material over the shoulders. The headmaster had a large cigar dangling from the corner of his mouth. His ill-fitting glasses appeared in need of a good clean. They were perched on his nose at an angle that was nowhere near being horizontal. The traditional tribal cap sat sideways on the left side of his head. He was a bit shorter than me, and possessed a face with delicate, unobtrusive vertical tribal marks.

'I can,' I replied in a flash. He did not ask and I did not volunteer the information that I had never driven a lorry before.

'OK,' he said tossing me the keys. 'I want you to drive that lorry round to the front of my house.'

'No problem sir,' I assured him, my face almost completely replaced by a wide grin.

I stepped on the foot ledge and, in one quick movement, had opened the heavy door and was in the driving seat. I stared at the huge steering wheel and the long fragile-looking gear lever down to my left. The bulbous nose of the lorry curved away to the ground in front. The ground seemed far away, compared to what it felt like to sit in the car at home. The headmaster told me the route to take, as it was not possible to turn the lorry round in order to reach his house. I did not know the way, and noticing the questioning look on my face, said he would follow in his car.

I sat high up in the lorry, a Bedford, looked at the distance to the ground through the driver's window, and I was excited by it all. I put the key in the ignition and fired her up. The noise vibrated my whole body. I pressed the clutch and engaged first gear by depressing it with more effort than I ever required in a car. I drove off without stalling and my excitement was palpable, and I felt my heart thumping. I was driving without a licence, and was about to join a busy main road.

The adrenaline coursing through my body provided a shield of fearlessness and immunity to the possible consequences of my actions. I could not contemplate anything beyond the next few, potentially exciting minutes. I drove fairly competently until I reached a narrow part of the road, and noticed a car coming towards me. I realised that there was not enough space for both vehicles; I pulled in behind a parked VW Beetle.

After allowing the other car to pass, I continued my journey; at least that was the intention.

Years of driving family cars had instilled in me the habit of turning the steering wheel with one hand. I did exactly the same in the Bedford and was surprised to see that the vehicle was still travelling in a straight line. I noticed that the Beetle was also moving, despite there being nobody in the driver's seat as I shunted the car gently into the ditch near where it had been parked. Realising what I had done, I panicked.

I must keep going and must not stop. Some Nigerians had a habit of beating you up first before asking questions. My mind was definitely made up when, on looking through the huge wing mirror on the passenger side, I saw many people running after the lorry, shouting and waving in a manner I assumed was asking me to stop. Do-gooders heard the shouts, and noticing what was going on, blocked the road, forcing me to brake. As people were banging on the driver's door, shouting all kinds of obscenities, I realised I had a problem. I was going to need all my powers of persuasion to prevent getting beaten to a pulp or worse. One of the guys banging on the door was dressed in military uniform, and on seeing this, I became truly afraid.

Nigeria had a recent history of military coups, and soldiers carried their guns in public. I looked down at this young soldier, who could hardly have been much older than me. Fortunately, he had no gun that I could see. I had an imminent urge to use the toilet, and at that moment in time, would happily have taken my chances in the oven-like toilets.

As I contemplated the best course of action, I heard the headmaster's voice before I could see him. My relief was immense. He apologised to the soldier who owned the car. Local people vouched for his identity when he offered to pay for any damage. He said that it was my first day working for him and I was getting used to the lorry. Amazingly, the short drive he had witnessed had assured him that I could drive, and so I was allowed to drive the rest of the way. That was the most exciting thing that happened to me in the six or so months spent at the college.

A close second involved the time when one of the other students challenged me to a fight which I avoided by talking him out of the idea. He had taken offence when I made a mistake and corrected his pronunciation of an English word. I had made him look bad. Looking down physically at this squat man, who was probably much older than me, and his battle-scarred features, convinced me that I had made the right choice. As Adebo loved saying, this man had muscles in places that I didn't have places. I knew that he would have won any physical contest.

I was kept busy writing letters in respectable English for those unable to do so and being available to read and translate the replies. The college appeared to be a money-making scheme for its owner as far as I could see. There were no school reports that I could remember, making it impossible for Father to assess how useful the exercise was.

I could not be whipped unless I was on holiday, failed to answer questions correctly, or for some other excuse. The thought of eventually escaping one day spurred me on. I did not agree with the methods employed by Father but could see the warped motive. He believed that his success in life was due to the way that he had been brought up. I did not think that my treatment at his hands was a result of him being malicious. Having convinced myself that I had an explanation, I was less likely to hold a grudge.

Punishment beatings I could just about take but mental cruelty, especially combined with a lack of affection, was much harder. In my later years, I came to realise that child abuse was not unique to me. Things went on behind ordinary-looking front doors that were truly awful. I felt that there was no worse punishment than mental cruelty. He never treated Yinka in the same way, and looking back now, could it be that he did not rate girls' education as highly? I totally refused to contemplate that beating us boys excited him.

We children finally accepted that maybe we were not adopted and shared the same genetic blocks as our tormentors. Even at such a young age, I believed that every child possessed an inherent and innate personality, which could, to some extent, be modified by the environment. In later years, an inherently good child can be turned bad with no chance of recovery should good forces never come into his or her early life. A potentially bad one can be modified to be good, provided the stimulus for good behaviour is never far away.

Looking at Bode's and my life, I could relate to articles that I had read in newspapers about prisoners who, while on the outside were difficult and bad, suddenly developed the ability to be on their best behaviour while locked up. The same applied to soldiers who, prior to joining the army, were difficult to control. They fitted in somehow once inside the armed forces. Father never considered that children might be different.

My parents should never have treated all their sons in an identical manner. Sometimes, a word is enough for a given child, while another might require physical punishment in order to get the same result. Ultimately, a growing child without love in his or her home environment will find it difficult, though not always impossible, to give the same later in life. Today, I am convinced that my siblings and I bear psychological scars from our past. These scars are of a different intensity in each one. We were moulded by the home environment we endured.

I wondered on many occasions how my life might turn out were I to ever have a family of my own. I smiled whenever I recalled an older relative telling me that he always prayed to God not to give him children like himself.

Since education was so important, I was prepared to invest in this. Father had many students for whom he was responsible for their postgraduate studies. One of his PhD students came to the house to give me extra tuition. He and I got on very well as he tutored me in Mathematics and English. Mr Okonye hailed from the eastern part of the country and was an extremely nice man. He would often sweat, as he never turned up without a jacket and his university tie, regardless of the weather. His once-white handkerchief almost matched the colour of his skin. I could not explain why his body odour smelt differently from Sunday's.

Considering he originated from a part of the country where ethnic differences mattered to some, he never once discussed politics with me. The part he came from was on the opposing side to the Nigerian government during the civil war of the sixties. As he talked about his home, my understanding of a place I had never visited as a young man growing up in Ibadan, was extremely positive. All strands of the nation came together in the Amure household. Mr Okonye taught me a lot about life and, as a well-educated man himself, imparted some valuable knowledge. It was he who planted in me the seed of never giving up. One day he quoted a passage from one of Henry Wadsworth Longfellow's writings, which has stayed with me. Longfellow (1807–1882) wrote, 'The heights by great men reached and kept were not attained by sudden flight, but they, while their companions slept, were toiling upward in the night.'

I realised then that few things in life came easy, and hard work was required to get what you wanted. The best actors, football players, concert pianists and so on, all practised to hone and perfect an underlying innate ability.

With no feedback from BHC that he could judge my progress by, Father decided that I needed to change schools yet again, and before long I was going to be attending my seventh school in my short life. As usual, my feelings were not considered worthy of opinion, but the prospect of leaving BHC pleased me a lot.

9

My new school, Ibadan Grammar School (IGS), was going to be a lot better than the previous one, as that was the impression I got on my first day. The long, tree-lined drive to the main buildings was impressive, and the building had windows, albeit wooden ones with horizontal wooden slats. By coincidence, it was about half a mile from St Luke's Primary School that I had attended ten years before. I was tempted to go and see whether the foster parent that had been so cruel to Olu and me still lived there but resisted the urge. I had come full circle in a geographical sense.

From the school gates to where taxis and minibuses touted for passengers was just over a mile. Walking in daylight was fine but walking at night was a different matter. It was pitch black, and various noises from nocturnal animals limited the occasions I walked through with fewer than three friends.

Tales were told about a psychopathic or madman loitering after dark in order to attack and rob the students. The man, folklore had it, was unshaven, had matted hair and had huge, unblinking eyes. He wore a sheet round his waist, leaving his upper body covered with a fishnet-type of singlet. His sandals were said to have seen better days. I did not wish to meet him.

All the students belonged to houses at the school. My housemates loved life and we enjoyed ourselves. The dormitories were strategically placed, located around the shower room, toilets and dining room. My dormitory had rows of bunk beds either side of the entrance, with a locker for provisions next to each bed. The concrete floor was never devoid of dust which created a mini dust storm when swept. I was taught by older students to sprinkle water on the floor prior to sweeping in order to reduce the amount of dust thrown up.

In each half of the dorm, either side of the entrance, was a naked bulb hanging from the ceiling by its plaited life-giving wires. The wires did not look up to the job and it appeared they might come away with the slightest gust of wind. The metal bunks stayed in the rooms at all times, with students bringing individual mattresses from home. Since they were usually folded in order to allow them to fit into the cars, everyone had the flimsiest mattress they could find. Bed sheets and covers, including blankets, were also brought from home.

It made sense to have a sturdy padlock for the lockers as things went missing at times and no one ever confessed to knowing anything about it. In my dorm, there were two sockets that we used for plugging in electrical appliances. This allowed us to make hot drinks and heat water to take to the shower room.

The classrooms were clean, well-stocked and spacious. Toilets were nearby, a far cry from BHC. They were not the most salubrious in the world, but were only a few yards from my dormitory. The stone-built toilets with corrugated metal roofs, consisted of six cubicles, each with a wooden door that could be bolted from the inside, although I never really understood why anyone would willingly lock the doors. The presence of electricity meant that they could be used day and night.

Once inside, the toilet was essentially a hole in the ground, over which one squatted and into which the waste was deposited. It helped to aim straight and to be as hunched as possible. Great care had to be taken in order not to lose one's footing as getting any part of the anatomy beyond the rim of the hole was asking for trouble. The six cubicles, though separate, had the effluent confluent, as it were. Every so often, a lorry came to empty the toilets. The smell was bad at the best of times, but with the stuff above ground as it was suctioned into the lorries, and carried on the wind, the whole school and probably those for miles around knew when the collection happened. I felt there must be a thing about toilets that attracted snakes because on many occasions snakes were killed in them.

The shower room was only slightly better; it was a brick building with a corrugated iron roof. The holes in the concrete blocks forming the side walls acted as windows that lacked any glass or plastic covering. I hated having a wash in the place for two main reasons. One was the dangerously slippery floor, which was caused by months of dirt and soap from dirty young bodies, never ever being hosed or washed down. The other reason was the fact that almost everyone bathed in cold water obtained, when they worked, from flimsy taps. The cold wind of the early mornings made the water feel even colder than usual; this happened when the electricity was off and I could not boil my own.

My parents gave me an allowance to buy provisions such as bread, biscuits and razor blades for shaving. I went without some of these things in order to be able to afford a small electrical coil that was useful for heating the water in the metal pails. The bucket doubled for bathing and washing clothes.

The students in school shared a tank just down from the dorm from where we all collected cold water. A council lorry brought the water regularly, just as another had done some ten years before. Had this community progressed at all since my previous residency, I wondered at times?

Some students soon learnt to remove the light bulb in the dorm and plug the electric coil in its place in order to heat water. This only occurred when both wall sockets were in use already. A warm bath was infinitely better than a cold one, and for some reason, the warm water made the floor of the shower room less slippery. I allowed some of my roommates to borrow my electrical coil.

The large, communal dining room provided three meals a day to the entire student boarders. The day students only ate with us at lunchtimes. The prefects summoned us at mealtimes by ringing a handheld bell. The food was nothing special but it was edible. Once the prefect rang the bell a second time, the black wooden doors were locked and those still outside for whatever reason went without food. We sat on wooden benches at long wooden tables. We were served at a separate table and the meal was placed on our individual shiny metal plates. Some, like me, were fortunate enough to have personal cutlery, otherwise using fingers was the order of the day.

I did all sorts of things at school that were daring. I ventured into town on a few occasions, knowing there was a military curfew in force, with orders to shoot on sight. It was a challenge dodging the soldiers we encountered, but I hate to think what might have happened if they had spotted us.

Some friends and I visited a local cinema from school on many occasions, without bothering with an exeat, which was a requirement of the school - a teacher had to be made aware that a student was leaving the school campus, and a signed written permission called an exeat obtained. We preferred the cheap cinemas. Our favourite one was located just a couple of miles from the school. A Lebanese businessman owned it. The film projected onto the white wall of a neighbouring house, most likely without the owner's permission.

The students from our school could not afford to go to Scala, a relatively expensive cinema to which Father once took the whole family to see *The Sound of Music*, (the one and only time the family went to the cinema together in Ibadan). When it rained at our preferred cinema, all the spectators attempted to take refuge by standing at the sides of the nearby buildings. It must have looked odd with a clear central area and everyone positioned around three sides of a square. Since refunds for bad weather was not on the agenda, the students tried as hard as they could to see and hear despite the rain. A large number of the films were made in India, and at school, some of the boys pretended to be the actor, Shammi Kapoor. Life was as good as it could be, with holidays being the only depressing times.

We sometimes bought pieces of skewered meat, known locally as suya, from vendors near the cinema. They grilled these on open coal fires and all of us loved buying them as snacks. Those of us who liked our meat spicy looked on in amazement as the vendors added the pepper in a unique way. They placed the dried peppers in their mouths and sprayed the cooked meat by virtually spitting over it while rotating the wooden skewers. As far as I am aware, none of us ever got sick.

I actually managed to fit my studies in somehow and got above average grades. I still had to contend with Sunday being called at home, and I wondered how much longer I could put up with things. I had, written in my diary, apart from the suicide prompts, how to run away from home and where I might go. I felt that Father did not like me. I tried everything within my limited powers to get close to him. After telling what I knew to be a lie, I sometimes went back to confess the truth on occasions, hoping that Father would have a better opinion of me. It never worked, as I heard him tell Mother one day as I was leaving, that the confession was most probably a lie as well.

For reasons never fully explained to us children, our parents used to believe that all dead animals went to heaven. Some sections of Nigerian society killed an animal just before it was required as a meal. Chickens, goats and so on had their throats slit by a sharp knife. The family went to town beforehand, picked out the chicken or goat that we wanted and took it home. We kept the chickens in a woven basket coop that had a small circular opening for entry and exit.

Getting them out of the coop required guile and care, as on too many occasions a chicken got loose and chasing after it to catch it was not funny or easy, though onlookers might have been amused. The person tasked with killing the poor animal caught it usually by its neck. He or she then folded the wings upwards, stood on them, placed the legs together, and stood on these. The defenceless animal thus placed on the ground with the butcher, for lack of a better word, having ensured that it could not escape. This freed both hands of the person doing the killing. One hand was placed over the poor bird's eyes while stretching its neck, while the other wielded a knife.

What followed next was not pretty. Having already dug an apology for a hole in the ground, the butcher trickled the blood into this hole after initially coping with it spurting from blood vessels in the neck. Once dead, the animal then had to have its feathers removed; this was achieved by soaking it in boiling water. Before the animal was killed, my brothers and I were encouraged to whisper in its ears to ask for anything. By doing this, the animal conveyed messages to heaven. We were convinced to believe that in this way, God received messages, as did all our relatives who predeceased us. Even then, Bode and I were not convinced, and after a while I used to stand next to the animal's ear pretending to say things.

Everyone we knew apart from a handful of expatriate lecturers killed animals in this way. As far as middle-class Nigerians were concerned, killing an animal just before eating it was normal practice.

IGS was co-educational, and my eye for a pretty girl was still intact. I had girlfriends but often did no more than hold hands because I was so afraid of what might happen if I misbehaved, as Mother always delicately put it. I felt brave sometimes and kissed a girlfriend. This simple act caused all sorts of hormonal wirings to discharge in my body. I enjoyed the feeling.

There was a most beautiful girl in the year below me. Everyone I spoke to admired her. I could see how beautiful Bisi looked but she just had no interest in boys. Bisi was of medium height, slim and elegant. Her bottom was perfectly rounded, and it was the first shape I noticed through her school uniform. Bisi's skin was so smooth that I wanted to stroke it. Her jet-black plaited hair nestled over her ears split into two identical rows separated by a front to back parting. When she smiled, it had an inexplicable effect on me and I would have done anything she asked of me at such times. The feelings engendered in me brought back memories of Janet.

Accompanying her smile was the habit of lifting her head and looking upwards. I noticed that she appeared to lack bra straps when I looked from the back and assumed that her perfectly formed breasts could defy gravity without external help.

Fancying my chances with almost any woman, I took on a challenge from my friends one day when they said that I would never succeed in getting her to be my girlfriend. As there was a financial incentive for me to succeed, I took on the bet. I had been involved in a friendly sort of way with one or two girls before this, and had reached the stage in my life, aged almost eighteen, that I felt able to confide certain things to Mother.

The usual response, after considering Father's possible opinion on things, was that the girl was from the wrong part of the country, or the wrong tribe or more astonishingly, their parents, usually the father, drank too much, or was a womaniser. At times I wondered who the prospective boyfriend was, and who was going to have to live with the consequences of any choice. It was with mild amusement that I wondered whether it would ever get to the stage where I would have to visit a prospective bride's family. I knew that some parents insisted their children did this. I had little control over the present. It appeared that choosing a partner in the future was not going to be in my control either.

In order to know whether I stood a chance of winning my bet, I had to do some initial research, bringing back memories of my matchmaking days. I found Bisi's best friend and asked her a lot of questions, of which the most important was, did her friend have any views about me at all? The answer was encouraging; she said that Bisi found me funny. Further research confirmed that Bisi was a practising Christian and attended regular Bible study meetings in the evenings in the school chapel.

To think that some friends and I had played jokes on the Christian Union members almost made me think twice about accepting the challenge. The Bible study evening meetings usually lasted about an hour or so, and some friends and I had found it amusing to creep up to the door, bolting it from the outside. The rationale being that they could have a bit longer with their God. Recollecting these acts of youthful exuberance created a slight problem, and my friends were certain that they had won the bet. There was no way that I could chat up this girl.

All I needed were a few days of weighing up the pros and cons. I decided that in order to win the bet, I would have to join the Christian Union as well. As far as I was concerned, joining was a means to an end, and if successful, I might even keep the friendship going. I did not know what my friends thought of me with respect to crossing this particular line. Would I actually go so far as to join the Christian Union? They did not know what I would end up doing. It surprised me when some mentioned that at least I could not catch gonorrhoea from her. They obviously did not know me as well as they thought.

I duly joined the Union and was surprised at the lack of animosity towards me. I felt ashamed of my previous behaviour. The visits to the meetings allowed me to talk to Bisi. It helped to know that she found me amusing, and I did nothing to alter that view. For the first few weeks, the Bible discussions went over my head and I could not recall the discussions whenever she asked me later.

I decided that there was no point going if I could not show that I was serious. I began to listen and concentrate on the discussions and to my great surprise, began to contribute. I could not believe the things I heard myself say, as I had only ever gone to Sunday school and church because it was expected and it allowed me to wear smart clothes.

Somehow, the lessons from the Bible began to get to me and I began thinking about things religious. Jesus' teachings made sense, and even for those who were not practising Christians, they were good rules by which to live. The longer time went on, the less important the original reason for joining became. Even as I collected my winnings from incredulous friends, it meant less to me than it might have done at the outset.

Under normal conditions, I would have left the Christian Union and found a way to jettison the girl, but for some reason, I did neither. I started to develop feelings for her and our friendship was to last for the rest of my time at the school. My male hormones played havoc with my urges, almost smashing down my wall of resistance, but being the sort of girl that she was, she kept me in check. Bisi was good for me in that she usually managed to talk me out of escapades that could have got me in trouble. School holidays became more of a wrench, as I knew that I would not be seeing or talking to her for some time.

My eighteenth birthday was coming up and both parents, for reasons that I did not understand, felt that this was a milestone. Mother managed to convince Father that I should be allowed a birthday party. You could have knocked me down with a piece of the cotton wool Mother had in her make-up cabinet. What was going on? I thought that leopards always kept their spots. I was totally confused. It was one thing allowing Yinka to have a party; it was another matter with the boys. On my birthday I received two presents, an act that was in itself out of the ordinary. Mother bought me a white transistor radio that became my pride and joy, and she also bought me a King James Bible. I still have the Bible some fifty years later, although it's now held together by Sellotape!

I listened to the radio more often than I read the Bible. I had to have the radio volume turned down low in my room at night, to avoid getting in trouble. I had been warned that it could be confiscated. At school, I was one of a select band to own a wireless. I dreamt of England and relived some of the memories from Bristol. I spent hours at night listening to the BBC World Service. I envied all those people overseas who had recorded messages to be played for their loved ones back in Nigeria. I invariably liked the music they chose to send their loved ones, like Diana Ross and the Supremes, James Brown, Wilson Pickett and Motown.

On the day of my party, for which certain rules had been set, the guests arrived by six o'clock in the evening and were given light snacks along with soft drinks like Coca-Cola, Fanta Orange and Sprite. Music was allowed but no dancing, and the party was not as I had imagined it would be when I was granted permission. The ultimate downside was when another proviso that I had been unaware of was suddenly announced. Everyone had to leave by nine o'clock! Nine o'clock? Some parties that I had sneaked to in the night had hardly begun rocking by nine. After it was all over, and everyone had left, my embarrassment was such that I was grateful that it was the school holidays. Hopefully, they would have forgotten the need to make fun of me by the start of term.

At this stage of my life, the beatings had reduced in frequency but I was still likely to be caught unawares at any moment. I persisted in trying to impress Father, working hard at school, despite his insistence that I was not doing well enough. If only he would talk to me, find out what sort of person I was. Some family friends had given me some money for my birthday and, determined to show Father how sensible I was, I decided on a foolproof plan, or so I thought.

I took a bus into town one day, did what I had to do feeling very pleased with myself, and returned home as happy as I had been in a very long time. On coming through the hedge bordering the driveway, I could see Father's car in its parking place. Normally, I would have been scared with an uncontrollable urge to urinate and defecate.

I entered through the back door that opened into the kitchen, as we were not allowed to use the front door; we could not be trusted with a key. We boys assumed that it was most probably because the parlour was always tidy, and it was preferred that it stayed that way. Father was sat in his favourite chair, and without looking at me, lobbed a question like a grenade with its pin still in.

'Where have you been?' he said in a voice that sounded soft enough. I could not detect the usual menace.

'I went to town,' I answered in a voice not as shaky as normal. I did not stammer.

'What for?'

'I went to open a bank account,' I replied with pride and a beaming smile.

'Why?' he demanded, and for the first time, I sensed danger.

'I wanted to save some of the money I received for my birthday.'

'Which bank?'

'Standard Bank of West Africa, sir,' I replied tentatively.

'Show me the book,' Father half shouted. It was then that I realised things were not good. Father snatched the book and looked at it, flicking through the pages despite the fact that there was only one entry. The solitary entry said ten shillings deposit, with the date of deposit written inside. For a few seconds, Father went quiet, but I could see from his screwed-up eyes that I was in some bother.

'You are a thief,' he said, waving the book so that I could feel the cool air on my face. That sentence made me feel like a fly that had just been whacked by one of Father's swatters. For a moment, I almost explained that I had not stolen the money. Then Father continued, 'I know why you have opened this account.' I knew why I had opened it; one reason was to earn interest, and the other was to try and show him that I could be sensible.

'You have opened this account in order to steal money. You plan to deposit one pound so that you can then alter the passbook to read one hundred. That is why, isn't it?' he demanded to know.

I was completely and utterly stunned and even if I'd wanted to, I could not have managed meaningful speech or response. Where were these ideas coming from. That bankbook was confiscated there and then and I never saw it again. I sometimes wonder whether interest is still being accrued or has someone taken the money after more than fifty years of inactivity. Years of being treated as though I was nothing but irritating flotsam should have inured me to events, but somehow Father still managed to surprise me. In reality, my confused mind could not understand his thinking. Altering the entry in a passbook should not fool any competent bank clerk, especially as there would be a way to confirm the amount written in the book. All banking would fail if staff had no way of verifying customers' accounts. No allowance was made for the fact that, had I been planning something shady, there would have been no way that I would have confessed the reason for going to town, never mind show him the book. But then he did have an extremely negative view of my intelligence. Bombastic fools could not be clever or devious.

I was the life and soul of the after-school events such as the dance and quiz nights. Watching me dance with Bisi must have been a sight because of the male urges over which I had no control. Dancing to a fast record caused no problem, but dancing to a slow one became a different matter.

As our bodies touched, it brought back memories of the feeling I got from touching the metal pail while heating the water using an immersion coil heater, the difference being that it was more pleasurable than that experience in the dorm. One of my roommates had thought it would be amusing, out of envy, to sabotage the wiring in the coil and attach a naked electricity wire to my pail of cold water. On touching the bucket handle, my body jerked as a unit and I was thrown back. Somehow, I escaped death. The culprit stood and laughed because he found it amusing. Fortunately, I landed on my bottom on an adjacent bed without any physical damage.

Dancing with Bisi simulated an electricity current that coursed through every building block in my body. There were stirrings between my thighs which created a stiff problem. In order to hide what was going on, I arched my lower half backwards, looking like a comma in the process. By bending like this, I was, of necessity, made shorter. This only compounded matters as my face then aligned with her breasts. I bought a jock strap as a consequence of these dance evenings.

Bisi and I occasionally went to see films together, with me desperately hoping that it would not rain. The simple act of holding hands had an effect on me like nothing I had ever experienced before. Love was not something that I could define easily, but I felt in love with Bisi. My best explanation of the word love when asked was to say that you loved someone when you were prepared to do anything for him or her. There was nothing that I felt I would not do for her at that stage of my life.

Fortunately for me, nothing much happened except for kissing and cuddling in one of the deserted classrooms late at night. The moonlight bathing the classroom allowed us to have our regular meetings in some secret. When she told me that she loved me, the feelings overwhelmed me and I could have walked barefooted on glowing embers. Sometimes, I returned to my room with an uncomfortable coldness in my trousers. I had to change on getting back to my dorm.

I was not in a position financially, to buy her presents although I would have loved to. Attending Bible study together was amazing and I became more of a Christian as time progressed, praying for salvation from the home environment most nights. Amongst the topics discussed at Bible study was the fact that Jesus said people should ask and it would be given to them. I spent many days asking for salvation, and to be free of the problem at home.

As far as I was concerned, some of my friends and I exhibited some crazy behaviour. Some of the things we got up to could have caused serious illness or death, except for the fact we were too stupid to notice. Once, we decided to hold a contest to see who could drink a whole bucket of water without being sick. Foolishly, I decided that I could attempt this successfully.

The buckets were filled with water from the tanks near the dormitories. It never once occurred to me that certain escapades were just plain dangerous. The buckets were of similar size and filled to the same level with water. All those taking part knelt down by their buckets and began to drink. One guy used a mug from his locker to scoop the water; another poured aliquots into a plastic beaker and drank that way. I opted to kneel and suck the water up from the bucket, and as I progressed down it, picked it up and tipped it like one would a two-handed jug, except it lacked handles. Multiple visits to urinate caused the oddest swishing noise in my abdomen as I walked along gingerly. Somehow, I won and claimed winnings that I had not been aware were at stake. For the next few hours, every time I moved, my stomach moved, not in unison, but with a time lag. My stomach appeared to be under the influence of its contents, behaving like a balloon filled with water. Many years later as I learnt about the human body, I discovered that I could have burst my stomach or died from cerebral oedema as the brain was not designed to be flooded. Maybe I survived this idiotic act because I did, in fact, possess, bombast.

At the end of my first year at IGS, I came top in English and was awarded a book, Darwin's *On the Origin Of The Species* which I have kept safely. I thought that I was doing well, but Father still needed convincing. He wanted me to attend university, and to study medicine. There was no other occupation that would do, and as for my having a say in the matter, this just did not exist. As professorial head of department of one of the medical sciences, everyone loved him, and we children never heard a bad word said against him. He was always helping someone else's child to progress up the education ladder. I did not mind studying medicine as I felt that I wanted to help those who suffer through no fault of their own.

He suggested that as I was not clever enough to get the A level grades required for entry to medical school, he would enter me for the Preliminary University medical exam at the local university in Ibadan. This exam, were I to pass, would be an A level substitute and I would read a preliminary year, studying pre-first-year subjects before joining the class of medical students containing those that took and passed A levels. In due course, I sat the exam with barely adequate preparation, and personally was not very hopeful.

Some weeks later, the results of the exams came out and I had failed badly. I could not even pass an exam not deemed too difficult by many contemporaries that sat it. I think that this failure might have been the final straw from Father's point of view.

There was going to be one last throw of the dice, and nobody would be able to say that he never tried or that he failed to do his duty as a father. The plan was to involve me once again as a central character, and again without discussion regarding any point of view that I might have had on the matter.

10

As I got older, I started to wonder how couples ended up with converging views. From the little I knew about Mother's upbringing, it was diametrically opposite to that of Father's. Maybe one partner moves closer to the viewpoint of the other; my opinion is that the weaker of the two is the one who shifts more. Mother, in my opinion, shifted her position but I did not hold this against her as she was up against formidable opposition.

Her upbringing sounded like the sort I would have wanted but never got. Strict but inside a protective shell of love and affection. Physical cruelty, as far as I was concerned, was less of a problem than psychological cruelty, and I had more than my share of the latter. Physical wounds can heal but I felt certain that psychological ones did not unless one develops dementia or loses the capacity to recall.

My physical scars triggered awful memories only when I viewed them, whereas the psychological ones were always in the background, silently waiting to be recalled when exposed to appropriate triggers. In my many quieter and reflective moments, I did a lot of crying alone, ensuring that no one could see.

Growing up, I had so many plans for getting even as I saw it, but the influence of the Christian Union put paid to such plans. If I professed to be a Christian, and accepted its teachings, then it would be hypocritical to behave otherwise. I realised that while I could do things where the victim may be unaware of me as the perpetrator, God would nevertheless see.

There were infrequent flashes of temper exhibited by Mother such as that shown on the day we visited Adebo at school and he was nowhere to be found.

We drove out of the school in search of this boy whose crime had been to leave school with permission on an exeat. Soon, Bode saw him walking along the dusty path beside the tarmac road. He was with friends and was laughing and possibly joking, walking along without a care in the world. I could see that Bode had spotted him and hoped he might keep quiet but he did not. I am certain that Bode did not act maliciously.

Mother ordered the driver to stop the car, flew out of it before it had come to a complete halt, and ran up to the poor boy. She slapped him so hard, that he stumbled and almost fell to the ground. With the movement, the outer lower half of Mother's traditional costume worked loose and fell to the ground. The petticoat underneath was visible to all who had turned round in surprise to see what was going on.

Traditional dresses were made up of two halves, excluding the headwear. The lower half consisted of two pieces, with the petticoat underneath the outer wrapper. The upper half was one piece. The headwear was usually made of the same material and wrapped around the head before being tied at the side or back.

Holding his hand to his face, Adebo looked round to see what was going on; the look of utter surprise on his face, would stay in my mind forever.

I had no idea what the poor boy was thinking, but I was glad that he did not react instinctively or Mother might have ended up on the ground from a flurry of punches. Adebo was stocky and muscular. Just looking at him, many people erred on the side of caution and avoided confrontation. His friends looked just as surprised, and with justification. Mother picked up her wrap and returned to the car. Adebo was then ordered into the car and driven back to the school. He sat in silence, and I observed him clenching and releasing his fists. He possessed a faraway look on his face. According to Mother, he had been sent to school to study, and there he was roaming the streets. A trifle over the top, one would have thought, but as experience had already taught us boys, this was no ordinary family.

He had been humiliated in front of his friends who were left standing in the dust as the car roared off, and who would no doubt be expecting some explanation later.

However, we boys preferred to be punished by Mother whenever we did wrong; we begged her not to tell Father when she threatened to do so. We were closer to her, and sometimes felt relaxed enough to tell her things, but then only after careful consideration and selection. She, too, was not having the sort of life one would have expected for her. She only had one close friend as far as we could tell.

That Father loved her greatly appeared not to be in doubt, but I felt that his kind of love could unintentionally stifle a person. I had once seen a hen smother a chick in her rush to protect it from a hawk circling overhead.

Father did not like her driving a car, but he had reluctantly agreed to driving lessons and subsequent test. Mother, being confident, passed the driving test without a problem. She drove without any issues for a while, and appeared to relish the freedom it offered. One day, she took Adebo and Yinka to a party in the university grounds, and on the way back drove the blue Opel Kadett through a puddle. Unfortunately, the water and the engine did not see eye to eye. On the other hand, maybe their eyes met and just disliked each other, because the engine packed up in protest. Mother could not restart the car and was late returning home as a result. Father went to look for her, found her not too far from home, and arranged for her and the stranded car to be towed back to our house.

We all heard the admonishment from our bedroom, as if it was her fault the engine got flooded. Her driving licence went the way of my SBWA passbook and she never drove again. Mother accepted this unilateral decision taken to stop her driving without too much fight.

I knew from personal experience that there are times when fear can be so great that one finds it impossible to protest at injustice. I also believed that everyone has a point beyond which they cannot be pushed. Unfortunately for us children, it seemed as if Mother's breaking point was off a measurable scale. We only ever saw her get really angry on one occasion, and that was soon after our return to Nigeria in early 1964. Before leaving for work, Father had said something that was really hurtful and this had been enough to propel Mother towards the end of her tether.

Bode, Olu, Adebo and I saw her drinking a lot in an attempt to blot out the memory. We recalled hearing the heated argument after Father returned home that evening. The end result was that we sat by the upstairs window watching as she waited for a taxi with a packed suitcase. Unfortunately for her (but fortunately for us), either none came or she changed her mind, for we saw her return to the house.

I honestly felt that she would have been better off if she had left that day. My brothers and I discussed later on how we might have fared in a family without a mother. We felt convinced that we would have survived, without any positive factors to back up this assumption.

On the day Mother discovered that I could drive a car she looked at me with her mouth opened so wide that a large fruit would have easily gone in. It looked like she wanted to say something, but no words came out. Despite my potentially tricky situation, all I could think of was that if she kept her mouth open much longer, an insect might enter. She was at her very good friend's house when I drove in after being collected from school. Her friend saw me first and Mother did not need much encouragement to come and see for herself. Eventually, Mother spoke and asked if I had been driving. Her eyes remained wide open with her lower jaw having submitted to gravity. Her eyes and mouth reminded me of an inverted triangle made up of circles. I confirmed that I had and she asked me to show her. I did so without hesitation, while feeling extremely proud of myself.

When I got out of the car, any semblance of pride evaporated in an instant, like a drop of water on a hot oven, when she threatened to tell Father. I started to cry and begged her not to do so. Her friend could see the state of the poor wreck in front of her and pleaded forcefully with Mother not to report me.

Luckily for me, Mother decided not to tell. Did this stop my surreptitious driving? Not one bit. I just resolved to be as careful as I could be in future. We children had to accept the lack of joint family fun and enjoyment. After all, we were still in someone's care. Mother, on the other hand, was a grown-up whom on occasions, was treated like a child. We felt very sorry for her. I distinctly remember asking her one day why she put up with it, and why not leave? Her reply made sense; because she thought that she had to stay for our sake.

I assumed from this that once all the children had left home, she would reconsider her position. It did, however, beg the question as to why she hardly ever intervened on our behalf when Father dished out severe punishment. I always gave her the benefit of the doubt and assumed that things might have been worse for us, and me in particular, had she not made behind-the-scenes representations. I had no proof that this was the case, but it allowed me to explain things to myself in a satisfactory manner.

There is only so much that a person can take, and eventually most people reach an inherent predetermined breaking point. I reached mine one evening after I had gone out without asking permission. Bearing in mind that I was nineteen years old, and would never have been given permission anyway, I decided to go and visit friends. On my return, Mother asked where I had been and I told her the truth. In reality, we both knew that I had gone without permission, and when she threatened to report me, I responded with a shrug of the shoulders.

When she invited me for dinner later that evening, I replied that I was not hungry. I hated being beaten on a full stomach, and besides I had by then honed the art of starving myself if I felt wronged. When Father arrived home, she told him what I had done. As I reflected later, I wondered whether Mother's mood at a given time determined her actions. She had not looked happy all afternoon, and I felt her reporting me reflected her state of unhappiness. I compared this to her response on the day she had caught me driving, when she had been relaxed and in an obviously happier state.

'Sunday,' was the next thing I heard; he hadn't even asked for an explanation. I looked straight at Father and spoke slowly and firmly.

'Not this time. NOT THIS TIME.' I moved my head from side to side while keeping a close watch on him. My arms remained taut by my side with my fists clenched, as I assumed a defensive posture. Father looked extremely confused and said nothing. I then went to the kitchen and ran out of the back door. I was not having it. I could only imagine the scene in the household as I ran up the road, heading nowhere in particular. By this time, it was dark and I was feeling hungry.

The adrenaline kept me going till I eventually reached the main gates of the university campus, some four or five miles from home. I sat on a wall watching the world go by. The streetlights reflected off almost everything. Car headlights, their size increasing as they approached me, and the cacophony from human activity was incredible. Such a simple scene and its effect made me realise how secluded our home lives had been. Sitting and watching it all calmed me down. The search party sent out by Father failed to locate me. I found out later that Father had said initially that he did not care whether I returned or not. That would have made two people prepared to accept any outcome.

I eventually got back home around midnight, determined that if he tried to beat me, I was going, and this time it would be for good. I entered the house, noticed the whips in the corner, and walked into the sitting room. No one asked me where I had been, and Mother offered me some food, which was devoured in double-quick time.

Those whips were never used. I forcefully told Mother the next day that if I ever got whipped or even threatened in future, they would never see me again. If they wanted to kill me, they might as well get on with it as that would be preferable to the life I had lived up until that point.

My attempted running away must have had an effect, as Father suddenly announced that he had been thinking of the

153

best way to help me. After a lot of consideration, he had decided that I was to be sent back to England. As Grandfather had sent him to Norwich for A levels, and this proved successful, he had been in touch with the college, who had offered me a place starting in September 1972. There was no more that he could do as I was not making the grade academically as far as he was concerned. My life was oscillating like an erratic pendulum between various places, as yet to find a place of rhythmic comfort.

I had very mixed feelings on being told this news; it felt similar to those I had when leaving Brislington Grammar School. On the one hand I was happy to be leaving the claustrophobic and stifling home environment, and on the other, sad to be leaving my friends at IGS, especially Bisi. Those I had left behind in Bristol had kept in touch for a year or so before the friendship withered on the tree of inactivity. I was conscious that here was another set of friends that could be lost forever.

IGS opened my eyes to a lot of things, and some would stay with me. It was there that I was finally convinced that God existed, and that the Bible was a most powerful book. I started to believe that God gives humans hints and nudges, and if fortunate, they do the right thing. I had previously spent years attending church and Sunday school without ever being truly involved. Why did God allow me to suffer as I did? I do not know the answer and most likely never will. But then, my opinion about suffering was purely subjective. I joined the Christian Union to chat up a girl for a bet! The place where this initial act led me to still causes me to shake my head in amazement many years later.

Religion was to play a major role in my life from then on. There have been numerous instances where I know that my faith has played a part. Proving these instances to sceptics is not easy, and I have never bothered trying too hard. It took me some months to begin to appreciate religion. It intrigued me that the beauty of religion is having the faith without the immediacy of proof. If it could be proven to all that Heaven and Hell are real places, all would be good, but where would the satisfaction be in that? I explained things to myself in simple terms. I loved the Christian religion because no one was forced to believe or accept its teachings. Everything about it was, up to a point, volitional. I don't understand quantum physics, but my ignorance does not invalidate its authenticity.

The relationship between God and humans, I mused, can be considered similar to that between a parent and child. Such relationships are built on trust, for without this, it is extremely difficult to have a meaningful relationship. A child placed on a table and asked to come to Daddy or Mummy will do so without thinking. Such a child would not be concerned about falling off the table despite observing a huge gap between the table edge and the parent. As they grow, experience would confirm that the faith is well placed, further enhancing the relationship. I felt that relationship with God should be seen on a similar basis.

I had some people who always asked me why, if God exists, does He allow bad things to happen on earth? I was certain that no one knew the reason. I tried answering this question by referring again to the relationship between a parent and a child. A ten-year-old might not understand the reason for being told not to walk home through a park alone at night, but the reasons become clearer as the child grows older. At the time, however, the child might feel that the parent is being unreasonable because in his or her world, knowledge is limited and restrained by lack of experience. If this thinking can be extrapolated to God and humans bad and sad events may seem awful at the time, but growing up in a religious sense, might make things clearer.

None of my non-Christian friends can answer the following questions when I ask them. How is it that almost any man can have a child by almost any woman on earth, yet scientists tell us that attempting to donate blood or other tissue from one person to another can cause serious problems with rejection. Where is human sperm in this equation? A single person can usually lift an unconscious, inebriated or anaesthetised person. However, once the person is dead, one person does not find it as easy to lift on his or her own. This is despite the ante- and post-mortem weight being identical. What has changed? Has something 'left' the body between the two states? Does what we call spirit make the live human body lighter than it should be? I don't know the answer, but I find these two questions intriguing. I am told that the term dead weight originated from the observation of this latter fact.

On telling Bisi that I was leaving soon to travel abroad, she became very upset and she promised to write every week. I also promised to write regularly and meant it. Deep down, I knew that after a while, the frequency of letter writing would drop before finally withering to nothing. I could not recall the last time I contacted either Italian or English John. Whoever said that absence makes the heart grow fonder?

Bisi and I still met in one of the classrooms, doing nothing too serious, and I felt able to confide in her up to a point. I never told any of my schoolmates or friends the type of life I had at home. The only ones with any idea were those who lived near us on the university campus. Two of these boys, being white and from England, could not understand why I was treated in such a manner. I wondered sometimes whether they told their parents. This thought scared me.

Seth, who lived next door, had a father who was professor

of biochemistry. Seth had blond hair and originally came from Seattle on the West Coast of the US. Whenever you spoke to him, he always had both hands placed in his trouser pockets. He reminded me of a young Gregory Peck, the actor. He was my age and still attended the expensive school I attended before BHC. He was sensitive enough not to tell his parents exactly what he knew. I am glad that he did not interfere. I found it easier to make friends with schoolmates who did not know too much about my home life.

Before long, it was time to leave for England. I radiated so much happiness that some people wondered what was wrong. Going abroad meant that I would be my own boss, able to go out and return as I pleased. Father sending me to England did not fit in with his usual behaviour and character.

When the time came to leave school for the final time, I said goodbye to Bisi and it was all she could do to stop crying. I did not know what to do to ease her obvious pain. We stayed in the classroom late on the penultimate night, not wanting to leave each other. I wiped her tears with my shirtsleeve and reminded her that I would keep in touch by letter. Even though, I too, felt emotional, I somehow managed not to cry.

I was proud that I managed to resist the urge to respond to the male yearnings coursing through my body and settling in my groin, especially as by that time she was all in favour of moving to the next step. I just felt that it was not right. Besides, what if she got pregnant and I was overseas? The next day, I made a conscious effort not to see her as I couldn't be certain I could handle it. In fact, it turned out to be a quiet exit; I just waved to those that saw the car leave.

My green suitcase that I was to travel with was barely full, despite containing some textbooks and virtually all of my clothing. I was sad that I was unable to take books that I felt might be worth referring to in the future. I left behind my copy of an early second edition of Darwin's *On the Origin of Species*, not to mention my James Bond, *Biggles* and Edgar Rice Burroughs's *Tarzan* books. While in Bristol, I had collected stamps and had amassed a decent assortment, which I left behind as well.

Very soon, the day came for me to leave for England. I was instructed on what needed to be done, and how to behave. To help me settle in, both parents would accompany me to England, and take the opportunity to have a ten-day holiday. I said goodbye to Bode, Adebo and Yinka, and hoped that I would see them all soon. As both parents were going to be away for a short time, the house staff would look after my siblings. Keeping in touch with them by letter was not the same as hearing their voices.

11

Parts of the journey to England were a blur because I was so happy to be leaving home that I could not think straight. Following an overnight stay at the airport hotel in Lagos, we travelled early the next morning and within what seemed a short time in the aeroplane, arrived at London Heathrow Airport. The airport appeared slightly cleaner than the one in Lagos, but people appeared just as busy as they hurried towards their next destination.

From the airport we then travelled to Liverpool Street station from where we took a train to Norwich. Once in Norwich, we made straight for a bed and breakfast hotel on Unthank Road, where Mother and Father had a reservation. I only stayed there for one night as the college had arranged for me to stay at the YMCA on St Giles Street.

The next morning Father and Mother accompanied me on the walk to the college and introduced me to the head teacher. Even though it was a sunny June day, Father thought that it was cold. The head showed me round the important areas of the college but I did not take any of it in.

I could not stop my internal smiles as I thought of the freedom about to come my way.

Once my parents had returned to their lodgings, I went and explored the YMCA and soon made friends. The building had many students living there as well as some young men who had steady jobs. Amongst the residents were a few from Nigeria. I soon got to know them all and worked out which were the ones to avoid getting too close to, depending on their attitude. It was a bonus that I could speak to others in Yoruba.

I was paying the YMCA five pounds and fifty pence a week, to include bed, seven breakfasts, and any four evening meals. Across the road from the back door of the YMCA was the Labour Club where I soon got involved in gambling on the machines, taking care not to put myself in a position where I had difficulty finding spending money. I was surprised to learn that one of the barmen was the city mayor. I did not understand how such a high-ranking official ended up serving pints.

My room in the building was on the second floor, reached via what seemed a like a warren at first but soon became second nature. The bathrooms were shared and well maintained by the cleaning personnel. The building also possessed a small kitchen where residents could cook light meals and heat prepared meals. I soon developed a taste for canned spaghetti and sausages. I bought bottles of milk for tea and the occasional cereals from local shops. In the winter months, being too lazy to walk to the communal fridge, I placed the milk bottles on the window ledge of my bedroom. I hoped that the bottles would not fall and hurt some innocent passer-by.

Out of the front door of the YMCA, and turning right onto St Giles Street, was the Wimpy and beyond that, the Guildhall, the market, the cathedral and Jarrold's bookshop. Between the Wimpy and Jarrold's was a small store selling everything one could need. I just loved walking around the local area, loving the cobbled streets that I came across, and I spent many evenings sitting on a bench at the bottom of St Stephens Road just watching the world go by. I did not feel truly liberated until my parents had left to return to Nigeria. Then I experienced real freedom, and anything that happened from then on, good or bad, would be solely down to me.

I was glad to find that the YMCA was not far from the cathedral. In fact, the YMCA was located centrally and not far from my new school, Norwich City College on Ipswich Road. The police station, not that I anticipated needing their help, and the Theatre Royal were also within walking distance. The food was so good that I gained weight. Lunch was anything that was not too expensive at Wimpy; sometimes, that meant eating little.

I attended the cathedral regularly. I hardly ever needed to visit the doctor I registered with on Upper St Giles Street, where Barclays Bank was also situated. The excitement of opening a bank account at Barclays could not be put into words. When the chequebook arrived, I could not stop looking at it. Every page had my name printed on it. I realised that this book was never going to be confiscated.

Having arrived during the summer holidays, I had no lessons to attend and was advised that I could earn money as a student by finding a summer job. I visited Manpower offices, whose function was to find jobs for people. I applied for a job at the Milk Marketing Board in Harford Bridge and got the job on a short-term basis. There was only one other black face there, and we both got on well with our workmates.

The other person, from the West Indies, was much older and had been working there for a few years. He was not as dark as some Nigerians and had a great manner about him. Nobody could feel intimidated despite his tall and muscular appearance. The factory produced yoghurts, milk and various cheeses. Unfortunately, I never developed a taste for cheese and so could not eat too much. The free pots of yoghurts of different flavours were a different matter. The money was not bad either and added to the fifty pounds a month that Father sent. I eased into a very comfortable life.

I had money, freedom and some new friends - things were looking great. After a ten-hour working day, my legs felt weak and I appreciated the chance to sit down on the bus on the way home. On getting back to the YMCA, all I wanted to do was go to the television room and relax. I thoroughly enjoyed the time at Harford Bridge and made many short-term friends. Some of these friends were forthright in saying what they thought and I was receptive to some of this. For some reason, a few of the workers decided to call me Sam. It took a few weeks for me to realise that it was in fact a shortened version of a derogatory word for black people. Personally, I was not bothered when I found out, being the sort of person who believed in changing attitudes in a gradual manner by my behaviour.

My gambling gene was reawakened in the work environment one day when I found workmates playing cards in the changing rooms after work. I asked what they were playing.

'We are gambling,' replied one.

'I can see that,' I countered, having noticed a pile of money on the table in the middle.

'It's called brag,' explained another. 'Three-card brag.'

'Can you explain the rules to me please, so that I can join

in?' The amount of money in the middle was the magnet and I wanted some. The rules were simple really; everyone bet once three cards had been dealt to each player, and betting continued until there were only two players left. The winner was the one with the better hand. A player could fold at anytime and discard his hand if the stake became too much. A further twist was that a player could bet blind, and pay only half the current stake, as he was betting without having seen the cards dealt him. I had received my wages that day and asked to be dealt in.

'Are you sure you want to play,' asked a fellow worker, looking concerned and possibly thinking that I might lose all my money. I insisted that I wanted to play and was dealt in the next hand. In what seemed to be a flash, I had put in almost thirty pounds and had little money left.

'What happens when you run out of money?' I asked, feeling a damp sensation on my furrowed forehead and palms.

'You lose,' was the succinct reply that made me feel extremely uncomfortable. I had worked for a week with not much to show for it. Staring at the money in the middle, which was well over one hundred pounds, I thought how stupid I had been. All my money would be gone when the round of betting reached me.

At that moment a supervisor entered the locker room, and asked what was going on. The boys were not quick enough to cover the stake money, negating the need for an answer.

'You know very well that gambling on the premises is not allowed. Can you please stop right now,' he asked.

'Sorry, boss,' replied one of the players. Everyone agreed that the best course of action was for everyone to show his hand, with the best one winning the money.

I could not believe it when all the money was shoved in my direction. I had the best hand. That narrow escape was enough of a lesson regarding playing brag in future. I had won with a low pair – two fours. Speaking to one of the older guys later, Jack warned me not to play cards with some of our fellow workers as they were likely to rip me off. I replied that I had already decided never to play again.

Jack and I became friends and he looked after my interests from then on. He was seventy years old and had a ready smile. Jack's wispy grey hair protruded from under the rim of his regulatory white cap. He had a matching grey moustache and looked physically fit. He walked, from my point of view, as if he had a weight between his thighs. His white boots, poking out from under the white overcoat we all had to wear, always pointed outwards as he walked. I was concerned that he might fall over and remained vigilant in readiness to catch him if he did. His steps were short and quick, and he had a habit of walking as if his centre of gravity was ahead of him. Jack had Parkinson's disease, something that I had no familiarity with at that time.

I understood one of the problems of the condition one day when I volunteered to make him a cup of tea during yet another break.

'How many sugars do you take, Jack?' I asked.

'Five or six please, Shoola,' he answered, making a huge effort to get the pronunciation correct.

I made the tea and handed it over. Jack took one mouthful and sent out a spray of brown liquid that created a mosaic pattern on my white coat.

'What have you put in here?' he asked.

'Six spoonfuls of sugar.'

'It tastes awful.'

'I am sorry,' I said, thinking that I must have misheard the reply about how much sugar he took. It turned out that I had heard correctly, but with his Parkinson's, it took him five or six attempts to get the amount of sugar he wanted when he made the tea himself but this didn't equate to five or six spoonfuls. I felt bad, but he was very good about it. Jack was another person with a saying that resonated with me. One day we were discussing life in general and I asked him about his past. He replied that the only advice he could give me was to try to do anything that I really wanted. Once old age arrived, it was easy to relive achievements. The problem, he said, was that it was irritating to think about things that you could have done but hadn't. That prompted me to say that in future I would attempt everything I wanted, within reason, in order not to have a canvas in old age punctured with lacunae of regrets.

I was surprised at the amount of prevailing ignorance concerning black people, especially as my father had attended the same Norwich school and lived in the area way back in 1949. Some of the questions such as what it felt like to wear clothes for the first time would have upset many people. Another asked how I had travelled to England and refused to believe that aeroplanes flew from West Africa. He appeared convinced only when I said that I had taken a canoe until I reached civilisation, before boarding a plane. The poor guy failed to appreciate my attempt at humour. I felt that much of the prejudice was built on a foundation of ignorance. I believed that it would help to try to explain things to people rather than become annoyed, as only the former had a chance of changing views and preconception. The latter, I felt, would only reinforce innate prejudices. Some people could not really be blamed for their ignorance, as many television programmes at the time played to stereotypes. The comedy shows on television such as *Till Death Us Do Part* only showed situations that reinforced prejudice and ignorance. Hardly any programme showed African cities with skyscrapers or multilane highways.

When college term started in September I realised that I was in a class mostly with people who had taken the A level exam already and failed. Only three of us in that class had not yet attempted the exam, with some others already having had at least two attempts. The class was taught as if everyone had experience of the exam. To give myself the best chance of passing, I started working hard from day one and ensured that I revised what had been taught at the end of each day. I then reviewed at the weekends what I had learnt during the week; the rationale was that when I came to revise, the information would not be totally new. Having only one year to prepare for the A level exams was another factor. I could not afford to fail, as that would prove Father right, and worse, might result in my being returned to Nigeria. I resolved never to be poor in later life. I had plans to help others. I also wanted an occupation where I could be of use to people.

While living at the YMCA, I watched some television and occasionally visited the cinema. The communal television room was packed every Thursday, as everybody loved *Top of the Pops*. The freedom was almost intoxicating and I felt the most relaxed I could recall in a long time. I received letters from Bisi to which I replied as soon as I had read them. Some were read three or four times. Gradually, the frequency of letters arriving and my replies waned, just as I had thought.

My studies were going very well and before long, it was time to apply for university. This was done through the Universities Central Council on Admissions. I read the UCCA booklet and decided to aim as high as possible. I applied to Cambridge to study medicine. Having sent off the application, I then received another application form to complete in order to be able to sit the entrance exam. I sent this off too. I sat the exam in due course and waited for the results.

I saw the Cambridge University postmark on the white

envelope as I retrieved my letters from my YMCA pigeonhole. I opened it and was shocked to find a letter inside inviting me for an interview at Pembroke College. It appeared that I had managed to do well enough to get an interview. Some of the written examination questions had been very difficult, requiring a great deal of working out but I soon realised that it was easy enough to break the questions down into parcels of facts that I knew from my revision. Having done this, they were no more difficult than any other questions.

I felt that the questions were designed to test the power of logical thought. In truth, the information required to answer the questions was all there. My favourite question was in the English paper; it asked for an essay on ivory towers. I decided that I would stand a better chance if I could appear different. I therefore answered the question in the form of a poem. I spent time counting the beats in each line, ensuring that not only did the last word on each line rhyme with one three lines down, but that the beats matched as well.

In December of 1972 I arrived at Cambridge railway station for the first time. I sensed the wall of history standing in front of me as I got off the train. I was not confident that I could make any meaningful dent in it. I felt sure that same wall would still be unaltered following my visit.

I was well wrapped up wearing a thick winter coat which came in handy. While waiting to change trains at Ely station the cold wind blowing along the platform was enough to cause my teeth to chatter.

I made my way from the station by taxi to Pembroke College, completely in awe of the many old buildings I saw on the way. The taxi driver was helpful in pointing places out to me when I asked what they were. I was shown to my room for the night. Having an idea of the age of the college, I wondered how many people had sat in that room over the years. Sitting on the long bench in the hall that evening, and having the food brought to the candidates on a tray in order to help ourselves, almost caused me to pinch myself. From a partitioned dining table in the family home in Nigeria to this. This was a different world, one I could not have predicted accurately given an infinite amount of time.

I listened to some of the other candidates talking in a manner that reminded me of the accents I had heard on the BBC World Service programs when I lived in Nigeria. No one at my college in Norwich spoke like that. Even though we were of roughly similar ages, these boys looked different. Some of them possessed an air of entitlement, as if they expected to be offered places in the college. I found out from their conversations that they attended fee-paying or private schools. I smiled to myself as they constructed sentences and used words and phrases that were not common to anyone, or to me, from my college. It appeared they already possessed an advantage over people like me. It was like running the 100 metres and they had a 20-metre advantage. I resolved to just do my best in the morning and leave it at that.

Either the occasion got to me or my sense of release was to blame, for at the interview the following morning, I managed to upset the admissions tutor. When asked why I had applied to read medicine I gave a standard reply about wanting to help people. I did not get told to join the fire service or the police as they helped people too, as I had been told some candidates had been advised. Another question was, why Cambridge as opposed to other universities? Like a fool, I thought there was no way that I was going to say anything along the lines of it being the best university in the world, something I actually believed then and still do. I replied that I filled in the application form as I came across them alphabetically in the UCCA handbook. When the tutor replied, 'That will be all,' in a firm tone, face stern and unsmiling, I knew that I would not even have to open the rejection letter when it arrived to know what it said. On the train back to Norwich, I reflected and thought that maybe that particular answer was not the right one under any circumstance.

By early 1973, Norwich City College had completed a new accommodation block next to it, called Southwell Lodge, and I applied successfully for one of the rooms. I moved into a brand-new room which overlooked the drive from the main entrance. It had a very comfortable bed, a desk, and a couple of chairs (excluding the one at the desk). The curtains were blue as were the doors of the medium-sized wardrobe. The carpet looked hardy enough to cope with use and not need replacing too often. The radiator provided more than sufficient heating. Some of my Nigerian classmates had also been given rooms in the building, and despite having to resit the exams, appeared more concerned with enjoying life. I used to sit at my desk and watch them as they went off to the nightclub most nights. I was still there on their return after two o'clock in the morning on most days.

Some Saturdays, I did go out with them to Scamps, a favourite haunt, to see whether anyone in the group could successfully chat up girls. I did manage to get some girls interested but because I was deemed too interested in bookwork, the relationships were short-lived, in a manner similar to a candle with a very short wick.

One event did stay in my mind, though. One evening, as we boys sat round the edge of the dance floor, watching girls dance in a circle around their handbags, two pretty girls caught my eye. The taller of the two, slim and blonde with a body that could not be bettered, appeared to smile at me when our eyes locked in the intermittent brightness caused by the strobe lighting pulsating in time with the music. At the end of one record, I approached her at the bar and offered to buy her a drink. She kindly declined but I persisted. In exasperation, she told me to go and utilise a dildo on myself. My face changed to a mixture of sheer surprise and confusion. I stood rooted to the spot, mouth slightly open as she walked off holding two drinks.

I slunk back to my friends who were all laughing and pointing at me. They all knew that she did not like boys; the girl she was with was her partner. I did not believe at first what they told me, but I soon learnt that some people preferred people of the same sex, as I noticed her kiss her partner long and passionately.

12

Despite living with fellow students in Southwell Lodge, I felt extremely lonely. My brothers were in Nigeria. I found the absence of close family difficult. However, I knew the importance of what had to be done. One of the things that had kept me going through the recent past in Nigeria was knowing the passage of time was inexorable. The lack of a domineering presence and the fact that I no longer had to put up with being beaten compensated to a degree.

No matter how hard I worked, I struggled with physics and did very badly in the mock examinations, which was just the kick that I required in that subject. Chemistry was my favourite subject; I found that perfectly straightforward. The physics teacher went so far as to suggest that sitting that particular subject was not only a waste of my time, but also that of the poor examiner who had to mark it. I was determined to prove him wrong.

There was little correspondence with home, although I attempted to write regularly. The longer I spent in Norwich, the less the urge to write home regularly became. I was grateful for the monthly fifty-pound cheques that Father sent. I walked up to Barclays Bank and paid the cheque into my account. Finding that cheques I wrote were honoured, took some getting used to. This was the same guy that was not trusted to open an account in Nigeria.

I tempered hard work at college with taking time off to do things I enjoyed. I went to the cinema on Prince of Wales Road, a beautiful street with wide pavements. Their width brought back memories of Nigerian roads, and I could not believe the difference between English and some Nigerian roads. Not many of the latter possessed pavements, something that possibly accounted for the occasional dead or dying bodies seen lying by the roadside. Drivers lacking licences had run others down. Some very unfortunate ones were not even on the roads when they died. They sat perched on the very top of whatever load a lorry was transporting. Either they fell asleep and/or failed to notice the electricity wires across the roads and fell down from their perch to certain death. Despite the presence of laws limiting how many passengers a lorry could carry, these were ignored in the main. The police officers meant to enforce them were so badly paid that a small bribe was sufficient for them to turn a blind eye to law breaking by drivers of lorries and cars.

I visited nightclubs and pubs where I was intrigued by the jukeboxes where music could be bought by putting money in a slot. One particular establishment had a few empty slots in the machines that allowed people to effectively buy approximately three minutes of silence. I also started smoking, which was a very bad thing to do. I was aware of the health risks associated with the habit. I started after one of the guys in the Nigerian group offered me one. The initial drag on the cigarette had such a calming effect on me that I continued to smoke. My favourite brand was Peter Stuyvesant.

On one of the visits to a nightclub, I met a beautiful blonde Norwich girl. She was tall, had a great figure and was approachable. Her loose hair cascaded down as far as her hips. Every now and then, as she shook her head from side to side, the hair reminded me of a sinusoidal wave. This thought made me smile, as I remembered that I was not supposed to know any physics. I marvelled at its sheen and length. Jane was nineteen years old and lived with her parents and younger sister above a shop her parents ran in the north of the city. She sometimes borrowed her father's red Ford Escort estate, in which she and I travelled when going out. Her eyes reminded me of the colour of the waters I had seen when travelling back to Nigeria on the Aureol, only bluer.

She always collected me from Southwell Lodge, or from the YMCA during the summer. The Nigerian students stayed at the YMCA during the holidays as it was cheaper. Jane at least liked boys and had a strong Norfolk accent. This accent made an impression on me, and before long, some local dialect began to find its way into my vocabulary. I enjoyed asking for help to light my cigarettes by saying, 'You got a loight buoy?'

Despite going out together to various places, she appeared reluctant to invite me to her house and I used to wonder why. She told me that she worked for her father in the family-run corner shop, as did her mum. Her younger sister sometimes helped out too. We met up as often as time allowed and when we went to Scamps, we went as a couple. I had met my share of ignorant people before, but some still managed to surprise me. Questions were asked of my girlfriend along the lines of was there not a single one of her kind she could have found? Things were said within earshot that came as a shock, as I erroneously assumed that the Britain of the early seventies was an age removed from the Bristol of the early sixties. As I write this today, in the twenty-first century, there are still pockets of surprising behaviour. Two slight differences are that people are less blatant and in-your-face, and many of the younger ones appear happy to mix with those who are different. I guess that an increase in international travel has a role in this.

I felt safe inside the club as we had become friends with all the bouncers, especially David. He had a nose like that of a boxer who'd been on the wrong end of too many fights. It was squat and pointed towards his right ear. His paunch prevented the buttons on his jacket from getting anywhere near the holes made specifically for them. His brightly coloured socks, always visible, made me wonder why he did not let down the hem of his regulation black trousers.

Some of the bouncers let us in, even when we had no free promotional tickets available for Mondays to Wednesdays. Dancing was something that the black boys all enjoyed, and we made sure that other club goers noticed us. We tended to agree on the colour of our clothes for the evening. The moment a record we loved started playing, we attacked the dance floor en masse, and danced as if we were peacocks putting on a show for potential mates. The Nigerian contingent from Southwell Lodge stood out with our agreed uniformity of dress. The DJ played along by switching off all lights except the spotlight focused onto the centre of the dance floor, where we were exhibiting.

One evening, we were all at Scamps, with me in my favourite expensive white jacket, relaxing after a strenuous exhibition of dancing, when a total stranger walked up to me accompanied by two of his friends. I was still wiping the sweat off my brow and talking to Jane when the stranger slowly and deliberately poured a full pint of lager over my head. From my knowledge of beer, it tasted like lager.

'This one looks like he needs a wash,' he said, exhibiting an oddly shaped array of teeth stained brown by years of heavy smoking. I did not say a word but looked up at him with a questioning gaze. I must have resembled someone after more vigorous exercise than just dancing, as I was dripping wet. I could feel my underpants slowly getting wet as the collected pool in my lap gradually disappeared. The gangly stranger turned round to look at his friends, almost as if he was asking them to admire his handiwork. When he turned back to look at me, he was still grinning.

'Why did you do that?' I asked eventually, clenching both hands rhythmically and fighting the urge welling up inside me to stand up and knock the guy's stained teeth down his throat.

'Want to make anything of it?' he responded, arms outstretched and leaning back slightly, while nodding his head up and down like a puppet. I shook my head slowly in a further attempt to dissipate the anger bubbling up inside. Jane started shouting at the guy and I told her it wasn't necessary. She was gesticulating wildly near the guy's face, her blonde hair contrasting with her red face. I noticed two prominent veins on either side of her neck that I had never seen before. Her response surprised and impressed me in equal measure. Judging by the behaviour of some boys in the past, she might even have been the reason for the assault.

If I had stood up then, I would have done serious damage and might have ended up being prosecuted. Fortunately, I believed that there was no point in retaliation, as sometimes I felt convinced that things would even out in the long run. I was proved right, because David and another bouncer suddenly appeared and, without a word, grabbed this guy by an arm each and threw him down the stairs. I am certain that he made contact with every step on his way down. The

175

grin on his face was soon replaced by a frightened look. His two friends tried to intervene, and as other bouncers assumed that they were about to cause trouble, they received similar punishment. On reaching the bottom of the stairs, the three guys were pummelled, and if it had been a wrestling match, they would have submitted. Since that option was not open to them, they had to endure the beating. Realising that they were getting hurt and in danger of more of the same, and still dripping, I went down and pleaded with the bouncers to stop. The one who had poured the drink on me now had blood all over his face and had a gap where a couple of teeth had previously been. My pleading was heeded and the three were thrown out of the club and told that they were banned in future. I thanked the bouncers for coming to help and went to the toilets to clean up as best as I could.

As I left for home just after one in the morning, I was wary that the boys might be waiting outside, as there had been previous instances of arguments being settled outside a club or pub. People had apparently been shot at with air rifles or beaten with bicycle chains. I had been lucky on one occasion when someone tried to pick a fight with some friends and me at a petrol station in Caister-on-Sea. I had approached the car to ask for directions but the young men sitting inside had other ideas. The guy in the driver's seat jumped out and made a dash for the boot. It was just as well that I hesitated and was able to see that he had picked up a jack and was threatening to attack me. I backed off, making sure that I did not turn my back to him, entered my hired Godfrey Davis car and drove off with the tyres sounding as if they had had an argument with the road.

Fortunately, there was no one waiting outside the club as we left. It was explained to me later, by a friendly giant of an Irishman at the YMCA called Mick, that even bad guys had a code of ethics. As I had not done anything to them, it would not have been fair to attack me. Mildly confused, especially as the assault on me was unwarranted, I nodded and pretended to understand. Where was the code when the guy decided to drench me in cold beer?

Living in Norwich taught me to be on the lookout for people who might have bad intentions. Looking out for car drivers mounting the pavement to scare me was something I could never understand. At least, I hoped they were only trying to scare me. To this day, I still try and walk on pavements so that I can attempt jumping on car bonnets if required.

I still did some things that a few of my friends considered crazy, such as the day that I bought a pamphlet from a young man standing at the end of St Giles Street near the market. Ignorance of what the literature contained was a factor in my buying it. The vendor took the money, glanced at it and then at me as if to check I did not lack mental capacity. The obvious look of surprise on the young man's face did not switch on any bulb in my brain.

When I got back to the hostel, I happened to show the pamphlet to one of my friends who burst out laughing straight away. He laughed so much that tears streamed down his cheeks and had to hold on to a nearby table in order to stay upright. The friend, through intermittent intakes of air to satisfy his lungs, explained that the aim of selling the pamphlet was to raise enough money to repatriate all those they did not like. Oh dear, I thought, contributing to my own fare! *The Bulldog* was not a riveting read and was subsequently discarded. I might not have bought it had I had a much closer look at the picture on its front, which depicted a black man with a bone strategically placed through his nose.

As the weather warmed up, I realised that the exams were approaching and I cut down on visits to the clubs and pubs.

Some of my friends did the exact opposite; they thought that I was making a fuss of the exams. I just refused to contemplate failure. I was focused to such an extent, that I resorted to unorthodox methods in order to aid my revision. I used to get tired around one or two o'clock in the early hours of the morning. To stay awake, as drinking coffee did not always suffice, I developed the idea of drying ground coffee granules in an oven, and then using the dry powder as snuff. I found my eyes, upon looking in the mirror, were very red, as if I was on drugs. In a way, I was, except that this drug was not illegal.

My friends persisted in telling me that the exams did not require the amount of effort I was expending. I thought, but didn't express, if things were that simple, how come they were resitting? One guy seemed to be there for chasing and bedding as many girls as possible. He received a lot more allowance than the rest of us, and hardly studied. He used to hire cars so that he could impress the girls, and it worked. The cars were almost new and he used to take other Nigerian students and me for rides. I quickly stopped travelling with him when I discovered that he did not even have a proper licence. I could drive too but had resolved to take driving lessons and try to pass the test once the exams were over.

Late one morning, I was called down to main reception and when I arrived, was surprised to see two policemen. I was afraid because the police had once stopped me on my way to college. I was shown a warrant card and advised that I looked like a wanted suspect. I was free to go after I showed them my ID. These two had some questions for me. My initial fear soon dissipated as a rapid trawl of the memory bank could not recall anything that I might have done wrong. The police officers, the manager and I went into the manager's office where they showed me their warrant cards.

'Do you know a man called James?' one of them asked.

'Yes, everyone knows James,' I replied, raising my eyebrows and nodding.

'Have you ever been in a hired car of his?'

'Yes, but not recently.'

I was dying to find out where these questions were leading but had little success at that point. One police officer was writing down everything that I said, while the other did most of the talking. Some more of my fellow students were called in for questioning after me. Later that day, some of the Nigerian students and I met in one of the bedrooms. We attempted to try and figure out what the problem might be. It dawned on us that none of us had seen James on the day in question and wondered whether he had been arrested on a charge related to a hire car. Had he crashed one? Had he injured someone? We all agreed that he often drove too fast, overtaking on blind corners and the brow of hills. It would not surprise any of us if he had been involved in an accident.

A few days later he turned up after having missed some lessons, although that probably was of little relevance from his point of view. He was coy at first and did not want to tell anyone what had happened. Eventually, we prised the truth out of his reluctant mouth.

'You know that I hire cars a lot,' he stated. Most of us nodded in agreement.

'How did that involve the police? Did you have an accident or hurt someone?' I asked.

'No, nothing as simple as that.'

Simple? I thought. What was he going to tell us?

'Well' he said, placing a cigarette in his mouth and lighting it. 'I felt that since they made so much money from me and the other hirers, I could get something for my money.' By this time, he had totally lost everyone, and he could see from our faces that more explanation was needed. Continuing, he said, 'The last car that I hired, I reported it stolen.'

'Ahhh!' a few of the group chorused in amazement while expanding the word as is the wont with many Nigerians. That would explain the police visit, glancing up at him from the bed as the smoke from the cigarette in his right hand wafted upwards, followed by perfectly formed smoke rings from his mouth. Watching as he struggled to keep his eyes open, while ineffectively attempting to wave away smoke with his left hand, I realised that there was more to the story.

'Go on, James,' I coaxed.

'The car had not been stolen; I painted it another colour, kept it and told the car hire firm a lie. I never thought that they would find out so easily.'

'How did they find out?' someone asked.

'The police carried out some checks, and discovered that it had not really been stolen. Something to do with being on the lookout for the number plate.'

'What happens now?' I asked as it dawned on me that James had painted the car but had left the original number plates on! With that level of intelligence, maybe it was better that he did not take the exams at all.

'I have been offered a choice of paying a fine or going to court. I have decided to pay the fine because if my father ever finds out, I will be on the first plane back.'

I kept my thoughts to myself regarding how stupid James had been – painting a car with emulsion, leaving the original number plates on, and hoping to get away with it. If he was that stupid, he should stick to doing anything but study. I never got over the James escapade. Virtually the whole group in my class, especially those from abroad, appeared not to understand the importance of the forthcoming exams and when I spoke to them, it transpired that they could not cope with the unshackled freedom conferred by coming to England as an independent.

There was nobody asking about their whereabouts, and no one asking whether they had done any revision. They were free to do as they pleased, something I thought the majority could not handle.

The exams came soon enough and we all went and did our best. I found the papers difficult apart from chemistry. I loved the practical exams as I found that marks could be scored more easily in them. There was little margin for getting average marks. You either knew the answer or did not. Practical biology for example, included placing lettered flags and pins in organs of a dissected mouse. (I did feel sorry for the animals but at that time I could do nothing about it). Provided the pins did not fall out on the way to the examiners, and one was certain of things, it was easy to get good marks.

On the days when I had no exams, I was back in my room studying. The contrast with some of my friends could not be greater as, for them, the free days were excuses to have a lie-in. Anyway, they needed to recover from the excesses of the night before. After the exams were over, I really began to catch up on those evenings of going out that I had missed. I got a full-time job again at the Milk Marketing Board, working an eleven-day fortnight. This involved working a sixth day every other week. This was great as my days off were rotated sequentially. It was great when two long weekends came together. Getting up at six in the morning initially bothered me, but I soon got used to it.

Jack and I had lunch together and he invited me to his house on a few occasions. His Parkinson's was getting worse and there seemed little that medication could do to help. I felt very sorry for him as the condition had by then started to affect his gait more. He shuffled along, unable to lift his feet off the ground. Remarkably, he had little problem climbing the stairs at work when going to the canteen. Management made allowances for his problems, although some idiots thought it funny to mimic his walk. He had learnt to never fill his cup or glass, because the shakes were so bad that half the contents were spilt during transfer. I noticed the dried tea and coffee stains on the walls leading from the kitchen to the sitting room at Jack's house. There were some stains on the carpets too.

Jack felt confident enough to talk to me about most things, and I felt upset as I listened to the difficulties he had doing things most people took for granted. Shaving, washing and cleaning up after visiting the toilet were all extremely difficult for him. Unless you were in his shoes, there was no way to appreciate exactly what he was going through. A once-proud man reduced to that state by something over which he had no control and for which there was no definitive treatment, at least not a curative one. This was so sad to see.

Jack's eyes welled with tears as he proudly showed me old photographs of his time in the army. Those photographs showed a healthy-looking and fit younger man. He could probably have run a marathon in those days. The difference between what the pictures showed, and the man that I was talking to, was stark. If anyone had said in his army days that he would turn out like he had, no one would have believed it. Jack was widowed and he and his wife had been unable to have a family. Fortunately, he had some very good neighbours.

The pay at work was very good, so much so that I could save money to buy things I wanted. I bought some long play records including Motown, as well as some in vogue at the time such as David Cassidy, Dave Edmonds and the Jackson 5. I possessed energy that I was unaware I had, because on some nights we returned from the night club after two in the morning and I still managed to get up for work at six.

On the way home from the club, we occasionally stopped off by the castle to buy beef burgers smothered with fried onions and drowning in ketchup. Arriving home did not always mean that we went to bed straight away; we sometimes stayed up smoking and chatting. To prevent tiredness and falling asleep at work, I drank cups of black coffee. None of the others who had jobs needed to get up as early as me, so it mattered less to them how many hours sleep they had. By the time I arrived at work, the milk tankers had long since left to make their deliveries.

I opened a Gateway Building Society account and paid money in regularly. The plan was to encourage saving and I paid in five pounds a month. As long as I kept the investment for five years, and made no withdrawals in that time, I received a decent rate of interest. Anyone willing and able to leave the accumulated money for a further two years, with no compulsion to add more by regular or lump sum investment, was rewarded with an equivalent amount of interest after two further years. This seemed like a good idea. No one confiscated the passbook and I was not considered a potential crook.

13

It was a wonderful summer holiday and for the first time in a very long time, I did not wish the holidays away. Work took up most of the day and enjoying myself with friends in pubs and visiting clubs in Great Yarmouth accounted for the remainder. On occasions, we missed the last train back from Yarmouth and slept in shop doorways. The best ones had a recess to provide respite from the wind and cold. The downside was the creation of a place for the wind to skim thereby creating a loud whistling noise. Fortunately, tiredness ensured our sleep was not disturbed.

I had many happy moments when looking at my life as it had become. I also knew that should I pass the A level exams, I would be going to Bristol University where I had been offered a place to study physiology.

Medicine would have been the preferred option, but the university was not prepared to offer a place on the medical course after one year's study. It was felt that I was setting myself too high a bar in attempting to attain the entrance requirements. The Cambridge interview had been for medicine. Maybe I should not have been too smart at Pembroke. I assumed that I would never have been invited for interview had I not been in with a chance of being made an offer. My career choice was between medicine and law. I just wanted an occupation where I could be useful to those going through a bad patch. I chose medicine in the end because I reasoned that, unlike law, almost all of your patients/clients would love you. I wanted to be loved as I couldn't cope with the alternative. I sometimes wonder whether I possessed innate ability as I had passed the 11-plus at the first attempt. It occurred to me that there appeared to be a direct correlation between my academic success and the presence of my parents. I might have done better at my Cambridge interview if I had been a full-time student getting adequate sleep and not working to earn extra money.

Both of my parents visited England every year, and on arriving in Norwich in the summer of 1973 they had Bode in tow. He too was going to attend the college, having done very well in his GCE exams in Nigeria. I was very pleased to see him. They stayed in a local hotel, where we met up on some days. Father had a love for Chinese takeaway meals and the hotel had no objection to our eating in the room.

Middle of August and the results were ready to be collected at the college. I had already arranged with my chemistry teacher that I would telephone and ask a single question. Whether I then went into college to collect the results in person depended on his answer.

I went to the communal telephone hanging on the wall in the lobby of the YMCA and dialled the college. I waited with rapidly moistening palms as the phone rang in the teacher's office. Any longer, and the handset would have slipped out of my grasp.

'Hello sir,' I said, holding on tightly to the phone, 'It's Sola here'.

'Morning Sola. How are you feeling?'

'Extremely nervous,' I replied.

'That's understandable'.

Oh dear, I thought. Should I have reason to remain nervous?

'Is it worth me coming to get my results in person?' I asked.

'It might be pleasurable to do so'.

'Thank you very much sir,' I replied, my legs and whole body feeling too light to support my weight. The prearranged coded response from the teacher was wonderful. Anyone passing by just then would wonder why I looked so happy. I was wearing a grin so wide that the creases at the corners of my mouth must have resembled quotation marks. I could not remember replacing the handset but do remember giving out a loud whoop of joy. I walked out of the back door, past the Labour Club, and virtually skipped my way towards St Stephens roundabout. I knew that I had not failed the exams, and despite not knowing how I had performed, I could not stop singing.

When I got to the college many students had arrived already, their faces showing a spectrum of emotions. The happy faces were illuminated by broad grins, while some of the others wore expressions of total grief superimposed on facial masks of incredulity. The latter group unsurprisingly included many of my fellow Africans and clubbers. These people had thought that my studying was unnecessary. Still unaware of the specific nature of my own fate, I did not stop to chat. I approached the classroom door and there was one of my teachers sitting at a desk outside. Laid out on the table in front of him were brown envelopes, arranged in rows according to surnames in alphabetical order. Scanning the envelopes, I could see my name, despite reading the names upside down.

The teacher did not need to ask me to provide ID and handed me the envelope. I opted not to open it there and sought a quiet corner near the canteen. I opened the envelope with trembling hands, and tried peeking inside to see whether anything was visible. I could not see anything meaningful so decided to pull out the piece of paper. The first thing to come into focus, were the words physics, chemistry and biology. I then saw that I had passed all three subjects. I involuntarily dropped the badly torn envelope on the floor, and just stared at the paper in my still-trembling hands. My feeling of joy was almost uncontrolled. A passing member of staff cleared his throat. I picked up the litter I had dropped and quietly gave thanks to God. On the way out of the front entrance, I missed my footing and grabbed on to a handrail. I felt lucky not to have fallen as I could have been injured when my soft and still joyous facial features met hard uncompromising concrete.

Outside, my friends were waiting to see how I had got on. I did not have to tell them. Some were genuinely happy, while others feigned unconvincing joy for my success. Here was this guy who had a year to study for his A levels and managed to pass them all. That was too hard to bear for some. It was not going to be the only time that my achievements were going to be envied. Asking them what they were going to do in the future did not seem appropriate, so I talked about nothing in particular.

Trying to remain calm inside was like a young man attempting to control a very powerful dog. I could hardly wait to convey the good news to my parents at their hotel. I left the college after chatting to some friends for a while longer and went straight to my parents' hotel. I don't recall ever seeing them as happy as they appeared that day. Mother hugged me so tightly that I thought that I would soon stop breathing. We agreed to meet later that evening to decide on where we could have a celebratory dinner.

After leaving the hotel, I went straight to the bank to withdraw some money. The next stop was an electrical store at the bottom of St Giles Street, and it was there that I treated myself to a present. I bought a Grundig music system, using some of the money I had saved from my earnings from the Milk Marketing Board.

Having passed the exams, relaxation became easier; I went out in the evenings without a care in the world. I got in touch with Bristol University to confirm that I had achieved the grades, and would be starting with them in September. Things were going well and on reflection, I could not help wondering what would have happened if I had stayed in Nigeria, twenty-one-years old and just passed A levels. All things having progressed normally, Italian and English John would both, by then, be about to finish three-year university courses. Somehow, along the way, I had lost three years of education since passing the 11-plus exam in Bristol some ten years before. To think that Bristol would be the next port of call in my life amused me, as it was not something I would have thought likely. The coincidences were amazing. Ibadan Grammar School was down the road from where the foster parents lived; Bristol, where I had gone to primary and early grammar school, was to feature again in my life. The way things were working out, I would not have been surprised if I ended up at some future date in Cambridge.

The relationship with Jane was intensifying to an extent that my girlfriend in Nigeria gradually assumed a lesser role. I was still extremely wary of doing anything too dangerous, as my home and school life had lacked any form of sexual education. All I had been told at home was that should any girl get pregnant, I would have to support her and any child by myself. Not being in a position to look after a family, it was my only motivation to avoid succumbing to natural urges.

As the time approached to leave for Bristol, I realised that I had no accommodation sorted out. I happened to mention my plight to the manager of the YMCA and was pleased when he told me that he knew the manager of the Bristol branch, and that he would have a word. This was how I got a room at the YMCA in Bristol next to Colston Hall.

Before leaving Norwich, I decided to surprise Jane by visiting her at home. I had only ever spoken to her dad on the telephone and thought he sounded like a great guy, a view reinforced by what Jane had already told me. I drove to her house in another hired car and knocked on the front door. A short, angry-looking man wearing a striped jumper opened the door, his right arm across the doorway in a manner one would expect if he were trying to prevent my entry.

'Can I help you?' he demanded in a tone and voice that told me that maybe I was not welcome. I knew that I had not come to the wrong house as it was the only one on the street with a shop underneath.

'I've come to see Jane,' I replied, my voice hesitant.

'And who are you?' he asked slowly and pointedly, with the emphasis on the word *you* an octave higher than the first three words. He sounded like an American southerner I had seen in films.

'Sola,' I replied even more hesitantly in a low voice as if unsure of my own name.

'You are Sola?' he said, with the index finger of his free hand jabbing to and fro a few inches from my face, without any attempt to hide his incredulity.

'Yes, that's me'.

'Wait here,' he ordered and bounded up the stairs, which were in line with the open front door, two at a time. As his back disappeared round the corner, I heard raised voices. He was asking Jane whether she had been brought up this way. I listened not knowing exactly what he meant by the question, but I could hazard a guess. Was this how she was going to repay their love and affection? Why had she not told him that I was black? What had this man thought about my name? Sola isn't exactly an English-sounding name. Judging by the noise and tone in his voice, even I recognised why she had not done so. He came back down the stairs, and brushed past me in a hurry. He got into his car and drove off causing the tyres to make a noise as though it was an expression of his feelings.

I was still standing when a meek voice invited me upstairs. Jane and her mum and sister appeared subdued. Her mother exuded kindness and apologised for her husband's behaviour. She was certain that he would soon get over it. Jane had inherited her mother's figure and looks. Her sister was different and obviously loved her food. I could not drink the tea that was offered but managed to stay for almost half an hour before I thought it prudent to leave. Jane was apologetic too but I understood without her having to explain. It did not affect our relationship, which continued as normal.

Over the succeeding months, my behaviour gradually brought Jane's father round sufficiently for him to trust me enough to bank the business takings. I used to offer to help restock the shelves in the evenings. We chatted about my love of sport, especially football. I narrated my experience of visiting Carrow Road with friends to watch Norwich City play home matches.

I knew that he had finally accepted me when he said that I could call him Malcolm. Malcolm was forty-eight years old and had a friendly face, so different from the one that I witnessed on our first meeting. His features could be described as being soft, contrasting sharply with those I met initially. His fair hair had a parting down the right side, and he made sure that he always used his comb, which was always in one of his pockets. He wasn't very tall. He was muscular and, when we accidentally bumped into each other in the small stockroom, I felt like a skittle. I marvelled at the way that he could pick up a crate of soft drinks as if it was empty. Over time, he even offered to pay my membership fees for the local golf club. Getting to know me better, Jane's father seemed to change completely, and confessed that never having met anyone foreign before, he had no experience against which to compare me. His views had been based on what he read and saw in the media, and from discussion with local friends.

Later on that summer, an incident occurred in a shop near where I had bought my music centre. Mike, one of the few successful students from Nigeria, and who had a place at Salford University, and I went shopping. Mike ate a lot of food and never gained weight. It seemed as if anything he ate stretched him upwards like a plant growing towards the light. His toothpick shape belied his muscular strength. I couldn't believe it the first time he beat me at arm wrestling. After paying for his goods, the assistant would not place the change directly in Mike's hand, dropping the coins from an indiscreet height. Mike was angry and threw the whole lot back at her.

'What is the matter with you?' he demanded in a voice loud enough to cause other customers to look to see what the problem was. Upon getting no reply, he spoke again in a louder voice.

'Do you think I have a disease?' His head moved forward and they almost touched noses.

'Mike, it's not worth it,' I pleaded, grabbing hold of his left arm.

'Let me go,' he shouted, tearing his arm away.

I bent down to pick up the coins while Mike was still shouting at the top of his voice. If he wasn't careful, I thought he risked bursting a blood vessel somewhere. I did not know what to do next. I was embarrassed as other shoppers stared, with the less brave casting surreptitious glances.

'I demand to see the manager,' Mike said, emphasising each word at a decibel that could not surely be louder. By now, we had an audience, some of whom were having their innate prejudices stoked and cemented.

The manager arrived, having been attracted by the commotion.

'Can I help?' he asked in a voice and manner that was inborn into the British. He would have made a decent ambassador somewhere, I thought. The voice and manner calmed Mike down.

'That girl threw my change at me,' he said, pointing and jabbing in the poor girl's direction. I thought about, but decided against, pointing out that she had not thrown anything at him.

'Is that true?' he asked the girl who by then was visibly shaken.

'Yes,' she replied in a very subdued voice.

'Can you please apologise to the gentleman.'

The girl apologised, Mike was given his change in a manner acceptable to him and we left the shop. He appeared satisfied at the outcome. I pointed out that he had done the wrong thing, but Mike would not agree. I tried explaining to him that he should have accepted the money and left. As it was, he got an apology, which did not appear genuine to me. I, too, would apologise to anyone to save my job. Whatever prejudices that poor girl had were definitely reinforced, in my view. The best way to change attitude was to act in a manner at variance with that already in the mind of the aggressor, I insisted. No matter how hard I tried to explain to Mike, he would not accept my argument.

I hated and still hate confrontation that might lead to aggression. I would rather walk away and not get involved unless my physical integrity was in danger. That is not to say that I have never been involved in some serious fights in my time, especially during those days when I had anger and aggression that required dissipation. Those experiences had taught me that such behaviour had a tendency to spiral out of control. I felt that a person cannot fight every single battle, and besides, it is easy to ascribe a given behaviour to a reason that might not be the correct one.

I was affected and influenced by a story I read as a young boy that was based on Welsh legend. It told of a faithful hound named Gelert who was killed by his huntsman owner because he thought that the dog had killed his infant son. On returning from a hunting trip and seeing his dog covered in blood, he shot him. As the dog writhed in agony and breathed its last, the sound of a baby crying came from the overturned cot. The huntsman, named Llywelyn, gently removed the bedding and there beneath the cot was his baby looking up at him. Next to the infant was a dead fox. Llywelyn, on realising his error, was inconsolable. I have a personal saying which is *A clock viewed through a mirror doesn't necessarily indicate the correct time.*

I packed my green suitcase I had brought to England the year before and got ready to travel to Bristol by train. Another chapter was about to start in my life. From this point on, faith, hard work and good friends were to be my companions and helpers as I travelled up the steep, uneven slope hoping for success and good fortune.

14

I arrived at Bristol Temple Meads train station in the afternoon. I was impressed by how clean the station was with not a piece of litter to be seen anywhere. I asked a member of the station staff how to get to Colston Street in the city centre. He suggested two options, which were to take the bus or to take a taxi. I opted for the latter as I was less likely to get lost. The sun was shining and the warm air enveloped me in its welcoming embrace. I felt happy, cossetted and contented, like fingers in a woollen glove on a cold winter's day. I spent a while just gazing out of the taxi's window, thinking how beautiful Bristol looked. Unlike Norwich, it appeared more cosmopolitan and people just looked happy as they went about their business.

On arriving at the YMCA, I noticed the external sign was identical to the one in Norwich. On my left was Colston Hall. This was the same Colston whose statue was recently pulled down in Bristol and thrown into the harbour. Edward Colston made his money from the slave trade in the seventeenth and eighteenth centuries, and had many things in Bristol named after him. Now, in the twenty-first century, attitudes are such that people like him are no longer seen as those to be venerated and honoured. In the United States, the Black Lives Matter movement has grown and certain historical acts, such as a lack of opportunities for blacks and minorities, which still persist, are seen as no longer acceptable. I remain to be convinced that change will occur without the support of the good men and women who live in the same ivory towers as the oppressors of minorities.

There are those who say that statues of people like Colston should be in the museum. Cecil Rhodes, too, was a slave owner who became extremely wealthy. He funded scholarships for students at Oxford, including for black students. Recently, some Oxford University students have demanded that his statue must come down too.

I think that if the statues are in museums, schools must also cover such people in lessons in order to educate the young people about what happened historically. Ignorance of history, it could be argued, makes its repeat more likely. The question remains that what if some not very good people in the past had a change of heart and realised the errors of their ways? Is forgiveness something that should not be considered because someone once had a belief that was extremely awful and led to the suffering of fellow human beings? Setting up scholarships and giving money to the arts and education may be a way some might have tried to make amends. Whether this action fully makes amends or not is open for discussion. Every single human being has a history from the day of his or her birth. How many of us, once we reach, say middle age, can honestly say that we are 100 per cent happy with every course of action that we ever took? On a personal level, I might not have had to do various jobs as a student if any benefactor had provided my funding. My focus would be on the good that I could offer others through my subsequent success.

I paid the taxi driver, gave him a small tip and thanked him. I pushed open the heavy, glass-fronted door and was surprised to see that the ground floor was empty. I climbed the stairs and found reception was on the first floor. The gentleman at the desk must have been expecting me as he addressed me by my name and welcomed me to the Bristol YMCA. He had a dark suit and tie on and wore dark-rimmed glasses. The glasses matched the colour of his thin and well-trimmed sideburns. I completed the necessary forms and collected an information pack.

He took me up a couple of flights and showed me to my bedroom. As I followed him up the stairs, I noticed that he had a problem and always placed his right foot first on every step. I assumed that he must have an arthritic hip joint. His limp on level ground was mild.

This place was to be my home for the next three years. The window allowed rays of the late afternoon sunshine to come through. I could see the small and normally invisible dust particles floating in the shaft of light. A brief glance indicated that my room was at the front of the building and since I loved watching the world go by, this suited me right down to the ground. The room was warm enough and I hoped that it would be sufficiently warm come the winter.

I was shown the communal bathroom and toilet, and advised to come downstairs once I had unpacked. I placed the two keys he had given me on a small desk in the corner of the room. The desk was scratched and looked old; it couldn't have been polished for a while. I lifted its creaky hinged lid and the space underneath was empty. I placed my loose change in it and put the pack he had given me on the desk. On the table was a lamp, which looked almost as old as the desk.

The wires leading from its base reminded me of the plaits of hair I used to see back in Ibadan. I wondered about what kind of people had sat at that desk in the years before me. I unpacked my suitcase and hung my clothes in the wardrobe. I put my shoes on the floor of the wardrobe.

After unpacking, I locked my door, walked down the well-lit corridor and went down the wide staircase back to reception. The man at reception, whose name was Bernard, told me that the two keys were for the main front door and my bedroom. He explained that the main door was locked at ten o'clock at night. He must have anticipated my question, as he told me that if required, there was a doorbell and the night porter would come downstairs if needed. He got up from his seat, led me round a corner not far from reception, and we entered a room through swing doors. He did not need to explain as I could see that this was the dining room. At its far end was a rectangular serving hatch and there were tables with four chairs at each. I was surprised to see that the tablecloths were made of what looked like cotton. Each table had a salt and pepper cellar on it as well as bottles of tomato ketchup and vinegar.

After confirming that I had no immediate questions, he left me to explore the building. I was surprised and happy to see that there was a snooker room with four tables. I had come to like playing snooker as the Norwich YMCA had had a table too, but now there seemed to be an opportunity to play more often.

On the way back to my bedroom, I stopped and asked about eating. My six pounds a week rent included all breakfasts and evening meals on weekdays. If I wanted to eat outside of these times, I had the option of paying for them.

I sat on my bed and thought about how far I had travelled in my life's journey. After a while, I decided to go for a short walk round the area. The university buildings and the Bristol Royal Infirmary or BRI as it was known locally were nearby. Not far from the YMCA was a flight of steps leading down to a courtyard where there was a fish and chip shop as well as a post office. Being almost six o'clock in the evening, the smell of fish and chips frying stimulated the receptors in my nostrils before my eyes saw the shop. I knew where I would be having supper that night.

The rest of the weekend flew by as I ventured further afield and played snooker with a couple of friends who also lived at the YMCA. One, named Simon, was a very nice man with long, brown hair, which most likely didn't often see a comb or water frequently. His hair almost reached as far as his waist and he occasionally tied it with a rubber band. He was always smiling, and said if there was anything that I needed, I should just ask. I was slightly taller than him by a few inches. He told me that his room was on the third floor and was number 16. I informed him that my room was on the second floor and was number 10. He replied that he was an aspiring musician who had yet to make it. I replied that I was about to start a three-year course at the university, studying for a Bachelor of Science degree in Physiology.

On Monday morning, I went to the Students' Union in order to register and see what clubs I wanted to sign up for. I was fortunate to run into a tall, blond young man named Chris. He had dimples in both cheeks, which were accentuated when he smiled. I couldn't believe it when he told me that he was on the same course as me. I told him I had travelled from Norwich and my parents were Nigerian. He lived alone in Bedford with his mother as his father had died. Chris was not keen on joining any club and neither was I. We signed up for our courses and collected our timetables. Chris had a room in Goldney Hall in Clifton. I promised to try and visit him.

My time in Bristol was great because I really enjoyed the city. I applied for and got a cleaning job at the BRI to supplement the remittances I received from Nigeria. I worked two evenings a week plus Saturday and Sunday mornings. The pay was good. The cleaning in the week was always after 6 p.m. I remember cleaning a room with a machine that hummed all the time. I think the machine was called a betatron, and I didn't know whether it had radiation associated with it. However, a fellow worker told me that it was a radiology machine that was built half below ground in order to prevent radiation leaking out. Looking back, I don't think the health and safety of today would allow unprotected young men to be cleaning around such places. Many years later as I lay on a couch in Cambridge undergoing radiotherapy, my mind went back to that machine in Bristol.

My funniest work experience involved the time we decided to go on strike for more pay. Our representative, Sheila, had met with management before coming back to tell the rest of us what had been offered. Sheila stood at the front wearing her overalls with her hair covered by a yellow scarf. We all sat in one of the lecture theatres as she stood up and cleared her throat while waving cigarette smoke away from her face.

'Comrades,' she said, as she took a long drag from the filterless cigarette in her left hand. 'We have been offered a ten per cent pay rise by management. What do you think about that?' The last word uttered as though she never wanted that kind of word to be even next to her tongue.

I listened, as various people offered their input. The majority wanted to refuse the percentage offered. They were willing to be guided. A small proportion thought that a rise of any sort was to be welcomed. Eventually, Sheila looked directly at me and pointed.

'Sola, you are the clever one with attending university, what do you think?'

I hesitated, looked around at my fellow workers who had thought that 10 per cent was an insult. I rubbed my forehead slowly as I pondered what answer to give.

'Well!' said Sheila as she took yet another drag on her cigarette. She coughed and her face went a tinge of blue, no doubt worsened by her coughing, For a second, I thought we might need a new representative. She regained her composure and wiped tears from her face with her sleeve.

'My opinion is that we should accept the percentage raise offered,' I said.

'Sola, Sola,' she said pronouncing my name as if it possessed three or more extra letter a's. 'You don't understand,' she continued. 'What you should be asking is this. If they only offer us ten percent, who gets the remaining ninety per cent?'

I looked around the hall in surprise. Some were nodding in agreement with her as they repeated the question. I thought it prudent not to say anything more. It was all I could do to prevent myself from laughing.

I really liked working at the BRI as it allowed me to save money and live a decent life at university. The extra 10 per cent pay rise that was later agreed on went into my Post Office savings. I frequented the Union with Chris when there was something we liked going on. In those days, we had pop stars come to play at some events. I liked listening to the band Wizard on my cassette player and could not resist attending the Students' Union when the band came to play. I arrived relatively early and was standing by the entrance when the bandleader, Roy Wood, arrived. He possessed a long beard and did not look like a pop star. I couldn't believe it when the security at the door refused him entry. I heard the doorman say that if he was a pop star, then *he* was the king of England.

Fortunately, one of the organisers came down and vouched for him. I felt like saying that we currently had a queen.

When I wasn't at the Union, I went to a nightclub below street level called The Dug Out on Park Row. Access to the club was down a steep set of stairs and the local joke was that those who could safely negotiate them must be sober. I enjoyed attending the club, mainly on Saturday evenings. The inside was very dim making it difficult to see another person clearly. The place lacked proper windows and it was usually filled with all kinds of smells. The overwhelming smell was of marijuana. If anybody was too poor to buy some from the young men at the club entrance, I felt certain that there must have been enough in the air, costing nothing.

The place was usually teeming, crammed full of sweaty young bodies moving, as best they could, in time with the noisy music. It was a truly United Nations environment with all kinds of nationalities present. Audible conversation was difficult, as you sometimes heard the last part of sentences being shouted as the music stopped. Catching only parts of a sentence occasionally made me smile as it was disconnected from whatever had gone first. I made a few friends, of all nationalities. We sometimes went up to street level in order to get some fresh air as well as to smoke the occasional cigarette.

A couple of the black people I met were surprised that I was at university. Some others even called me a traitor for wanting to be educated. This sentiment shocked and surprised me. It was one of these two people who warned me to be careful. Apparently, people they knew were out to beat me up for letting the side down. This was what made me start carrying a metal Afro comb, which ostensibly was for my hair, but in reality, was a defensive weapon. Fortunately, I never had to use it.

I enjoyed attending lectures and I got on very well with

201

Chris. He was much smarter than me and he helped explain things that I didn't understand in physiology. On our course was another young man named Steve. He came from Norwich and owned a Hillman Imp car which took us both to Norwich for many weekend breaks. Fortunately, I was able to stay at the YMCA during these trips as well as during university holidays. Steve was short and wore glasses. He was very funny and always made me laugh. Whenever he drove his car, he appeared to be straining to look over the steering wheel. With Chris much taller than Steve and me in the middle, we looked lopsided when the three of went out together. Steve always spoke in a quiet voice and I had to concentrate in order to hear him clearly.

During my first year, Jane visited me at Bristol on some weekends and as the YMCA frowned on ladies sharing our bedrooms, we stayed in a local bed and breakfast in Clifton. Our relationship appeared not to have been affected by the separation. There were a few girls in Bristol who made advances that I managed to reject because I felt that I had to be faithful.

At the end of the first term of my second year, I went to Norwich for Christmas, as usual. Adebo and Yinka had arrived in England that summer and had started their studies in King's Lynn and a girl's school in Norwich, respectively. We met up with other Nigerians including Mike, who travelled down from Manchester. I did have some savings but I was still careful with money. Mike had started going out with Jane's best friend and being from a family that sent him more allowance than me, he bought his girlfriend a fur coat for Christmas. I went to H. Samuel and bought a reasonably priced necklace for Jane.

The girls must have discussed their presents because on Boxing Day I received a phone call from Jane. My legs went weak as I stood at the communal phone in the YMCA. Jane told me calmly that our relationship was over. She accused me of being a skinflint because all I could buy her was jewellery compared to the fur coat her friend received. I couldn't believe what she was telling me, and I was still talking before it dawned on me that she had put her phone down. I went up to my bedroom and cried for a long time. The next day I visited her house to try and get her to change her mind but she refused to see me. I had bought a present that I could afford and it wasn't enough. I am not sure how I would have coped if I had been in Bristol when she phoned. Much later, some friends told me that I was lucky to have discovered the type of person she was at an early stage. This helpful piece of information did not ease my pain. I found out later, through mutual friends, that Malcolm was very upset by the fact that we had broken up.

In the summer of 1975, Chris suggested that we go on holiday to Majorca. I agreed readily as I had not been to many places other than Nigeria and England, not counting the occasions when aeroplanes were refuelled. We drove to Luton Airport in his Ford Escort. I was very excited at the thought of going abroad. Owing to a traffic jam caused by an accident on the road, we almost missed our flight. That experience is the reason that I now arrive at an airport either the night before a flight, or many hours early. My family still make fun of me, but all I can say is that until they miss a flight or cut it fine, they cannot appreciate my views.

Our one-week break was the most enjoyable thing that I had done in a very long time. We stayed in a resort called Cala Millor and had the sea and sand next to our hotel. We swam in the sea and hired yellow motorcycles in order to explore further inland. We visited the caves of Drach, where the further we progressed, the more scared I became that we might get lost or run out of oxygen.

The week's holiday flew by so quickly that I wanted to stay on. We met two girls on the island and that could have been the reason for my wanting the stay extended. We exchanged addresses with them and as far as I know, neither Chris nor I followed up.

My studies progressed fairly well despite my playing snooker for the YMCA's second team and working as a cleaner at the BRI. I spent many nights trying to keep up with my work, especially as I knew my future depended on managing to get qualifications which would allow me to earn an independent living.

In my third year, I had to write a dissertation on something called coupling in nerve cells. We used frog skins for the experiments and pithing the frogs made me feel extremely uncomfortable. Pithing involved inserting a very sharp object down the spine just behind the eyes. We had to use this method to kill them because any other method might have been painful or interfere with the study. It was known that nerve signals travel down nerve fibres in a given manner, and we wanted to find out whether neural messages sent down one nerve could be picked up by another nerve supplying the same area of the frog skin.

One scientist had worked on something similar many years before; my supervisor suggested we wrote to him in order to read his published papers. This was the reason I found myself writing to the Reverend Dr John Habgood. He had long given up being a scientist and was, in 1976, the Bishop of Durham. He went on to become the Archbishop of York. He was extremely gracious and wrote back. With his input and my experiments, I managed to present a decent dissertation.

I was happy, in the very hot summer of 1976, to be able

to attend the graduation ceremony for my year group. Both parents travelled from Nigeria and I could see that they were proud of my achievement. I wasn't too happy, though, as I could only scrape a second-class degree. But everything considered, I couldn't really complain, as I possessed a qualification that could help in advancing my life. Many photographs were taken of my parents and me. I ordered a few so that I could give them to Father and Mother to keep as mementos of their eldest son achieving a BSc in Physiology.

As soon as I could, I set about considering what I should do next and decided that I would still like to qualify as a doctor. I didn't feel my degree and where I was then could compete with young boys and girls applying to medical schools. I thought that I would apply to universities in order to study for a PhD in Physiology, especially as I had enjoyed doing the dissertation. I wasn't in the same position as my father had been in in 1950 when his A levels were good enough to get him into medical school. I wrote to many universities asking whether they had any lecturers who were carrying out research on the brain. If I ever made it to medicine, I loved the idea of being a brain surgeon.

I received only two replies from Aberdeen and Cambridge. I opted for Cambridge, as I wanted to make up for my error of December 1972. The fact that it was close to Norwich was also a factor as I knew the place and still had friends there.

I arrived at Cambridge train station in late July 1976 and made my way to the physiology department on Downing Street. I looked smart in my light-grey suit and Bristol University tie. I had bought the suit and shoes from C&A near Norwich market. My tie was new, having bought it at the post-graduation events in Bristol. It had two crests on it celebrating the fact that the university was one hundred years old in 1976. In 1876, it had been known as University College.

As I entered the department, I looked at the photographs lining the wall and couldn't believe my eyes. On those walls were photographs of people that I had only ever read about in textbooks. My body appeared confused as it tried to balance the gravitas of the place with the awe that I felt. Some of these people were Nobel laureates. I made my way to reception and told the gentleman there that I had come for an interview with Professor Shute. He made a phone call and within minutes, someone came down to confirm that I had come to see the professor.

'You must be Sola,' he said. 'Please follow me.'

I followed him through dimly lit corridors and eventually reached an office. The room was cluttered with all sorts of books and papers. His appearance mirrored the state of the office as he was wearing crumpled, brown corduroy trousers, with a matching brown jacket. His shoes were brown as well and I wondered whether this was his favourite colour. His shirt was unbuttoned at the top and I glimpsed chest hairs matching the colour of those on his head. He was thinning on top, with more grey hairs than dark, and was slightly shorter than me. As I sat looking round and thinking, I mentally rehearsed answers to imaginary questions. My thought process was interrupted when he asked me if I wanted a cup of tea. I said that I would and he left the room. He returned after about ten minutes.

'I hope that you don't mind sugar and milk, as I forgot to ask.'

'I am fine with both thanks.'

'Now, I see that you didn't do as well in your degree as your supervisor Dr Matthews, expected,' he said. He must have seen the look of surprise on my face. How did this man know? Goodness, he had already spoken to my supervisor in Bristol.

'I am Professor Shute,' he announced.

I never would have guessed this was the man himself. I had assumed, from his appearance, that he worked for the great man.

'I have a topic that I would like investigating by a PhD student. As your letter said that you were interested in the workings of the human brain, I thought you might be the right person. It is called the McCollough effect and I hope to find out more about it.'

'I am happy to work on it as you think it is important enough to investigate further,' I said. 'Can you please tell me more about it?'

'It involves looking at how the visual pathway is utilised in learning and memory by studying the effects of various factors on this process.'

He handed me a paper on the topic and told me to read the method and conclusions from an experiment that had been published. I read the piece of paper a couple of times in order to make sure that I understood it. More importantly, I felt it was crucial that I could ask a decent question, which I managed.

After almost an hour of discussion, he offered me the chance to be his PhD student. I was so happy that I couldn't stop thanking him.

'Do you have a college yet?' he asked. 'You need to belong to a college in order to be a student here'

'No sir,' I replied.

'No problem I will have a word with the responsible tutor in college tonight'.

That was it; interview done and I had places in the department and at Christ's College.

I don't recall much of my return trip to Bristol. I was so happy that I cried most of the way. I can't understand why

I resort to crying when someone is kind to me. Maybe there is a research topic in there for someone. I managed not to cry while crossing from King's Cross station to Paddington. I decided to stay in Bristol for the summer as I didn't want to have to pack up twice by travelling to Norwich first. I found a summer job via Manpower working on a building site and earned very good money most of which I saved in my building society account. This was to prove useful as Cambridge was going to be a more expensive place to study and live. Thoughts of returning to Cambridge to study excited and scared me in equal measure.

15

It was about four in the afternoon on a sunny September in 1976 that I drove up to the front of Christ's College in my hired car. I parked the car half on the pavement and half on the road. I entered through the heavy and ancient-looking wooden gates and entered the porters' lodge on my left, just before an immaculate-looking lawn in first court. One of the porters, who had a completely bald head, was sitting at the desk. The ceiling lights reflecting off his head made it resemble another light bulb. I introduced myself and he checked names on a list in front of him. He found my name and welcomed me to Christ's. He told me that his name was Peter and that he originally came from Poland. Peter was much taller than me and he was much bigger physically too. I guessed that if he ever played rugby, he would have been at number eight. I assumed that he must have had dark hair at some point judging by the colour of his eyebrows. He pointed out my allocated pigeonhole on the wall for letters I might receive.

Peter helped me unload the car and asked me to move it

to the back of the college on King Street, as I shouldn't be blocking the highway. I could then walk back so he could show me my staircase. Initially confused, I then recalled that at my interview at Pembroke some years before, my allocated room had been on a staircase.

On my return to the lodge, having walked down Hobson Street and past the gates to the Master's Lodge, Peter was waiting. He carried my suitcase as we walked round the first court lawn, pointing out places as we went past the entrance to the library, the buttery, the formal dining hall and kitchens, and then into second court. There was another immaculate lawn here too. He pointed out the entrance to the informal dining hall and then we arrived at staircase C. On the wall were names painted in white of all occupants on that staircase. There it was: C5 Sola Amure. Seeing this caused a sudden gush of pride to rise from my toes all the way to the top of my head in much the same way I guessed a geyser functioned.

Room C5 was at the very top and my window overlooked Drummer Street bus station. The room had a sink and a single bed as well as a desk and wardrobe. I thanked Peter after receiving my keys, and he left. I couldn't stay too long as I had to return the car to the hire company before a certain time so as not to incur extra charges.

I learnt later on that C5 was the room that Earl Mountbatten of Burma, great-grandson of Queen Victoria, was allocated when he attended Christ's College in 1919 to study English literature. I could not prove this definitively. That room is now used for housing overnight guests to the college. Two of the other students on my staircase were from Zimbabwe and Pakistan. It was a standing joke that we were placed there on purpose, as the staircase had a boiler on the ground floor making the staircase pretty warm.

On my return, I went to my room and put my things away.

I then went for a walk to explore the immediate surroundings. Walking round reminded me of Bristol as I saw faces of different shades. I loved the market, and most of the shops and old buildings looked great. I even managed to walk as far as the Downing Street site in order to see how far my department was on foot. Many times, I still found it difficult to believe that I was a Cambridge University student.

Over the next few days, I familiarised myself with the college layout. I discovered the common room for postgraduate students and located the squash court and New Court. New Court was the newest of the student accommodation and the rooms were tiered in what could only be described as staggered layers similar to a typewriter.

Walking round the college one afternoon, I met two faces I recognised from Bristol. One was a Nigerian man and the other a Welshman. I wasn't clever enough to work out the odds of three Bristol undergraduates ending up at the same college in Cambridge, studying for a PhD, but needless to say, I was glad that I had familiar faces to talk to. To complete the coincidences, I ran into Chris just outside college on St Andrew's Street. He told me that he had applied to join the Lloyds Bank management trainee scheme after obtaining his degree from Bristol. The bank he worked at was just across the road from Christ's on Sidney Street. Chris was the reason that I closed my Barclays Bank account and opened one at Lloyds in the autumn of 1976.

Many of the new intake of graduates and undergraduates frequented the buttery, which served all kinds of drinks and snacks. The payment system was a new one to me in that we purchased booklets containing different denominations of monetary values. Therefore, if a round of drinks came to £1.50 for example, we tore off little stubs not dissimilar to cloakroom tickets, equal to the amount owed.

It was in the buttery that I met the young man who became my very best friend. He just came up to me and held out his right hand for a handshake.

'My name is Stephen. Who are you?' he said.

'My name is Sola,' I replied as I felt his firm grip in my right hand. It felt firm enough for me to feel that I couldn't easily withdraw, but not so tight that it hurt.

'What is your subject?'

'I am starting a three-year PhD course,' I said. 'What about you?'

'I am studying natural sciences, pharmacology.'

We bought drinks and went and sat down. He never once asked me where I was from which impressed me a great deal. We chatted for a good while and agreed to go upstairs to eat in the cafeteria. He was significantly shorter than me and had a boyish-looking face that had no blemishes. His hair was blond and I noticed that he was wearing white clogs on his feet. After dinner, we returned to the buttery and chatted some more. It was only at closing time that we left. He went to his room in third court and I went to mine.

Once I had been shown my office in the department and discussed with my supervisor what the aim of my experiments were, I decided to treat it as a job. My office was at the end of a corridor that overlooked the classroom where undergraduates were taught. I devised a timetable so that I arrived by eight o'clock in the mornings. I worked until five in the evening before going back to college. I was extremely fortunate in that my experiments progressed well and I did not come to a dead end that would have meant starting again or charting a new course.

I loved doing research and I was fortunate to be given a grant by the Medical Research Council for my second year. The extra money made things easier for me and I no longer needed to work. Things improved further when I was asked to supervise undergraduates in physiology, because I received payment for doing this. It was while supervising that I came across a gentleman who some people referred to as a Soviet dissident. He had spent many years in prison back in his homeland and was an activist in his youth. His name was Vladimir Bukovsky. He died recently, in 2019, in Cambridge. All the questions that I felt I wanted to ask him were kept to myself.

I cajoled some of my undergraduate friends from college to act as volunteers for my study on the McCollough effect, or ME as it became known.

Scientists already knew from previous research that in the occipital cortex, the part of brain at the back of the head, cells were coded for vertical and horizontal lines. We also knew that viewing any orientation was associated with colours of the visible spectrum. The important facets of the research were discovered, in the United States, by Dr Celeste McCollough when she noticed that if black and a colour was associated with an orientation such as vertical lines, subsequent exposure to black and white vertical lines made the white lines appear as the complementary of the original colour. Subjects were asked to look at a grid containing vertical or horizontal black lines associated with the colour red or green. We used a simple slide viewer with background lighting to observe the patterns we inserted in them. The colours were filters placed in the grid thus allowing the white parts in the slide to appear the same colour as the filter.

When subsequently presented with a vertical and horizontal black and white pattern, the white areas were associated with the complementary colour of the original exposure. Therefore, if originally exposed to vertical black and red pattern, they saw black and green when exposed to vertical black and white pattern. The intensity of the complementary colour in the white part faded over time. Certain factors, such as drugs and degree of tiredness, also affected the rate of loss, or not, of the complementary colour.

We postulated that the presence of a colour that was not actually there was a learnt response and by understanding the nerve connections of the visual pathways from the eyes to the brain we could assess what factors enhanced this learning and which ones accelerated its decline or forgetting. In those days, I had my friends as volunteers who agreed to take medication in a double-blind trial. Looking back now, I cannot believe what we did. Nowadays such experiments would have to be sanctioned by an ethics committee. Fortunately, no one came to harm. Cigarette smoking enhanced the learnt response, and in order to assess what component of cigarette smoke was responsible, I obtained some nicotine and placebo tablets from a scientist at the University of Reading. My findings from those who were given nicotine tablets confirmed that the responsible ingredient in cigarette smoke was the nicotine. As I was looking at the effects of different types of drugs on the ME, my supervisor thought it would be nice to see what effect ginseng had on the phenomenon. We wrote to Sun Myung Moon who had established the Unification Church of the United States (known as the Moonies in the mid-1970s), and asked if he could send us some samples of ginseng. I was completely thrown when some samples arrived in the post. My supervisor tried ginseng but we opted not to give this particular drug to any of my subjects as we had no idea of possible adverse effects.

My research progressed very well indeed and I held regular meetings with Professor Shute. Sometimes, these meetings took place in his house next to Christ's Pieces, a Victorian park in the centre of Cambridge. One day I visited him and the front door was unlocked. I announced my arrival and he answered by saying that I should follow his voice. I did as directed and was surprised to find him lying in the bath. I didn't know what to say or where to look. I was nonplussed and sat on the toilet seat while we discussed an aspect of my research.

Carrying out research on the human brain led me to read various papers on the hippocampus. It is named the hippocampus from Latin because it looks like a seahorse. This part of the human brain is involved in the storage of memories including long-term ones. It was while reading scientific and anatomical literature that I came across its role regarding the effects of childhood trauma on the growing brain. I was surprised to read that there was scientific evidence that emotional and physical child abuse caused measurable changes in the physical structure of the brain, visible when the brain was subsequently scanned. Physical changes were noticed in the area of the hippocampus in the brains of young adults who were mistreated. These changes were thought able to lead to future vulnerability to depression, post traumatic stress disorder (PTSD) and addiction. It made sense to me that like a scar on the skin, the damage, while healed on the surface, is permanent. Furthermore, as the physical brain changes are located in the part responsible for memories, it doesn't surprise me that anytime in the future that an awful memory is triggered and recalled, a person could revert and have difficulty coping with a given situation.

Published papers have indicated that the long-term consequences of abuse include low self-esteem, persistent mental health problems, suicide and suicidal thoughts, difficulty trusting anyone and permanent, debilitating brain changes. Reflecting on my life, I wonder to what extent feelings of low esteem and worthlessness contributed to my inability to fight back. I also had thoughts of ending my life as a young child and I did find it difficult to trust people. The way Jane ended our relationship did not help me with building trust.

I must consider myself lucky that I did not end up in prison or worse. Some studies have shown that child abuse increases the risk of ending up in prison. Studies showing a correlation between abuse and incarceration range from 9 to 75 per cent (National Institute of Justice, 1998).

A Cambridge University retrospective study from Australia published in the *British Journal of Psychiatry* (December 2018) showed a high association between child abuse and subsequent psychiatric morbidity. I believe that my religious faith and meeting a great girlfriend while at clinical school helped me. Lizzie had left school early and had a decent-paying job in the centre of the city. I met her while working in a pub in Cambridge. She came in one summer's day after playing tennis. The mistake she made was turning up in her tennis outfit which was enough to make me try and find out more about her. My friends wanted to know whether a poster which was popular at the time had influenced me. Many young men had this poster on their walls. It showed a lady wearing a tennis outfit and seen from the back.

I asked the pub landlord Alan who she was, and he told me that her name was Lizzie, and she had been coming to the pub for some time. Lizzie was about average height and had ginger hair and freckles. She was athletic partly because she rode her pink Eddy Merckx cycle everywhere. When I first met her in the summer I asked her for her phone number. I finally telephoned her six months later to ask for a date.

Following my experience with Jane, I had many friends who were girls, and it took me about six months to gradually end all these relationships. Before meeting Lizzie I took comfort in having many girlfriends because, I assumed the hurt would be less if one ditched me. Something made me think that she was different from all the others. With my flashes of temper that persisted at that time in my life, Lizzie was one person who took my behaviour in her stride. I could not believe that someone could accept me as I was without getting upset.

We decided to give up our tenancies in our individual rented accommodation after a few dates, and Lizzie and I rented and shared a flat located above a firm of architects on Chesterton Road. As she was earning money in her job in town, the bulk of paying our bills fell on her shoulders. I am always grateful for this act of kindness on her part all these years later. She made our flat very nice indeed. It was small with a sitting/dining/study area opening onto a small balcony. The kitchen was tiny, as was the toilet. Our bedroom was large enough for a wardrobe and our bed - a mattress on the floor because we could not afford a proper bed.

As for my religious faith, I attended church regularly and soon realised that my life must be in the hands of a greater power. Things happened to me that I felt could not be down solely to luck. Managing to study for my A levels in nine months and getting an interview at Pembroke College Cambridge were two examples.

Fortunately, child abuse is not a guarantee of continued psychological problems. It is possible that, provided one is removed from an adverse environment before things are set like concrete in the brain, the chances of reaching a stage of irreversibility are reduced. I also believe that abuse without love and affection is worse than that which is interspersed with some love and affection, regardless of the source of the love. As mentioned above, studies have shown the possible devastating consequences of abuse in those less blessed than me. Lizzie was instrumental in helping me and she was the most perfect counsellor that I could have had.

My work was going to plan so I had time to join the university boxing club, volleyball club and the college chess and croquet clubs. I ended up as the croquet captain, which came as a surprise as I didn't think that I was the best player. Our croquet president was Lord Todd the college Master at the time, who had won the Nobel Prize in chemistry. There were times that I felt that I must be in a parallel universe when I recalled my days at BHC. Lord and Lady Todd were two of the humblest people that I have ever met. They had a way of putting students at ease. They were both very tall and Lady Todd was the daughter of a Nobel laureate, Sir Henry Dale.

In the physiology department tearoom, I sat with people whose intellects were way above mine. I remember being in discussions with some physiologists including Mr Patrick Steptoe, a gynaecologist working at Bourn Hall, and Dr Robert Edwards, who was a member of our department. I even managed to put in my miniscule contribution one day. Mr Steptoe and Dr Edwards were working on the early stages of in vitro fertilization or what was known by non-scientists as test tube babies. The main question I asked was, how did they know that, compared to natural selection that they were picking the best spermatozoa. In 2010, Dr Robert Edwards was awarded the Nobel Prize in physiology for his work on in vitro fertilisation.

Many years after my PhD, as I treated a lady who had been born as a result of their studies, I marvelled at her baby daughter who had been born naturally. I then wondered whether the awarding of the Nobel Prize might have been delayed until 2010 because those on the Nobel committee were waiting to see whether babies born by in vitro techniques could have babies themselves naturally.

I was also fortunate to meet the Duke of Edinburgh on two occasions when he visited our department in his role as chancellor of the university. The first time was in 1978, one year after he became chancellor. On both occasions, he asked me the same question. Having visited Nigeria, he wanted to know whether I liked eating yams. Of course, my answer was yes on both occasions.

I managed to get a couple of research papers published in reputable journals such as *Vision Research* and *The Journal of Physiology*. As a result, I was able to present papers at conferences held in Cambridge. I still cannot believe that Nobel Prize winners and eminent scientists from around the world were raising their hands in order for me to pick them for questions.

It so happened that I was reasonable at boxing and the coach actually suggested I give up my studies and turn professional. I opted to stay in academia and just enjoyed my boxing. My very first fight was held against Sandhurst Military Academy in Berkshire. I was fighting at middleweight, and I tried to psych my opponent out by performing rapid push-ups while waiting to be called into the ring. It must have worked because he was knocked out in twenty seconds. I still have the newspaper cuttings describing my win. That weekend, the Irish Guards were visiting Sandhurst, and, as fate would have it, they were to be our next opponents in Cambridge in a few weeks' time. They apparently decided that the Sandhurst fight could not have been my first ever fight and swapped my original opponent for their experienced captain. Needless to say, he beat me up well and good in our fight. I spent many seconds sitting down on the canvas but he didn't knock me out. There were times during that fight that I thought I was fighting identical twins. A rapid shake of my head got rid of one of them.

In early February of 1978, I had a deciding fight with another middleweight at the club in order to see who would be chosen for the university team to fight against Oxford University. I won and was chosen for the team. I felt bad for beating my opponent as he was a decent boxer and a friend. I was pleased that he subsequently earned a Cambridge Blue in cricket and went on to play cricket for Somerset in the company of Lord Ian Botham and Sir Viv Richards.

My Oxford opponent on the evening of the varsity boxing match was a medical student named Steve. I beat him on points and the home crowd displayed their annoyance at the verdict. The next thing I knew, sugar lumps, cutlery and napkin holders entered the ring. I still wonder whether this behaviour was the reason that having a three-course meal while waiting for the fights to start was ended. I was awarded a full Cambridge Blue for representing the university. Steve and I are still friends and he is gracious enough to keep telling me that I was a very stylish boxer.

There are many people who are against boxing and I understand their reasons. I maintain that the aim is not to injure an opponent, but to try and score points by hitting designated areas. If the aim were to cause injury, there would be no need for rules and referees. I used to say that it was the poor man's fencing. Personally, I would sooner box than play rugby because being hit in boxing shouldn't come as a surprise. I accept that this is a difficult topic but in the end, I feel that, provided nobody is coerced into doing something they don't want, and that the inherent risks are understood, then why stop people. I admit that there is a world of difference between amateur and professional boxing.

College life was very good and I belonged to a group of friends who were mostly undergraduates. We went to other colleges' functions and occasionally to a local nightclub. We ate sometimes at the local Greek restaurant in Lion Yard called the Eros.

We liked a very cheap restaurant on King Street called the Corner House. The odd thing was that it was in the middle of a row of shops. It was nowhere near the corner of the road. I loved eating there and usually opted for beef curry and rice. It was obvious that the meal had been precooked and only reheated once ordered. None of us students cared because it was inexpensive and never upset our stomachs.

Two of our group invited me to their homes in Rochdale and Leeds respectively. I enjoyed going up north for the first time, but sometimes found it difficult to understand the local dialect. My enjoyment was not spoilt by my car breaking down on the motorway in the dark and pouring rain. As I belonged to the AA, I was rescued and felt embarrassed when all the man did was to push what I think was the distributor cap back into place. It had somehow worked loose. After this experience, I purchased a *Haynes* manual and learnt a lot about servicing my Audi 100 myself.

My visit to Rochdale was an eye-opener as the friend who had invited me used to have his hair cut either short or his head completely shaved. Some people referred to this look as being a skinhead. He invited me to his local pub and I agreed. As we approached in the evening darkness, I could hear jollity and laughter coming from the pub. He stopped suddenly and said that I should go in first while he waited outside.

'Why do you want to do that?' I asked in all innocence.

'You'll see just go in first,' he replied with a grin on his face.

I approached the door, opened it and entered. All of a sudden, as if a switch had been flicked, all conversation ceased. I felt about thirty pairs of eyes looking at me in a way similar to my experience in Caister-on-Sea. I felt as vulnerable as an antelope encircled by lions. As the people looking at me were attempting to decide my fate, my friend walked in with his grin even wider than before. He laughed out loudly, placed an arm around my shoulders and said, 'He's a mate.'

The solid silence was suddenly pierced by laughter and speech. Some of the tough-looking guys who, a minute earlier might have been contemplating rearranging my physical structure, started patting me on the back, asking me what I wanted to drink. My friend's sense of humour was something that I gradually got used to. It turned out that he was a respected member of the group and was looked up to for making it to Cambridge.

More than forty five years later, most of my close friends from Christ's still keep in touch and we try to meet once a year in London for drinks and a meal. Our partners have fitted into the group without a problem. Even the Covid pandemic of 2020 couldn't stop us meeting online. People logged in from Scotland, Wales, France and the United States.

Before I met Lizzie I avoided getting too close to any particular girl as I didn't want to be hurt. Getting hurt would reawaken too many memories that I would rather forget, or at least park in a faraway recess of my consciousness. I had a few friends who were girls and, as a result, I got a reputation as someone who played around. I was happy in the knowledge that I never lied to any of these girls.

I once met a beautiful girl named Julie in a nightclub on St Andrew's Street, not too far from Christ's College. Her figure and face could not have been more beautiful, and for a moment, I was tempted to go for the serious option. We sat in a corner of the dimly lit club and chatted.

'What is your name?' she asked.

'Sola.'

'What a lovely name,' she replied. 'What do you do?'

'I am a student at the university, studying for a PhD.'

I sensed something as I watched her facial muscles go

through some kind of gymnastics as she tried to assimilate and decipher my response. After what seemed like a long time, she spoke.

'Do you have O levels then?' she asked.

I didn't know what to say but just answered yes, meekly. On the way home, I pondered how much of a chance any future relationship might have. This episode, though, was not sufficient for me to draw back from my thoughts of maybe making a go at the relationship. However, the decision was made for me following a dinner in formal hall. Graduates were allowed to invite a guest to formal hall dinner on Tuesdays, so one Tuesday evening I invited Julie. I wore my gown as was the rule, and we had drinks in the buttery before going in for dinner. I swelled with pride at all the admiring glances my fellow students cast in Julie's direction. Her dress looked as if it had been stitched on while she was wearing it. Fortunately, the college started admitting women the following year which made those males realise that women must be respected and were not to be gawped at.

Formal hall had a tradition that a scholar read the grace in Latin prior to dinner being served. Just before grace was read, a bell was rung and all was silence. In the gap between the bell being rung and grace read, I had seen Julie looking at the portraits on the wall, obviously impressed. I am not sure that she recognised Lady Margaret Beaufort, Charles Darwin, the poet John Milton, or any other person. All of a sudden, the silence was broken by a voice that I knew was not in Latin.

'Who are those people in the paintings?' asked Julie.

I could have died as all the Fellows on high table looked in our direction. There was nothing that I could say. I just looked down at the table in front of me. That episode ended what could have been a promising relationship. Maybe I should have warned her about the need for everyone to be silent.

My PhD research did not lack volunteers and I managed to get answers to all the questions that I was trying to prove. Professor Shute helped me greatly and was very instrumental in reading and checking my draft thesis. Things went so well that I had all my data ready by the end of year two. I wrote up my thesis without rushing and basically had a proportion of my third year free. I assumed that a PhD was three years in length in order to allow for time to restart or change direction if one hit a dead end in their experiments or research.

Before my viva, which was set for early in the summer of 1979, some friends who were postdoctoral fellows had scared me. A few told me tales of their vivas starting in the morning, and continuing after breaking for lunch, While I knew that I had enough data and I was confident of my work, I worried about a long viva. My thesis was barely one hundred pages long, including the references at the end.

I shouldn't have worried, though, as my viva was about one hour long. Professor Shute told me that as I had a couple of peer-reviewed papers appended to my thesis, and having presented papers at international meetings, I had proved my mettle. I was so happy following my viva and having been told by one of the internal examiners that I had passed, that I went and bought a bottle of whisky that I shared with some friends. I was now able to refer to myself as Dr Amure. That feeling took a while to be assimilated. My chequebook would have to be changed to incorporate my new title.

I told my supervisor that I would still like to become a doctor and asked for advice. He spoke to a friend of his in the college and it was suggested that I apply to study anatomy at the University of Surrey in Guildford, a one-year course. I already had all the other subjects required for medical school, apart from pathology, from my undergraduate studies at Bristol. Stephen, still wearing clogs after three years at

Christ's, also wanted to change to medicine, and that was how the two of us ended up at Guildford.

Stephen became like a brother to me and we never had to explain things to each other in our relationship. He too had had a difficult childhood and his parents had separated. Despite his outward bubbly character, I knew that inside he was a shy and quiet person. He was very scared of his mother and he tried to avoid seeing her without someone else being present. There were times when I visited that he would ask me to accompany him to visit her. Fortunately, she appeared to like me. Stephen was the only friend whom I have visited at every house that he lived in after our first meeting. I visited his residences in Cambridge, Chilworth, Norwich, Leicester, Bristol, Oxford and Dorset! Junior doctors did a lot of moving about while ascending the ladder.

Our year at Guildford went very well indeed. Stephen rented a room in a village near Guildford called Chilworth, and I was allocated a room in Cathedral Court next to the cathedral. I got a job as a barman at a pub in Chilworth, and, according to Stephen, the clientele increased in number as many wanted to see the novelty of a black man working locally. I don't remember getting a pay rise for any extra profit that the landlord might have made. Most of the people that frequented the pub spoke like some of the students I met at Pembroke College in 1972. There was a lot of wealth around but then Charterhouse, the public school was only five miles away.

We played snooker and studied hard. We came up to Cambridge on some weekends so that Stephen could visit his girlfriend. The way that he drove his short-wheelbase Land Rover must have hardened my nerves. He took chances and rather than queue at traffic lights, he would drive on the pavement in order to get to the front.

One day, while having lunch in the dining room of the university, a lady came up to our table and sat down after asking whether it was fine to do so.

'I am sorry to intrude on your lunch, but I want to ask you a favour,' she said. She looked intelligent with her spectacles perched on the end of her nose. She had silver stud earrings on and, protruding from her off-white headscarf, I could see that she had dark hair.

'No problem,' I replied. 'How can I help?'

'I have been listening to your voice as you spoke.'

I wasn't sure what to say in response and just stared. She went on and said 'I am in charge of finding Bible readers for the Christmas carol service at the cathedral, and I wonder whether you would mind reading the first lesson.'

'What does it involve?' I asked, completely overlooking the fact that reading a Bible passage should be straightforward.

'We will need to practise a couple of times in the cathedral.'

'I am happy to do it,' I said.

'Brilliant. Can I please have your contact details?'

She produced a pen and a piece of paper as if by magic and wrote down my name and room number.

'By the way, the service is being broadcast on BBC Radio 4,' she informed me.

This was how I came to read the first lesson in Guildford Cathedral for the Christmas carol service in December 1979.

In the spring of 1980, Stephen and I sat the anatomy exams and while he passed, I failed and had to resit. The end result of this was that Stephen was now a year ahead of me. I secured extra anatomy lessons from a very good Fellow in anatomy from Clare College. I also made sure that I visited the dissecting room in order to familiarise myself with in situ organs.

Stephen felt sorry for me and surmised that despite my parents being thousands of miles away, and that I had to work to earn extra money, were factors not conducive to studying properly. He told me that he was always afraid to fail an exam because he did not know what the reaction from home might be. I resolved to persist as I did not wish to be recalled to Nigeria.

16

I made it to Addenbrooke's Hospital Clinical School in the autumn of 1981. As the Cambridge Clinical School course was only two years and three months long, as compared to three years everywhere else, I resolved to work as hard as I could.

Money was now tight again after my PhD, so I had to get a job during term time. Cambridge University has students paying the university as well as the College fees. I managed to secure a post as a barman at a pub near my lodgings. The Fort St George is the oldest pub on the River Cam in Cambridge. Parts of it date back to the sixteenth century. One side overlooks the river, and the other overlooks the Midsummer Common. When the annual Strawberry Fair was held, we were very busy and made a good deal of money. The fair attracted all kinds of people, including some unable to hold their drink. As the evening went on, fights occasionally broke out and the police had to be called. The landlord was extremely kind to me. Alan was tall and looked fit and always appeared happy.

He was strong, which might have had something to do with carrying and moving full beer barrels around in the cellar.

We got on so well that he bought me a second-hand car after he found out that clinical students needed to travel to hospitals in East Anglia and Suffolk as part of our clinical specialties attachments. The pub manager later told me that not only did the landlord like me, his daughter did too. I laugh now at the thought that the car might have been a form of bribe. He and his wife lived in a house next door to the pub just beyond a small bridge crossing the river. After they emigrated to Portugal, where he taught English as a second language, the house eventually became a Michelin-starred restaurant called Midsummer House. I can afford to eat there now, but only on special occasions. Before emigrating, Alan gave Lizzie and me some furniture from their house.

The car Alan bought me made it easier to go to places like Luton, Ipswich, Norwich, Papworth, Huntingdon, Newmarket and Bedford. It was a beautiful silver and blue two-tone Austin. In the summer, it was very hot inside as the control for the heating system had broken. Lizzie had to place her feet on the dash to prevent her legs getting too hot. The winter months were bliss.

We were divided into groups of seven and I loved visiting the different hospitals with my group. We all had individual blue badges that said 'student doctor' with our names on. I enjoyed all the clinical attachments and working in the delivery suite in Newmarket was just amazing. Watching a baby being born is a privilege. Despite having spent six years studying physiology, and being on the periphery while discussing in vitro fertilization, I was just in awe watching babies come into the world. I had to watch six babies being delivered, and then deliver a minimum of twelve under supervision. I was taught how to examine and suture episiotomies. Some ladies required post-delivery suturing, and, as the Matron taught me, if you can place your first suture at the apex of the tear or cut, you couldn't go too far wrong. One abiding memory involved a young man possibly in his twenties, who sat with his boots resting on the delivery couch while his partner delivered their baby. When he saw the suture trolley being prepared, he asked what was going on. After it was explained to him, his response shocked me. 'Hey, doc, please put in a couple of extra stitches for me as I like 'em tight'. This was not the most appropriate thing to have said under the circumstances as far as I was concerned. He looked sheepish after Matron told him off and he apologised and placed his boots on the floor.

While the hospital community was by and large good, the same cannot be said for some of the local establishments such as pubs and restaurants. In 1984, while working under Dr Dickinson who was a consultant physician in Huntingdon, I went for lunch at a pub near the hospital. The landlord possibly did not like seeing a black man and a white girl together because he must have added something to my prawn cocktail. It tasted odd but not enough for me not to eat it. For days afterwards, every time I burped, it smelt of engine oil or something similar. Fortunately, I don't think I suffered lasting damage. I decided to stick to drinking and eating in the staff bar and canteen from then on.

Even this did not work out as well as I had hoped. I was on call one evening, and I made the mistake of having half a pint of lager. I was called to assess a lady for admission. I clerked her in and everything went well as far as I was concerned. The next morning on the ward round, I presented all the patients admitted overnight to my consultant. Without warning the lady said to my boss, that she had been clerked in by the drunk doctor – me! She said that she smelt beer on my breath. From that day on I stopped drinking whenever I was on duty.

We had a patient come in one day who had a lot of trouble controlling his blood sugar and hence his diabetes. He owned a caravan park and money was no problem, judging from the conversations I heard him taking part in with some of his visitors. I spent a lot of time with him recording his blood sugars and making sure that I allowed for the fact that his readings would be different from those recorded at home. It was one thing lying in bed, but a different scenario being at home, mobile and physically active. He would burn off more sugar at home, so I had to adjust his treatment to allow for the fact that the readings would be different in hospital. This patient was so impressed by my care that he asked me to make sure that I saw him prior to his discharge as he wanted to give me some money. This made me uncomfortable and I resolved to be absent when he left the ward.

I walked onto the ward after I was certain that he had gone, and Sister called me over to the nursing station. She handed me an envelope and said that the patient asked her to give it to me. I opened the envelope and inside was two hundred and fifty pounds. I couldn't believe my eyes; my first reaction was to wonder how I could return it. This was not possible, so I rang the Medical Defence Union, insurers of doctors, for help. Their advice was that I could accept the money as long as I did not ask for it and the patient was not on a psychiatric ward when I treated him. I donated the money to Hinchingbrooke Hospital; as far as I know, it went towards the purchase of a couple of special mattresses that reduced the chances of getting bedsores.

Prior to graduating I attended Bedford Hospital South Wing for my thirteen weeks of senior surgical attachment. I was in Mr Hadfield' firm. Mr Hadfield was a most wonderful man and we got on very well. He was much shorter than me and he was blunt and to the point. He was an extremely clever and intelligent man who was brilliant at surgery. He was a general surgeon with an interest in urology. He had already had two hip replacements from injuries sustained playing rugby. At the end of my thirteen weeks, he asked me whether I would like to come and work as his houseman once I graduated. I thanked him and accepted the offer. After qualification, every doctor had to do six months each of surgery and medicine prior to being admitted onto the full Medical Register.

My studies went as well as they could and before long, it was time for the first set of clinical exams. I studied hard and felt as ready as I could possibly be. A few of my friends and I met in each other's homes to revise. One person would answer a given question from past papers to the best of their ability, and the rest of us would add bits of knowledge that we felt had been omitted. As it was April, many of my friends and I resisted the urge to go out much in the evenings.

In those days, the examination results were placed on a notice board in the clinical school. We all sat three exams in April and they were labelled A, B and C on the results sheet. Many eager faces peered at the piece of paper pinned to the notice board. I looked and found that next to my name, the one thing that I did not want to see. The letters A, B, and C had black ink marks through them indicating that I failed all three exams. Four of us out of about sixty or so had failed all three. On getting home that evening, Lizzie was magnificent.

Some of my closest friends expressed sympathy and surprise that I had failed everything. All that I could think was whether I would ever qualify as a doctor having travelled so far. I was extremely upset but put on a brave face for my friends. In the following weeks, the Dean called all four of us into his office individually. From what I gathered from the other three, it appeared that I was the only one allowed to resit the three subjects I had failed along with the four exams due in December of that year. The remaining three had to defer until the exams in May, meaning that their course was effectively three years long. The Dean, I assumed, realised that putting me back would cost me money.

I studied even harder after this disappointment and made sure, after returning home from working in the pub after eleven at night, that I studied for a minimum of two hours. In order to prevent myself falling asleep, I used ground coffee as snuff again having decided that the oral proprietary Pro Plus was inadequate. My eyes went very red as a result, but I stayed awake. I was determined not to fail everything again.

I still managed to enjoy myself; I had some downtime by going to the cinema with Lizzie and playing poker with my clinical school friends on those nights when we were on call under the supervision of a senior doctor. I played space invaders a lot on the machine in the clinical school bar and became very good at it.

A few weeks before the exams in December, I was summoned to the Dean's office. I owed a few thousand pounds in unpaid fees to the university and a smaller amount to the college. I did not have this money and said so. The Dean's response was to tell me that I couldn't sit the exams. I pleaded and asked to be allowed to sit them but they could withhold my results until I paid. This was not acceptable. I spiralled in slow motion into a dark vortex of despair and hopelessness. That was the lowest point in my clinical studies. I dropped so low that I felt I had to stand on tiptoe to simply breathe. I don't know what made me think of it, but I decided that I would go to my bank manager and ask for a loan or overdraft of almost £3,000.

I sat in the large, beautiful foyer of Lloyds Bank in Sidney Street waiting to be called into the manager's office. The central ceiling is possibly the most beautiful ceiling that I have ever seen outside of a place of worship. I was very nervous, praying that things would go well. Prayers had become integral to my life by this time. I joined the Christian Union at Christ's and attended regular Bible study meetings. I had even decided to be baptised and confirmed, which was carried out by the then Bishop of Huntingdon.

'Dr Amure, the manager is ready to see you now,' said a young man who looked as if he should still be in school.

I followed him through solid-looking doors and up some stairs to an office. Standing outside was a very tall gentleman wearing a dark suit and smiling. Mr Montgomery looked like the headmaster of a school, and he just seemed like a decent man. He still had a good crop of hair, and as we entered his office he pointed out the chair for me to sit on, I noticed that his hands were smooth and indicated a life possibly devoid of much manual work.

'How can I help you?' he asked. He was looking at a folder with my name on the front.

'I...er... um, need to borrow some money please.'

'What do you need the money for and how much are we talking about?'

'I need about ... £3,000. I have to pay my fees otherwise the university won't allow me to sit the finals.'

'Do you think you will pass the exams?'

'Yes, sir,' I replied.

'In that case, you can write the cheque.'

My thanks came tumbling out; I couldn't believe what had just happened. I expected to wake up any minute. This man had just helped me in a way that I never expected. How did he know that I would pass? How could he be sure that I wouldn't just go back to Nigeria after the exams? The journey home was a slow-moving blur of actions and I am not sure how I got back to my lodgings on Chesterton Road without getting knocked down by a bus or car. Lizzie was very happy for me. Mr Montgomery is one of the main reasons why I am still with Lloyds Bank over forty-five years since I opened the account.

The exams were extremely difficult but I was determined as apart from anything else, I could not afford any more fees. My parents did the best that they could, but Father was still in the habit of judging financial adequacy by the standards of the early 1950s. I managed somehow to graduate as a doctor, helped in no small part by Lizzie who was a source of propulsion in an encouraging way. Whenever I felt despondent, she was there with words of encouragement. I am convinced that without her, I wouldn't be where I am today. I was now qualified as a doctor, and had a negative bank balance, but overall, I was very happy.

I was fortunate in having both house jobs lined up at the hospitals where I did my senior clinical student attachments. The first was back to Huntingdon for six months followed by six months in Bedford. It was while working in Bedford Hospital that Lizzie and I decided that we did not want to keep paying rent. We applied for a joint mortgage and got one with Nottingham Building Society. We had a mortgage on a new development further up from our flat in High Street, Chesterton. We saw the small house being built from the laying of the foundation stone to completion. Every month after completion, I visited the building society with my paying-in book in order to pay the mortgage, often in cash. The need for money was the reason that I stopped smoking cigarettes. After Lizzie and I returned from a holiday to Pula in Yugoslavia, as it then was, I placed all our duty-free cigarettes in the dustbin. I hope that my action did not cause some poor bin man to take up smoking.

The holiday was remarkable in that a local man, despite seeing I was with Lizzie, offered me sex with a teenage girl provided that I was prepared to pay. I could have beaten the guy to a pulp because the young girl was a victim of abuse and she probably had no one to defend her. I estimated that she was about thirteen or fourteen years old. My life experience growing up and that of the girl is one reason I go out of my way to help children and women to this day.

Once the house was completed, we moved in and felt so proud. We had been allocated car parking spaces and had a small garden. I drove to Bedford and only stayed away when it was my turn to be on call. Weekends were tough as I was on duty for eighty-hour stretches, from Friday morning until Monday afternoon. After some weekends I was so tired that I fell asleep driving home after my shift.

By this time, I owned a yellow BMW 3 series that I bought while on a weekend trip with Lizzie to Bristol to visit Stephen and his girlfriend. Lizzie and I had driven down in her father's car and returned with two cars. My two-tone Austin had long given up working.

Life as a junior doctor can be difficult. I recall a doctor friend of mine who fell asleep at the wheel and drove off the road into a small pond. On the occasions that I actually fell asleep, I was grateful for the rumble strips that woke me up. Working up to 136 hours on some weeks did not appear safe to me.

17

South Wing hospital was a wonderful place to work. Driving from Cambridge in the winter months was not fun, but things improved markedly in the spring and summer. The ward nurses were extremely helpful, especially the ward sister. I soon learnt that while they might not be doctors, the experienced nurses had seen and knew more than a fledgling doctor. I made sure that whenever I was unsure that I sought a sister's opinion.

On call sessions were difficult, but we got through them and learnt a lot. I was on a one-in-three rota, which meant that I covered every third weekday and every third weekend. I never bothered to get in the bed in the on-call room, and never took my white coat off. Some nights, even after working all day, sleep was non-existent. I got so tired at times, that I placed my summoning bleep on the lapel of my white coat. I had missed some calls because I had not heard it go off. GP calls could come at anytime so the on-call doctor had to be prepared. Occasionally, the calls came from one of the wards I was covering.

One night, I had a call from the night sister on Elizabeth Ward. I struggled up the stairs to the ward, which was a couple of levels away, ensuring that I held on firmly to the railing. Any residual sleepiness disappeared as soon as I was shown the patient. He was lying in bed sweating profusely despite being hooked up to an intravenous drip. I picked up the chart at the bottom of his bed and looked at his recordings noting the temperature, blood pressure and pulse. The BP was down, looking at the plots made by the staff, his pulse rate was up, and his temperature was up slightly too. I checked his name on the piece of paper above his bed.

'Hello, Mr Davis. My name is Dr Amure. How are you feeling? Do you have pain anywhere?'

'I feel pretty rough, doctor. There is some pain in my tummy.'

'Do you mind if I examine you?'

'Not at all,' he said, wincing.

I gently pulled the sheet covering him back a little, while preserving his modesty. I could see that he had a vertical scar running from below his navel to just above his pubic hair. Staples instead of sutures held the scar together. Mr Hadfield preferred staples instead of sutures sometimes, which was just a personal choice. Even allowing for the swelling associated with recent surgery, I thought his abdomen looked slightly distended.

'I am going to examine you gently; please tell me if it hurts.'

I knelt down by his bed and placed the flat of my right hand on his abdomen. I pressed gently while looking at his face all the time. I always did this because some people did not like admitting to pain, but their facial expressions usually told the true story. As I pressed gently, I noticed his expression change. Something was not right. I percussed the abdomen gently by tapping the middle finger of my right hand on the middle finger of my left hand, which lay flat on his abdomen. The dull sound I heard indicated that there might be fluid beneath my hand. I listened with my stethoscope and there were minimal bowel sounds. As I was about to stand up, it was then that I noticed an area of bruising near a couple of the staples. This was not the typical bruising I associated with post-surgery, in my limited experience. After putting sterile gloves on, I gently tried to test the integrity of the staples. To my surprise, the wound gaped open. On closer examination, I could see that not only was the bowel visible, but one of the staples had caught part of the bowel.

The hierarchical ladder in hospitals was such that I, at the bottom as the houseman, had to seek help from the next doctor up. I phoned him and he refused to come. He asked me how many of these kinds of situations I had seen before. I was advised to place sterile gauze soaked in saline over the area until the morning. I wasn't happy with this suggestion and apologised for waking him up. The next guy on the ladder was one step up again. I bleeped him and told him what was going on, and that the patient most likely required returning to the theatre. He did not like being woken up.

'Why have you called me? Why not call the guy below me?' he asked the questions in rapid succession.

'I did call him first and he refused to come. He advised me to put a wet gauze on the area until the morning.'

'Do what he suggested then.'

'I am not happy and would like someone more senior to come and assess please,' I replied.

'How many of these types of situation have you seen before?'

'This is my first one,' I responded hesitantly.

'Sola, I've had a busy day.'

'Are you coming or not?' I asked, getting somewhat irritated as I thought of the poor patient lying in bed in pain.

'No, I'm not. Do what your immediate superior suggested.'

'Why are you not coming?'

'Because he's not my dad.' The line then went dead.

I told Sister about both immediate seniors refusing to come and we looked hard at each other. I decided there and then that I had no choice but to get Mr Hadfield out of bed. The switchboard, after some hesitation and pointing out to me that it was three o'clock in the morning, put me through to his house. Mr Hadfield did not sound too pleased but he calmed down after learning that I had called those I should have called first.

He arrived on the ward and I could see that he still had his pyjamas on under his coat. He examined the patient and told me that he required immediate transfer to theatre. Back in theatre, Mr Hadfield couldn't praise me enough as there were two problems. One was that the man was bleeding into his abdominal cavity, and two, a couple of the staples had inadvertently pierced the bowel. If I had not insisted, Mr Hadfield told me that the man could have suffered an infarcted bowel, which could have led to bowel gangrene, and most likely his death.

On the ward round the next morning, Mr Hadfield made it really clear to the two doctors how displeased he was with them. From that day on, they always came when I called and worked very hard to make sure that Mr Hadfield wrote them decent references for their next jobs.

I learnt a lot from my six months at Bedford. My work reached the stage where Mr Hadfield trusted me sufficiently to allow me to do appendectomies and cystoscopies - examining the bladder under his close supervision. I assisted him sometimes by holding a heavy piece of metal known as a retractor. The retractor pulled large organs such as the liver out of the way so that the surgeon could have a decent view of the field of operation. I showed nervousness, but Mr Hadfield reassured me that the ends were smooth and that I couldn't cause any damage by tugging on this piece of sterile metal.

He invited Lizzie and me to his house in a nearby village some weekends when I was not on duty. The house had a large garden and also had a swimming pool. I was introduced to his family. His wife worked as a nurse at the hospital and she was so kind and understanding that I grew to like her a lot. She had blonde hair and always greeted people with a smile.

After one such visit, we decided to stop at a kebab shop that we frequented. We made our orders; I loved my pieces of lamb with lots of chilli and sliced onions and diced lettuce. Lizzie and I stood at the counter waiting for our orders. From there, we had a view straight into the kitchen through the open door. I noticed that the guy preparing our takeaway food was just about to sneeze. It was that unmistakable sign of inhaling deeply, which was followed by a sneeze. Lizzie and I watched in horror as the man opted to stop his thousands of bacteria particles from hitting the meat on the skewer by using my pitta bread to halt their travel. Lizzie and I exchanged sideways glances and no spoken word was required. We waited until our meals were delivered, wrapped in foil, ostensibly to keep the kebabs and the bacteria warm for the trip home. As soon as we were out of view of the shop, we placed the kebabs in a waste bin. It made me think about the fact that if we had not seen what happened, we would have eaten the kebabs and probably enjoyed them. We never went there again.

Sometimes, when I was not on duty, my friends and I visited a pub just across the road from the hospital. We never went for drinks, in truth; we only went to rile the landlord.

Everyone knew that he was a racist and hated anyone who looked remotely foreign. Behind the bar were faded copies of old newspapers showing him with leaders of very right-wing parties and copies of *The Bulldog*. I would walk up to the bar and order a round of drinks, making sure that my order was different from that of my friends. He pulled the pints without hesitation, but he then spat in my pint before handing it over. I always shook my head in surprise and, of course, refused to drink it. I also refused to pay for the adulterated pint and we invariably didn't stay too long. I convinced my friends to finish their drinks and I watched as the barman seethed. I always wondered what he did with my drink after we had left. Why he never barred us from coming remains a mystery.

Lizzie and I loved our Cambridge home and felt proud to own it. We made friends with our next-door neighbour who worked for the British Antarctic Survey and was away for lengthy periods. We kept an eye on his house for him, and occasionally tidied the garden. Our house was a two-up two-down. Downstairs had a sitting room and a small kitchen/dining area. Upstairs had two bedrooms separated by a small, windowless toilet. Lizzie's older sister visited sometimes with her husband and young son. During this time, Lizzie had a job in a store in the centre of Cambridge and our combined annual income allowed us to live a comfortable life.

Lizzie's parents visited us sometimes and I got on very well with them. They were the parents that I never had. They couldn't have been nicer. Her dad, Clive, was an Englishman and her mum Megan was part-Welsh. Her dad, a retired academic was approximately my height and possessed a well-trimmed moustache. He wore spectacles for reading, was extremely intelligent and had worked for the government in a technical capacity during the Second World War. He had also published scientific books that were used in some secondary schools. Whenever I accompanied him to a pub, he always ordered a pint of Guinness. At home, he was a dab hand at tackling *The Times* crossword.

Megan wore spectacles all the time and only took them off for close work like embroidery or while completing the crossword in the newspaper. Megan was about an inch or so taller than Clive. They both had just the right amount of fat and muscle. Megan's was as a result of her genes, and Clive's having been active in sports when younger. We visited them on some Sundays and had a great lunch whenever we went.

Lizzie's grandmother on her mother's side, whom we met sometimes on visiting Lizzie's parents who lived in a village to the north of Cambridge, was a lovely lady who lived independently in the northwest of England. Despite being in her eighties, she was as sharp as a person forty years younger. She was short and always had her hair tied in a bun at the back, and a friendly, smiley face, behind her spectacles. I couldn't imagine her ever losing her temper.

My six months at Bedford went so quickly that it caught me unawares. One day, while in Mr Hadfield's office, he asked me what I planned to do in the future and I told him that my wish was to train as a surgeon if possible.

'Sit down,' he said.

Before my gluteal muscles were resting on the chair, the telephone was in his hand.

'Hi Anil Jimmy here,' he said. 'I have this great young man with me who needs a six-month stint in accident and emergency. Can you accommodate him? Thank you very much. I will send him to see you.'

Having attended to see patients referred by GPs to casualty, I knew that Anil was the head consultant in A&E.

I was halfway through expressing my gratitude, when he picked up the phone a second time.

'Sister, it's Jimmy. Is Mr Pearson there please?' He then turned to me and said 'I am trying to get you a six-month post at the private hospital in Biddenham, as I feel you will need this job in order to study anatomy for the first part of the surgical exams.'

'Hello, it's Jimmy. Do we yet have someone for the post of house physician at Biddenham? Good, I have a great guy here who is suitable for the job. I will ask him to come and see you. Thanks.' Biddenham Manor was a private hospital that regularly employed budding surgeons in order to let them combine working there with teaching anatomy at Cambridge University.

Just as I was thinking that my next year had been sorted, he picked up the phone again, and spoke to his friend at Queen's Medical Centre Hospital in Nottingham. Before I knew it, I had eighteen months of jobs arranged without having to apply for them. This sort of thing cannot happen these days because trainees require a government allocated number in order to be able to pursue a career path. I couldn't thank him enough and just mumbled that I promise not to let him down. Mr Hadfield was one of the nicest doctors I have ever met. He proved how sympathetic he could be one day while we were on a ward round.

The firm including Mr Hadfield, the senior sister, the registrar, SHO and I were on a ward round and our final stop was the intensive care unit. Our only patient on this ward had suffered a catastrophic brain injury in a horrific fall from a building. Mr Hadfield had sought a second opinion from a consultant neurosurgeon from the nearest tertiary centre in Cambridge and was told that surgical intervention was unlikely to help. We walked up to the bed where this gentleman, who was only in his mid-forties, lay. If I had not known how ill he was, I could have imagined that he was just taking a nap. His well-toned physique was at odds with the clinical condition. The ICU nurse gave us an update and shook her head slowly. All neurological tests since admission were unfavourable.

The man's wife sat next to his bed gently holding his hand. It was obvious that she was mentally and physically drained and I really felt for her. Both eyes were surrounded by puffiness and the surrounding skin had lost its normal colour. I wondered what their situation in life was; whether he was the main earner and whether they had children. If it had not been deemed unprofessional, I would have given her a hug. Mr Hadfield asked whether he could talk to her outside for a minute and she agreed. I sensed she had an idea that the news was not going to be good.

'It is never easy to say things sometimes as a doctor,' said Mr Hadfield.

'I don't want to hear it, doctor, I really don't,' she said as tears trickled down her cheeks. He held her left hand as he continued.

'All the tests indicate that your husband's brain is irreversibly damaged. We need your permission to turn off the machine that is keeping him alive,' said Mr Hadfield.

'Is there nothing else that can be done?'

'I am afraid not. He has been in this state for over three weeks and there have been no signs of any improvement. I am so very sorry, but I need to ask you a difficult question. There is evidence from your husband's GP that suggests he would like to donate his organs.'

'I know. He is kind in that way.'

'Do you have any objections to your husband's organs being donated?'

'No Mr Hadfield, I have no objection so long as none of them are given to a black bastard.'

The ensuing silence was so audible it almost hurt my ears. I looked at Sister, who looked at the floor. The registrar rubbed the side of his nose and the SHO gently tugged the lower lobe of his right ear. The only person who appeared unfazed was Mr Hadfield, who slid both thumbs behind his braces, inhaled slowly and spoke.

'In that case, we will not be using any of his organs.'

Whether he was annoyed or upset, I never knew. When we got back to his office on the surgical ward, he could see that I was upset.

'I can understand you being upset,' he said. The registrar and SHO nodded in agreement.

'I am very upset, but not for the reason you think,' I replied.

'What do you mean?'

'I am upset because not a single person who might have benefited will now get the chance. Personally, I would have been happy that someone gained rather than nobody gains.'

'There was no way that I could agree to her request. I wanted her to reflect at some point about what her response has resulted in,' said Mr Hadfield.

All these years later, I am still of the opinion that I would have preferred that someone benefited, but I completely understand the stance Mr Hadfield took.

Thanks to Mr Hadfield, I spent six months in Biddenham at the private hospital and combined this with travelling to the anatomy department in Cambridge to teach undergraduates and learn at the same time. Many budding surgeons followed this course of action, as a good knowledge of anatomy was critical in becoming a surgeon. My time at Biddenham went very well and I rediscovered what it was like to sleep through most nights. Almost all of the patients paid for their care, and the responsible consultant was usually the first point of contact by the nursing staff.

In the February of 1986, I was back on site at South Wing as an SHO in accident and emergency. This was a six-month post, and it was very busy. I and the other five SHOs, worked 24 hours on and 24 hours off. I usually arrived at eight in the morning and worked first on call until four in the afternoon, after which I went to my rooms and only returned when it was busy while acting as the second on call. I returned at eight in the evening and worked as first on call again until morning. A&E was not a single specialty and the next patient could present with anything. We received calls from the good GPs at times to warn us of an imminent arrival. We also referred patients on to doctors with specialties that were better suited to dealing with certain problems.

I was surprised at how many young people presented with histories of self-harm which mainly involved having taken overdoses of tablets. Paracetamol overdose was a common one. Some of my fellow doctors occasionally jumped to conclusions about the reasons. I tried very hard to speak to these patients in order to understand and show empathy. I wanted them to feel that they were not truly alone. As far as I am concerned, very few human actions are taken without some sort of reason. While anybody may not agree with the reason, it is still valid from the involved person's point of view. I always recall my favourite poet Longfellow writing: 'If we could read the secret history of our enemies, we should find in each man's life, sorrow and suffering enough to disarm all hostility.' Virtually all patients were given something to make them vomit if they had ingested tablets within a specific time frame prior to being seen. Some had their stomachs pumped out in a procedure called gastric lavage. This looked uncomfortable but many nurses were convinced that the experience prevented a repeat in some patients. What pleased me the most was that almost all of the young people attempting self-harm were referred to some form of counselling service.

I still sought the opinions of the senior nurses regarding some things such as X rays for example. I am certain that this prevented me from making too many mistakes. When not busy, we sat in the nurses' room chatting and eating late-night pizzas, thanks to the preponderance of Italian restaurants nearby.

My worst experience occurred one afternoon when a young man aged about nineteen came in after his motorcycle hit a car head on. The two middle-aged ladies in the car were shaken and attended the A&E department as well. I was allocated this young man who was already waiting in a cubicle. I entered and drew the curtain. Before I could say anything, he spoke.

'Ain't there no effing white doctors left in this country anymore?'

'I am sorry, but I am the one on duty today.'

He looked me up and down and moved to and fro like a giant frond being blown gently by the wind.

'If you weren't wearing that white coat, I'd smash your face in.'

It was my turn to look him up and down. I thought for a minute and then removed my white coat.

'The coat is off now, so feel free,' I said, as I assumed a pose that I had learnt at boxing.

'Its OK, doc, just kidding,' he said. I encountered many people with similar views to this young man in my medical career. I was sorry to learn later on that some of them assumed that a foreign doctor had prevented an indigenous student from becoming a doctor. Some others just hated foreigners, regardless of how high a qualification they attained.

I took his medical history and examined him. I wasn't

happy at the discrepancy between his blood pressure and his pulse. While he had a raised systolic BP, his pulse rate was less than sixty beats per minute. I went to look for the two ladies whose car he had been in a collision with and asked them to tell me exactly what happened. I was shocked when the car driver told me that following the collision, the young man had gone over the car. She distinctly remembered looking in the rearview mirror and seeing him land headfirst on the road, with his feet in the air and his helmet still on.

I ran back to the young man to tell him that I wanted him seen by another doctor as soon as possible, and then went to search for a radiologist attached to the department. I told her the story and my concerns, and the young man was wheeled away quickly for a brain scan. About half an hour later, I learnt that he had died in the radiology department. I was so upset that I asked to take the rest of my shift off, as I knew that I wouldn't be able to concentrate thereafter. The half day I took off contributed to the one and a half days in total that I took off work in about thirty years of working as a doctor. Even when I was undergoing radiotherapy treatment for prostate cancer in 2009, I arranged the sessions around my work timetable so as not to let any patients down. My time as an in-patient and that following my surgery, I took as holiday. I hardly mentioned the diagnosis to my patients and, when some discovered later, I informed them that there was no way that I wanted to be the focus of discussion when they had come to see me about their own problems. As radiotherapy induced extreme tiredness, I had a few early nights during my four weeks of treatment.

Back in our flat following the young man's death, Lizzie could see that I was very upset. I explained to her what had happened and she did her best to reassure me that these things will happen in medicine. I had to explain that it wasn't his death that upset me so much as the fact that I was ready to fight him because of his attitude. What if he wasn't always like that? What if he was responding to the slowly increasing pressure on his brain that the scan showed was due to a brain bleed? I sent him for a scan because I remembered from my training that a raised BP associated with a low pulse, or Cushing reflex, could indicate a raised intracranial pressure. I was grateful that Lizzie was there that day to console me, as I still think about that young man over thirty years later. Could he have been scanned sooner? Medicine is not always a precise entity, and a boss once told me that in order to cope with the job, one must learn to live with uncertainty. That sentiment is not as easy as it sounds.

18

One of the things that I found difficult as a junior doctor was the fact that on finishing at one hospital on 31 January or 31 July, we had to be ready to start work at the next hospital on the first of February or August. So it was that I arrived to begin work at Queen's Medical Centre Hospital in Nottingham on 1 February 1987.

We were allocated a very nice three-bedroom flat in Florey Court. I loved this flat because all the heating bills were paid by the hospital and the place was always warm. We had an adequately sized sitting room, kitchen and bathroom. Lizzie and I made many friends and I was glad that she had people to socialise with when I was at work. I was on a one-in-three rota in the neurosurgical department. We now had a son aged ten months and we travelled up to Nottingham with him lying in a carrycot on the back seat of the BMW. These days, nobody would think of placing a carrycot on the back seat of a car without the good baby seats and harnesses.

He was born in Cambridge and Lizzie woke me up in the

night so I could drive her to the hospital. He looked so fragile that every time I held him, I was scared in case I dropped him. The labour was long and the consultant obstetrician actually considered carrying out a Caesarean section. Becoming a father made me feel responsible; I slowed down and didn't drive as fast as I used to. I got up in the nights to see to him as I felt that Lizzie had done enough during the day. The one thing I couldn't do was to breastfeed him. Fortunately, Lizzie, at age thirty, had a lot of energy and didn't show too much tiredness. I felt guilty when I had to do the eighty hours on call every third weekend. Similar to Bedford, I was on site and could nip home when things were relatively quiet on the ward.

I loved neurosurgery, and to this day, Lizzie still says that was the happiest that she saw me on any medical attachment. I enjoyed telling people who asked what I did for a living that I was a brain surgeon. My boss, Mr Jonathan, was a very clever and smartly dressed man. He always wore a dark, three-piece suit and usually had a brightly coloured pocket handkerchief. I can actually say that his dress sense was immaculate. He always stood upright as if a rod had been inserted in his back. He did not brook sloppiness and he made that clear. For reasons unclear to me, he trusted my judgment and on a couple of occasions allowed me to run his outpatient clinics when he was unavailable. This was despite the fact that there were three immediate seniors to me available. When I couldn't do it, he mostly cancelled the clinic. There were three neurosurgical consultants and one of them was Mr Hadfield's friend who had secured the post for me. Mr John was a very nice man. He only spoke when necessary and, unlike Mr Jonathan, he preferred to wear his white medical coat at all times on the ward. The only times he didn't wear a coat was when he had just come from theatre in which case he had theatre blues on. I assisted all three consultants in theatre, as did the other two SHOs.

I always smiled at one of the consultants because he was so short that he couldn't see to operate, and usually stood on a wooden step in order to be able to see what he was doing. The six months that I spent on the ward were truly brilliant, and I learnt a lot.

The first time that I assisted Mr Jonathan, I couldn't stop sweating beneath my mask. He was operating on the pituitary gland, which is located in a hollow called the pituitary fossa. Sitting above the gland is a collection of blood vessels known as the circle of Willis. The circle of Willis comprises two anterior cerebral vessels, two middle cerebral vessels and two posterior cerebral vessels. These vessels plus a few other smaller ones lie beneath the brain and supply it with blood. In order to have a good view of the gland, my job was to use a retractor to gently pull back the six vessels. Unlike the heavy-duty retractor I had used to hold back the liver in Bedford, this was much smaller. All I could think of as I held that retractor was that I must not jerk or sneeze. The resulting damage that I could see in my mind's eye was sufficient to stop me moving. To make matters worse, the optic chiasm, containing nerves carrying messages from the eyes was close by. If I did not kill the patient by rupturing the delicate blood vessels, then I might cause them to go blind.

To reach the brain, the theatre staff shaved hair off the patient's scalp, following which the surgeon used a drill to cut through the skull in order to allow access to the brain. I marvelled at the shiny *dura mater* under which the grey and white brain tissue laid. *Dura mater* is derived from Latin and means tough mother.

I wear helmets every time I cycle now, and encourage others to do so, because of an incident that I saw while doing neurosurgery. A lady in her early thirties had been knocked off her bicycle and subsequently developed a headache. Friends noticed a change in behaviour. She was brought to our ward and a brain scan confirmed a bleed into the brain. Mr Jonathan took her to theatre in order to remove the blood and reduce the pressure on her brain. Unfortunately, she died on the table. Looking at her lying there, she looked a picture of health. The devastating result of cycling without a helmet had not been immediately obvious. I want to stress that I only ever saw two patients die after bleeding into the brain secondary to head trauma, and this included the young man in Bedford. Quite a few were saved by surgical intervention. Seeing people die was not something I ever got used to. We had another patient die because he had refused a blood transfusion, should it have been necessary. He objected on personal religious grounds, and nobody could convince him otherwise. I am not sure I understand why the operation was even carried out, as we all knew that if something went wrong during the operation, transfusing him would have been seen as an assault. The only way I could explain it to myself is that it is possible non-intervention might have had the same result.

Wards D9 and D10 were adjacent in QMC, and we sometimes did joint ward rounds. One of the neurology registrars on ward D9 told me one day that a patient on our ward was a close friend of Diana, Princess of Wales. He had also found out somehow that the princess was going to pay a visit to our ward to visit the friend. I was late going for lunch one afternoon when I noticed activity at the nursing station. I watched as the most beautiful person I had ever seen walked past. I realised that it was the princess. She had the smoothest skin, and her smile served only to enhance her beauty, if that were even possible. She held her head ever so slightly to one side while at the same time barely looking down. The lady she had come to visit was a patient whom we had admitted after she fell of her horse and suffered a mild neurological injury. Fortunately, the injury was temporary. I guessed that the two ladies must have been really close in order for Princess Diana to visit her in hospital. I was so overawed that I couldn't tell you whether she had a security detail of more than two people. All I know is that there appeared to be a lot of people with her. It is possible that some of the hospital's administrators were also there.

Mr Jonathan was the one who explained to everyone what the problem was and he was very optimistic that the friend's stay in hospital would not be too long.

Mr Jonathan asked me what my plans were after finishing my six-month stint in neurosurgery, and I told him that I had applied for the two-year rotation in ophthalmology at QMC. When I was younger, I always thought that losing your sight must be the worst sense to cope without. I saw too many blind people while living in Ibadan and Lagos. I didn't know then why they were blind, but subsequently learnt that many had a condition caused by the bacteria *Chlamydia Trachomatis*. The saddest thing is that, with adequate and prompt treatment, the blindness is preventable. Being born in a country without free and available healthcare is in some way akin to being born into an abusive family. Both sets of people had no choice in ending up where they did.

He wished me luck as I explained that as my PhD was on the visual system, and coupled with having done neurosurgery, ophthalmology, which I have always loved, seemed a logical step. The joke was that looking inside the eyes was akin to looking at the external brain. This sentiment arose from the knowledge that the eyes in embryological development are outgrowths of the brain, reminding me of the tentacles protruding from the heads of snails.

I was very happy to get a letter saying that I had been offered a place on the ophthalmology rotation. My next two years were sorted and it meant that Lizzie and our son did not have to move across the country again for a while.

In my final month of working on ward D10, I was asked to come to the casualty department to assess a lady in her late twenties who was complaining of a headache. Her background history was of having fallen down the stairs and hitting her head. Doctors, regardless of their specialty normally examine all the different systems in a patient. I went and clerked the patient in and after taking a verbal history including asking about double vision and nausea as she had banged her head. I also asked about shortness of breath, chest discomfort, and when her last menstrual period, or LMP in doctor shorthand, was. She had had a period in the past four weeks; it was normal in length and in the amount of blood loss.

My examination was thorough and I carefully checked that all her paired twelve cranial nerves were in working order. I examined her chest for heart and lung functions, and these were normal. When I came to examine the abdominal system, I was struck by her distended abdomen and examined her carefully. When I pressed gently on the left upper area, she demonstrated that it was painful. I percussed that area of discomfort by tapping. The unmistakable dullness that I heard told me that something solid was under there. My brain went into overdrive and I began to worry. I put together the fact that she had given a history of falling down some stairs, the swelling and percussed dullness. I arranged for her to have an urgent ultrasound scan and booked theatre after discussing this with the on-call surgeon. I took blood samples for tests and also arranged for four units of blood to be cross-matched as I was convinced that she would need a transfusion.

I was sure the young woman had an enlarged spleen. The

spleen is an organ that lies below the diaphragm on the left side of the body. It plays a role in fighting infections. I remembered from lectures that damage to it can cause internal bleeding. What made splenic rupture dangerous in some patients was that, because it was enclosed in a sheath, any bleeding can be contained up to a point, before sudden rupture if damage is undetected. I was feeling pleased with myself as I sat in the casualty office while waiting for the radiologist to return and tell me that I had been correct in my diagnosis. I didn't know whether to laugh or cry when the radiologist informed me that the ultrasound scan showed that the lady was pregnant and that she was in labour! Nobody knew that she was pregnant as she had hidden the fact from her family and friends.

Before I left the neurosurgical unit to go and start my ophthalmology stint, I had to go up to Edinburgh in order to sit the primary part of the exams required to become a surgeon. The initial exams cost a decent amount to enter and had a low pass rate. Those who passed the multiple-choice questions part of the exam got invited for a viva or oral examination in Edinburgh. I enjoyed my trip up to Waverley Station in Edinburgh by train and had booked to stay at the North British Hotel just above the station on Princes Street. Looking out of the train windows as we travelled north showed the beauty of parts of the United Kingdom. I felt good at being able to afford to stay in a five-star hotel. The night before, I had practiced answering questions with a friend from Cambridge who happened to be up in Edinburgh too. I smiled when he told me that my depth of knowledge was much more than his. The location for the orals was within walking distance of the hotel. The sunshine reflected off the water like sparklers as I walked over North Bridge, making me feel good about my upcoming exam.

The waiting area in the old science buildings reminded me

of the physiology department in Downing Street, Cambridge. A lady wearing a bright red dress with matching red lipstick came and called me to go in for my turn. I was nervous as I entered the room where I could see tables with pairs of examiners at each. I counted six tables and worked out that at ten minutes per table, it was going to be a long hour.

'Dr S Amure?' asked one of the two gentlemen at table one. He ticked off my name on a list after I confirmed it. 'Sit down, please.'

'This is the pathology viva,' the same man said. The grey hairs nestling on the tip of his nose distracted me. These hairs matched the colour of those protruding from his earlobes. He peered at me over his spectacles as if mentally dissecting me.

'Where did you train?' asked the second examiner. His crumpled grey suit appeared as if it had never been introduced to any cleaning products. His light-brown tie was covered in what I assume must have been part of his breakfast that never made it with its mates to his stomach.

'Cambridge,' I replied. This caused them to exchange glances.

'Where are you from?' asked the hairy one.

'I am British,' I replied. Another sideways glance followed.

'Where were you born?' asked Crumpled Suit.

'London, sir,' with the sir added as an afterthought in an effort to ease the path I sensed that this encounter was heading.

'Where were your parents born?' asked the one with the grey suit. I could see that they were both getting exasperated. They didn't even bother to exchange glances by this point.

'Nigeria,' I said. For the first time since I sat down and having taken a fair chunk of my examination time, they smiled. This allowed me to see that Professor Crumpled Suit had virtually all his teeth matching the colour of his tie.

'That's where you are from,' said the hairy one. 'Now we have established your nationality, we can ask you about tuberculosis. You get a lot of that over there, don't you?' I felt like saying something but held back, despite knowing at that point that I had failed. I had studied very hard and any optimism that I had that I would pass the exams were obliterated by this experience. It all seemed totally unfair.

Back in my hotel room, I felt an amalgam of anger, sadness and confusion. Almost twenty-five years since seeing signs in B&B establishments saying 'No Blacks', it seemed that little progress had been made. Despite having a good idea of my fate, I congregated with other students in a huge hall near the main university building in order to hear the list of the successful candidates being read out.

The guy reading out the list looked like he relished this part of his job as he rattled through a list of those who had passed.

'Number 7, number 42, number 47, number 76,' and so on. Between the numbers being called out, many people walked out upon realising that their exam numbers nestled within those that were omitted.

My journey home was not as enjoyable as my trip up. Life went on and I soon determined that I would just have to resit; many successful surgeons had multiple attempts before passing. I tried to console myself with the thought that if I had answered every exam question correctly, then it would have been difficult to fail me. One friend did tell me later on that there was a specific examiner who failed everyone he examined regardless of who they were.

Lizzie was brilliant in consoling me, as usual, and it helped that we had a young baby boy to look after. Baby Sola had very curly hair and if the light caught it just right, I could see a tinge of red mixed with the black. Looking at this young boy added to my determination, and I was able to pass the Diploma in Ophthalmology at the Royal College of Surgeons in Glasgow in due course. Scotland was therefore instrumental in helping me obtain a postgraduate surgical qualification.

Sitting here today, I have twenty-six letters after my name, and considering where I started from, I am very pleased. I hold a Bachelor's degree (Bristol), a Doctorate and medical degrees (Cambridge) and a surgical specialty degree in ophthalmology (Glasgow). These notwithstanding, I sat the Royal College of General Practitioner's exams on three occasions, and could barely break 40 per cent in the three sections of the examination. I cannot state for a fact that prejudice played a part; struggling to get 40 per cent could just be a reflection of my IQ. One Nigerian friend once told me that to succeed in medicine as a black man or woman in the UK, one had to be like the boxer who, in order to get a draw, had to knock out his opponent. I laugh at this but there are good people out there like Professor Shute, Mr Hadfield and Dr Dickinson. I could name more people of similar disposition – Clive, Megan, Lizzie, Stephen, etc. Despite the presence of decent white people, not enough appears to have changed in medicine.

As Covid raged in 2020, a study published in the *British Medical Journal* (December 5 2020 – No. 8271) reported a poll of 3,693 doctors carried out in June and July of 2020 that showed 46 per cent of ethnic minority doctors responded that the sharing of knowledge and experience had been positively affected by the pandemic. This compared with 61 per cent of white doctors. I accept that progress is being made, but we seem to have a long road still to travel.

Fortunately, I was not squeamish about operating on eyes. My introduction in the early weeks involved having to go and collect two eyes from a dead body in the morgue. My consultant told me over the phone in the middle of the night what to do to remove them, and he didn't repeat the instructions. I remembered what he said and successfully harvested the eyes. I admit that I was extremely nervous, and woke a colleague up in order to accompany me. The cornea is the clear part through which we see the coloured iris, and is the only part of the human body without a blood supply. This fact meant that one could transplant corneas without the fear of rejection of the tissue by the recipient.

Operating on eyes was a close second to neurosurgery as far as enjoying my work went. The first time that I performed cataract surgery was nerve-racking. Everything appeared big under the microscope, but the fact that I knew the correct dimensions made life difficult. The distance between the back of the cornea and the iris, the coloured part of the eye varied between about one and a half millimetres and over three millimetres.

While performing cataract surgery, one cannot inadvertently touch the inner surface of the cornea, which is lined by cells called endothelium. These cells are one layer thick, and what we are born with lasts our lifetime. I was nervous as damaging these cells could mean a loss of vision. There was a saying in some ophthalmology circles that general surgeons bury their mistakes, while eye surgeons continue to see them in the clinics. This saying was not one that I appreciated. Another thing that I disliked was the habit of some doctors to refer to patients by their diagnoses. I would rather say 'Mr X in bed 6' rather than the 'gallbladder in bed 6' or 'the kidney stones in bed 8.'

I cannot describe the joy that I felt on seeing a patient who had come in one day barely able to see, and who, when the bandaging was removed the following morning after surgery, could see things much more clearly, especially colours. There was no joy to be had when a relatively simple operation went wrong. My waking nightmare was the one where a patient with eye cancer, usually a melanoma, came in for enucleation or total removal of the affected eye. As this procedure was considered relatively easy, it was left to the juniors to do. The procedure is similar to that used to remove cadaver eyes for their corneas. There were cases of where the good eye was removed instead, and one had to go back and tell the patient that the diseased one had to go as well. Fortunately, I never had this problem.

The day before such operations, I made sure that I saw the patient and dilated the pupils. Dilated pupils allowed a decent view of the internal structures of the eyes. I also used a marker to draw an X above the affected eye. I also wrote LEFT or RIGHT in capital letters in the patient's medical notes. I never abbreviated which side by writing L or R. If anyone asked me if I was going to operate on the left eye, for example, I always said 'correct', and not 'right', for safety reasons.

Medicine, as far as I am concerned is a privilege, and a fair number of patients are anxious about being ill. I try very hard to explain things to patients in non-medic speak. In fact, I developed a reputation as the doctor who always drew diagrams. Being able to empathise is a prerequisite, as far as I am concerned. One cannot get angry or lose one's temper with a patient. Laughing with a patient is fine, but laughing at them is a no-no.

The only time I did laugh was during an incident involving a patient who was concerned about the effects of ingesting petrol. He had contacted me in a panicky state and explained that as he was siphoning petrol from a friend's tank, he inadvertently swallowed a mouthful. I couldn't see what the problem was, until he asked me how long it would be before it was safe to have his next cigarette. After regaining my composure, I suggested that he buy a can of Coca-Cola and drink it quickly. Once his burps no longer smelt of petrol, he could most likely light up.

One day, I had to draw blood from a confused elderly gentleman and as I spoke to him, I could see that he was agitated. He was a nice-looking gentleman in his seventies who had been a professional in his working life. I sat down on the chair next to his bed and explained what I was going to do. I wanted him to confirm that he understood and he nodded. I rolled up his shirtsleeve, and applied a tourniquet in order to make the vein stand out.

Having checked that he did not find the tourniquet too tight, I unsheathed the needle and placed it over a juicy and well-filled vein. As I placed the needle in the vein he jerked his arm away and let out a cry of discomfort. As I sat there looking at the red fluid dripping down his right arm onto the bed sheet, he suddenly spat straight into my face. Stemming the blood flow was more important than wiping away the spit, and I released the tourniquet as fast as I could and placed gauze over the bleeding site. I asked one of the nurses to help me apply pressure to the arm while I went to the sink on the ward. There was no way that I could get angry with the patient. When I returned later to draw his blood, I made certain that Sister was on the other side of the bed, chatting to him and holding his right hand in an attempt to distract him.

We had sad times when we had to break bad news to patients or their relatives, and in over thirty years of practice, it never got easy. How does one cope in the telling or the receiving? I was called to the casualty department once as a man in his thirties had suffered a catastrophic injury to his left eye while playing rugby. When I arrived, I took a history from him and then examined him on the slit lamp, which allowed for detailed eye examination. I was very upset to see that he had an extremely serious injury. The left eye had been irretrievably damaged and the sight in that eye would never recover. My upset increased exponentially when I found out that he was already blind in his right eye. He explained that a friend had accidentally shot a homemade arrow into it when they were playing cowboys and Indians as youngsters. It was one of the saddest days of my working life when I had to tell him that his job as a schoolteacher might no longer be possible. When I asked why he played rugby, he replied that he did not want to live a less fulfilling life just because he only had one eye.

Thankfully, there were happier moments too, as continually getting only bad news could affect a doctor's mental wellbeing more than that already associated with the normal stresses of the job. Things such as seeing a healthy baby arriving in the world and getting people's lives back on track were the counterbalancing weights on the scales. We sometimes had episodes that made us laugh too. One afternoon, I was doing my stint in the eye casualty, when a patient arrived having been referred by his GP.

'Good afternoon sir,' I said.

'Hi, doc,' he replied. Glancing at his notes, I could see that he was sixty-two years old. He had on a white boiler suit and I assumed that he must have been at work before seeing the GP. His face had a fine dust-like covering which could have been from his job.

'My name is Dr Amure. Do you mind if I ask you a few questions?'

'Go for it, doc.'

'What is your occupation?'

'Painter decorator.'

'Have you been at work today?'

264

'Yes, and all of a sudden, I realised that I couldn't see so well, which is why I hurried to the surgery'.

'I just need to check your eyesight. Can you please look at the chart on the wall opposite and cover one eye? How far down can you see, starting with the top letter, please?'

'Not very far, doc, I can only make it to the third line down.'

'Now the other eye.'

'No better, doc. In fact, I can only make the second line.'

'Now, look through the hole in this instrument, please. Each eye in turn.'

When looking through the pinhole, he managed to read all the way down the chart with each eye. This told me that his problem was one of refraction, which made me ask whether he wore glasses. He said that he did and took them out of the top pocket of his boiler suit. One look at his glasses and I could see that they were caked in similar dust to that coating his face. I got some spectacle spray and a lens cloth and cleaned his spectacles. When I checked his visual acuity again, he had perfect vision and read all the way down the chart with both eyes.

Even the patient smiled as I told him that I didn't think that he had a major problem with his eyes. The best part was writing my letter to the GP.

'Dear Dr Y,' I wrote, 'Thank you for referring this gentleman with reduced vision. Treatment offered: I cleaned his glasses.'

I wish that I had been present when the GP read the letter. I did not blame the doctor because most medical schools only offered a few weeks in teaching ophthalmology.

By the end of 1987, we had become a family of four with the addition of another son. Becoming a father again made me feel even more responsible somehow. It was one thing being two adults as boyfriend and girlfriend or husband and wife; it was on a totally different plane being responsible for a human being who, as a child, completely depended on adults. We decided that the two-door BMW was no longer adequate and so we bought a four-door car.

Clive and Megan drove up from Cambridge to stay with us on some weekends. Lizzie appreciated this as it allowed her some respite as I was not always able to give her a break. As a junior doctor, I worked long hours and I was constantly aware of how difficult it must have been for Lizzie looking after the children on her own. Her attitude was nothing short of brilliant. I tried sneaking home when I could when I was on 80 hours of continuous duty over the weekend. I had many private chats with Clive that I appreciated. Talking like this to someone I trusted was very good. He seemed to understand me without asking questions to discover what kind of person I was. Megan was brilliant too and as the old adage goes, before marrying someone, check out the mother first. However, I was happy even before I met Megan.

Lizzie's Welsh grandmother expressed her feelings without fear. Even though she wore small sized shoes, one deduced that it was wise not to cross her. I got the impression that her family was in awe and that her opinion mattered.

This was confirmed when she visited Cambridge to stay with Clive and Megan one weekend in 1985. Megan had told her that Lizzie and I were planning to get married. We decided along with Lizzie's parents, not to tell her that Lizzie was pregnant. In order for things to progress without a hitch or maybe just to get Grandma on board, it was arranged that I would spend a little time with the family having lunch in a pub near Clive and Megan's house.

We all went to the pub in the next village and the five of us sat at a round table. Out of the corner of my eye, I noticed that Grandma appeared to be studying me. I pretended not to notice as I playfully twirled one of the beer mats between my fingers. After looking at the menu, we ordered drinks and our meals. We ate while chatting and Grandma Morag asked me a lot of questions about my job as a doctor and my views on current affairs. I answered the questions as best as I could. I learnt beforehand, while speaking to Lizzie, that this lunch was a sort of interview. At least she didn't say what a Scottish friend's mother asked me when I visited Fife to spend Christmas with them in 1978 on learning that I was a PhD student in Cambridge, she wanted to know if I could write in English.

From my perspective, judging by the fact that my appetite was unaffected, the afternoon went very well. After lunch, Lizzie and I departed for home and left Clive, Megan and Grandma in the pub. Later on, I had a good laugh upon learning from Megan what Grandma thought of me. Megan said that she was waiting to hear what her mother thought and was anxious in case Grandma did not approve. Apparently, after a period of silence while she appeared to be weighing things up, she announced, 'You quite forget he's black, don't you?'

Those present took this as a sign of approval. I am not sure what would have happened if she had said that I did not reach the standard required in order to join the family. I was glad that I had passed the test and was accepted by the matriarch of the family who, as far as I was concerned, was a great lady.

19

Working in eye casualty showed me more of the sort of damage that humans can inflict on each other, especially once excess alcohol was factored in. As a result of one person smashing a pint glass in another person's face, I was invited to court as a professional witness. When he had arrived in casualty, his face was covered in blood, some of which had already congealed, making good visibility difficult for both patient and doctor.

Once the excellent nursing staff had cleaned his face, the damage was obvious. He still had pieces of glass embedded in his face. More worrying was the fact that I could see that one eye had been completely damaged and my guess was that the damage was irreparable. This was a Friday night and the department was used to seeing patients who were the worse for wear. Many in the latter group had drunk so much that they hardly felt any pain. This poor patient, who said that he was a student at the university, was actually sober and I felt sorry for him. I asked the consultant to assess him before I attempted to suture his facial cuts in case something could be done for his sight. Suturing jagged ends caused by broken glass is not possible and those ends were left to heal naturally. However, where there existed clean edges, suturing was possible. The consultant examined him and told him there was no chance of saving his left eye. I removed, as carefully as I could, pieces of embedded glass. I then carried out the suturing where possible after this, knowing that I wasn't losing valuable time that might have been beneficial to him.

I arrived at Nottingham Crown Court about forty minutes before the time stated on my letter of invitation. I looked smart in my suit and wore my University of Bristol tie. My shoes had been polished because I felt that, as I had been invited as a professional witness, I had better look the part. I entered the imposing doorway and felt scared even though I had not broken any law. It was odd as I could feel my heart racing. I could not see any signs indicating a waiting area for court seven. The receptionist had been curt and just pointed in a vague direction which I followed. I gingerly pushed open a well-polished wooden door and entered an empty room with chairs set around three sides. I stood contemplating whether to sit down, when somebody, possibly a lawyer, appeared.

'Hello, can I help you?' she asked in a tone of voice that switched on a recognition trigger in my brain. With experience, you learn to recognise those that think less of you.

'Yes please I am looking for court seven.'

'This is the waiting area for court seven but you aren't supposed to be here.'

Slightly confused, I was about to ask her where I was supposed to be when she spoke again.

'The entrance for defendants isn't through here.'

'I am a doctor attending as a professional witness.'

'Uhh,' she said and walked off.

I see that this sort of judgment and reaching a conclusion based on one's appearance still happens in law courts thirty years after my experience of the 1980s. The solution, in my view, depends on teaching people when they are young that differences should not immediately result in prejudicial thoughts.

I love a story that I read recently about a primary school teacher teaching her class about prejudice. On Monday, for example, she asked the children not to play with anyone wearing glasses and on Tuesday asked them not to play with anyone with blond hair. She chose a different trait each weekday, and at the end of the week, asked the children in the ostracised groups how they had felt on the days they were ignored. Not one child said that they liked or enjoyed the experience. She then told them that the way they felt was the same as that experienced by someone who was excluded from a group based on some perceived difference. I would like to think that the teacher sought the permission of the parents beforehand!

There is prejudice everywhere and if we are honest, we all have things we believe that others might find distasteful. I believe that every society has good and bad people in them, and it would be unfair to judge a whole race or community by the actions of a few. After all, I made a decent life due to my faith and also from helping hands from white people. I might have struggled without people like Professor Shute, Mr Hadfield and Dr Dickinson. These three, amongst others, helped me a great deal. I am in touch with Dr Dickinson currently; we get to play golf together most weeks now. Professor Shute always comes to mind whenever I visit Christ's College, something I try to do as often as possible as I only live about twelve miles away. He had a massive effect on my life because the best friends I have now were all met while at Christ's. He was the first solid human piece in the jigsaw of my successful life, and I would go so far as to say that without him, my current life would probably not exist.

It is human nature to focus on the bad events, sometimes to the exclusion of the good ones. My feeling is that all these gentlemen and some others were innately good and decent, or maybe that they saw something in me that prompted them to help me. History is replete with examples of people who have helped others who a neutral observer would not expect them to help.

Regardless of the reasons, my helpers might have been prompted to help me by a higher authority, especially as I am a man of faith. Looking back after all these years, I don't recall seeing too many ethnic minority faces where I ended up, after their help.

As was the way of life for doctors in those days, it was soon time for me to leave Nottingham for a three-year stint in the north east of England. I had been offered a post rotating around hospitals including North Tees in Stockton, South Tees in Middlesbrough and Darlington Memorial Hospital to train as a General Practitioner.

By this time, our family had grown to five after the arrival of a daughter. Each child affected me in that I took progressively fewer chances than before each arrival. I reduced my driving speeds on the motorways even more and stopped driving as if late for meetings. I worked really hard in order to be able to give these children the best life that we could. I found it difficult in the beginning to not shout at them or even to smack them. I am proud that I have only ever smacked one child on the leg for not being truthful.

Studies have shown that abused children tend to turn out as abusers themselves in a lot of cases. Credit for my not being like my dad or grandfather goes in a major part to Lizzie who guided me and possessed huge forbearance. Looking back today, I am convinced that had I married anyone else, I would have been divorced long ago. I might even have been competing with my grandfather in the numbers stake, the main difference being that my wives would have been sequential.

Watching Lizzie give birth to our children was enough to make me promise to myself that I would never cross the line and have an affair, no matter how tempting. Standing in the delivery suite on three occasions and seeing what she was going through was sufficient motivation. I concluded that she was going through all that pain for the two of us. I remember our wedding day when I also promised before God, friends and families to be a faithful and good husband. I must say that temptations were many, and some were really blatant. A nurse once told me that she would love to have sex with a black man – I was standing next to Lizzie at the time! I hoped that alcohol played a part in her behaviour; there are some people whose inner thoughts are unlocked by the key of alcohol. My faith and my promises were enough to prevent me going over an irreversible and unseen line in the sand. That unseen line in the sand has been visible at times, but thankfully has never been crossed. Certain actions once carried out, can never be undone no matter how many apologies are offered, as far as I am concerned.

Stephen was my best man and I had been his best man a couple of years before when he married his long-term girlfriend. My best man's speech was recorded and the family still played the recording many years later.

I was nervous in the church on our wedding day in early November 1985, especially when the vicar got to the bit asking if there was anybody who knew of any reason why we could not get married. I had visions that my parents, who were invited but refused to come, had sneaked in at the back. They knew the date and which church, but because I had chosen my own partner and not one they chose for me, they were against it. My father's reaction surprised me, as I knew that he had white girlfriends while he was at university in Bristol. Later on, when I challenged him on the matter, he replied that it was one thing having a white girlfriend, but a different proposition getting married.

I was glad that Bode, Adebo and Yinka all attended and were genuinely happy for me. Clive was extremely generous and paid for our wedding reception. We had a very good wedding breakfast at the Post House Hotel just outside Cambridge with sixty people attending. I was allowed less than one week off work but, as we couldn't afford to go abroad anyway, it didn't matter. Included in the package from the hotel was a free night at any Post House Hotel in England so we drove to Coventry for our free night.

When we woke up in the morning, we were amused to find that during the night, someone had added the number 1 before the number 2 so that our breakfast brought to the room was too much for two. We then drove to Alveston Manor in Stratford-upon-Avon for a few nights.

My father had told me before the wedding that I was taking on a foolish experiment that was bound to end in failure. He gave the marriage a maximum of five years before it fell apart. Writing today, we have celebrated over thirty-seven years. I believe that I was destined to meet Lizzie because, had it been anyone else, my father's prediction of five years would have been an over-estimation! My behaviour in the early years of our relationship left a lot to be desired. However, Lizzie's almost saintly behaviour helped me a great deal.

Human nature can be difficult to understand sometimes. I recall asking a racist acquaintance whether he would allow his only child to receive an organ donated by a black donor, and I cannot say that I was surprised when he said that he would allow it.

For ten years after we got married, neither parent spoke to me despite the fact that I wrote letters regularly to Nigeria. I cried when, out of the blue, I received a letter from my father. He told me that as his seventieth birthday was coming up, he would like me to attend. I visited them in Nigeria and our relationship restarted.

That trip, after so many years, did surprise me. I couldn't afford to fly direct to Lagos from the UK so I bought a cheap ticket through a travel agent offering student discounts.

The trip back to Nigeria involved flying to Copenhagen, staying overnight in a hotel, and then flying to Lagos the next day. Despite initially travelling north, and all the other expense, it was cheaper than a direct flight from Heathrow. On the Copenhagen to Lagos leg, flying with Scandinavian Airlines, I met a black American on the plane. Bruce was much shorter than me, but he was stocky and well filled out in a muscular kind of way. He wore a multicoloured beanie hat. He wanted to visit his ancestral home, having done some family history investigations. I liked him and as he said that he had nowhere planned to stay in Nigeria, I invited him to travel with me to Ibadan. It seemed a natural thing to do. When I met my father at the airport and introduced my American friend, I was very surprised that he did not fly off the handle. To his credit, he not only allowed my new friend to travel with us to Ibadan, but he also arranged for him to stay in a small local hotel and put the driver at the young man's and my disposal.

I was really involved in helping organise the birthday party and I was glad that I had taken enough Traveller's Cheques with me! My experience of that trip was extremely positive.

I saw him genuinely laugh one night while we were sitting on the balcony outside his bedroom, chatting and looking up at the sparkling stars in the perfectly clear sky. The part of Ibadan we lived in did not suffer from man-made light pollution. The homes of middle-class people were a magnet for crooks, so my father had employed a night watchman. All of a sudden we heard him snoring. My father said, 'I am paying him to sleep, and it's not even midnight yet.' He laughed so much that it relaxed me and I joined in. We both had tears streaming down our faces. I wondered whether this other persona had been hiding in some closet while I was growing up.

Father and my mother visited England in the summer of 1997 and I took the whole family to meet them. The first thing he said to Lizzie when we met was, 'Does he beat the children?'

Unfortunately, having been brought up to distrust everybody, including close relatives, I found it hard to encourage our children to reach out to their relatives, even though a few lived in the UK.

As our relationship grew in subsequent years, I began to understand why he was the way that he had been. He was successful because of harsh discipline and he told me that he would have gone off the rails otherwise. I politely disagreed and said that I think that children respond better to explanation and examples set by older people. I have eternal respect for him because of something that happened before he died. He was ill and I was visiting Nigeria to see him. He was in the bath and I was washing his back because he couldn't reach it himself.

'I have never done anything bad to anyone in my life,' he said suddenly.

I listened and said nothing. He turned round to look me

straight in the face and said, 'Except for the way that I treated you.'

That day was a very good day as far as I was concerned because I believed that he was sincere. These words came from a man who hardly ever apologised and was never wrong. There are too many people I have come across who are ready to apologise in a way that I deem a reflex. Some of these people are not really sorry or genuine in my opinion.

Mother was and remained until her recent death, extremely religious and she prayed regularly. I thought that this was impressive considering the difficult times that she had gone through. She had only been allowed, briefly, to drive a car on rare occasions, despite possessing a driving licence. She was not allowed many friends and did not regularly visit many of those she had. Living with Father was not easy but she stuck at it having taken a marriage vow for better or worse. Mother was extremely strong in many ways. When Father's will was read after his death in 2005, everybody was surprised to see that he left everything to Bode, Adebo, Yinka and me. His wife of over fifty years got nothing. I have yet to meet anyone in Nigeria who thinks this was normal behaviour. I remember asking him once if he loved his children, and his response was that if he didn't love us, he would not have spent money getting us educated! Perhaps he had a different opinion of what love meant. Fortunately, the four of us looked after her, making certain she did not want for anything. We telephoned her in Ibadan six days a week and paid for her travels to visit England.

Our children have turned out well and level-headed, and they are our pride and joy. They all have jobs that they enjoy. I readily admit that a lot of this was due to Lizzie as I was hardly at home because of my work. Counselling is very important part of treating people with mental health issues.

In my professional life, I have seen people counselled who responded very well, and there are some who went on to self-harm or worse. For counselling to work, and I have done a small course on it, I think that the depth of the effects of the causative factor is important. If a person is fortunate enough, as I was with Lizzie, they might meet someone who is just the right one able to help disperse the hazy fog of dark despair.

Medicine is seen by some as a glamorous position from the outside. Not many doctors wake up in the morning determined to go to work and injure someone. Most of us are dedicated and went into medicine because we want to be of use to people who are going through a difficult time. We try our best, but we sometimes fail. It is the right of patients and their relatives to be offered a truthful explanation as to why things didn't turn out the way that was expected. I have had personal medical friends who took their own lives following a complaint from a patient or their relative. One brilliant doctor, following seventy-two hours of continuous duty, placed the decimal point in the wrong place while working out a dose. The end result was that she injected the baby with ten times the paediatric dose, causing the baby's death. No matter how much everybody tried to tell her that it was not her fault and could happen to anyone, she gave up medicine the very next day and that was that. It was a shame that the NHS lost a good doctor. I think the NHS has improved its support for doctors who exhibit mental health problems. When I was a junior doctor, we were used as cheap labour. I once wrote a letter to management when I was the only doctor on duty for a week. Someone had given the other two doctors the week off as holidays, and no locums were appointed. Nothing was done to help me.

Junior doctors used to be happy when a job came with what we called *umties*. The proper term was Unit of Medical

Time or UMTs. What this meant was that the first forty hours of duty might be paid at three pounds an hour, for example, and each extra hour above this was paid at a third of the usual rate, that is, one pound an hour. On a one-in-two rota for example, a junior doctor worked 136 hours a week every other week. Ninety-six of those extra hours were paid at one third of that of the initial forty. The beauty of this, despite its apparent unfairness, was that doctors with jobs having UMTs earned more than the basic salary paid to those in jobs without them.

After returning home, I found it difficult to not worry about patients that I had seen while on duty. I especially hated Monday mornings and brown official-looking envelopes. I always sat down at my desk before opening these envelopes, because I did not want my legs to give way after reading that a patient that I had seen and reassured on the Friday had died over the weekend.

I am ashamed to say that I did not always stand my ground when I felt that a patient's condition did not warrant a prescription or referral. I relented when it was inferred that a written complaint would be put into the authorities. I recall a patient of mine who drank more than was good for him, and as a result, developed depression, a recognised association of alcoholism. Whenever he consulted me, he couldn't stop himself from crying in the waiting room. His wife asked if there was something that I could do to help. I ended up going to the car park on many occasions and sitting in the passenger seat of their car in order to carry out the consultation. After he lost his job, I wrote a reference letter in an attempt to help him find another.

You can imagine my shock and despondency when I informed him that he did not require referral for a complaint that he presented with, and his response was to put in a written complaint about me which was three sides of A4 long. He said that I failed to refer him because I was trying to save the government money, as the NHS was cash-strapped. As a consequence, I drank more alcohol at home and had difficulty sleeping. To rub salt in the wound, he and his wife continued to ask to consult with me. My practise of medicine became defensive and I carried out more investigations than I normally would have done. My contemporaneous notes became copious. My white colleagues appeared not to have similar problems and could be more forthright in turning down inappropriate requests.

I knew that the authorities were happy when you were working hard, but if things went wrong, it was assumed that the doctor was at fault. This assumption rose exponentially for black doctors. It is very sad that nothing appears to have changed much in this respect in the early twenty-first century. More ethnic minority doctors are still ending up before disciplinary panels than their white counterparts. Legislation such as the Race Relations Act is fine but it is the heart and innate prejudices that need changing. Many doctors soon realise that each one of us is totally dispensable when the brown stuff starts flying. One action that really irked me was the action of suspending a doctor from work. This was referred to as a neutral act. Neutral for whom? The suspended doctor, still on full pay, sat at home slowly going into a depressive state in a manner not dissimilar to watching water go down a sink's plug hole. I think the longest suspension I was aware of ran over two years. It is said by some that an aim of long suspension was to de-skill the doctor thereby making it difficult to return to work. I confess I do not know the veracity of this suspicion.

Some doctors hid their feelings well, and it was only at their funeral that one understood what was going on inside their bodies. Inside the physical exterior they projected was a jelly resulting from a blending of induced fear and anxiety. It would not surprise me if some considered themselves to have failed.

My best friend Stephen is no longer with us, having hanged himself at his house in September 2012. I am not sure what led him to this disastrous course of action, but I feel I now understand where he felt he was.

Not long before he died, I spoke to Stephen on the phone more in a month than I had done in the previous year. All he could say to me when I visited him in the final few weeks was that his life, and something in his head, resembled a train which had jumped the tracks. He never elaborated but I surmised he was comparing himself to the train driver. I felt he had lost control over an aspect of his life and couldn't cope. He had reached the status of a hospital consultant, had successful children and yet, something made him decide that life was not worth living. Not a single day passes without me thinking of him.

As Longfellow wrote, 'A torn jacket is soon mended, but hard words bruise the heart of a child'.

Stephen's death had a massive effect on me especially as I had harboured thoughts of suicide as a child. Having seen the effects of his action on his wife and children, I do not think I could do something similar to my own family. I am grateful for a wonderful family and I also have my strong faith, both of which preclude my taking such a drastic step. Even though I am very happy with life now, I look back and sometimes cannot believe that I successfully negotiated the road I have travelled. Fixing on the horizon, metaphorically speaking, ensured that I never gave up.

I am now completely retired from medicine after thirty years of working for the NHS. I try and play golf once a week, and I am the health and safety officer on our Parochial Church Council. I am currently vice chair of a new Special Educational Needs school near where I live to the north of Cambridge.

Life is very good and our two eldest children work in London in financial services and our daughter works in media. I feel that I must have done something right in my professional career as, more than eight years since retirement, I still get patients knocking on my front door seeking a second opinion!

Acknowledgements

I would like to thank Sarah and everyone associated with Goldcrest Books who has contributed to helping me with this book. I am very grateful and will never forget your help. Sarah has been extremely kind and always answered my questions with patience and understanding no matter how small they were.

I also want to thank Lynn Curtis who has been helping me for some years, and who gave me editorial and other advice. Lynn supported me when I was close to thinking maybe I would never get the book published.

Finally, I want to thank my family and friends for putting up with my idiosyncrasies over the years.

About the Author

I retired as a doctor after serving three decades working for the NHS as a GP and ophthalmologist. I qualified initially as a scientist and obtained a Bachelor of Science degree from Bristol, followed by a PhD from Cambridge. My PhD researched an aspect of learning and memory in humans. After this, I qualified as a medical doctor from Cambridge, which then led to my gaining a post graduate Ophthalmology degree from Royal College of Surgeons in Glasgow.

I love music and trying new things. I passed Grade 4 clarinet in my sixties having never been able to read a note before this and performed a 25 minute stand-up comedy routine at the Edinburgh fringe in 2017.

I am currently on our church parochial council and I am vice chair of a local school for children with special educational needs.

One of my Nigerian names is Lanre, and friends in the early 1970s found it difficult to pronounce, hence we agreed on Larry.

Milton Keynes UK
Ingram Content Group UK Ltd.
UKHW031134070924
447976UK00001B/22